Tourism Enterprises and Sustainable Development

Routledge Advances in Tourism

EDITED BY STEPHEN PAGE, *University of Stirling, Scotland*

18. Tourism Enterprises and Sustainable Development
International Perspectives on Responses to the Sustainability Agenda
Edited by David Leslie

Tourism Enterprises and Sustainable Development

International Perspectives on Responses to the Sustainability Agenda

Edited by David Leslie

Routledge
Taylor & Francis Group

New York   London

First published 2009
by Routledge
270 Madison Ave, New York, NY 10016

Simultaneously published in the UK
by Routledge
2 Park Square, Milton Park, Abingdon, Oxon OX14 4RN

Routledge is an imprint of the Taylor & Francis Group, an informa business

Library of Congress Cataloging in Publication Data
Tourism enterprises and sustainable development : international perspectives on responses to the sustainability agenda / edited by David Leslie.—1st ed.
    p. cm.—(Routledge advances in tourism ; v.18)
Includes bibliographical references and index.
1. Tourism—Environmental aspects.   2. Tourism—International cooperation.
3. Tourism—Government policy.   4. Ecotourism   5. Culture and tourism.
6. Environmental policy.   7. Sustainable development.   I. Leslie, David.
G156.5.E58T68 2009
910.68'4—dc22
2009003760

ISBN10: 0-415-99332-6 (hbk)
ISBN10: 0-203-87358-0 (ebk)

ISBN13: 978-0-415-99332-6 (hbk)
ISBN13: 978-0-203-87358-8 (ebk)

This book is dedicated to

Dr Phillip F. Hall
Professor of Obstetrics, Gynaecology, and Reproductive Sciences,
and
Director, Fetal Assessment and Manitoba Obstetric Outreach
Programmes

"A Man for All Seasons"
1948–2008

As Phil may well in mischief like to play
his part and spar in discourse:

"What is he that builds stronger than either the mason,
the shipwright, or the carpenter?"
Hamlet Vi: 46.47

Contents

Figures

Plates

Tables

Preface

Over the last decade there have been a number of texts that discuss tourism and sustainable development/sustainability (see Hall and Lew, 1998; Mowforth and Munt, 1998 & 2003; Aronsson, 2000; McCool and Moisey, 2001). However, more often the focus is orientated to the destination locale and promotion of best practice at the destination, e.g., "sustainable tourism" (for example, Middleton and Hawkins, 1998; Swarbrooke, 1999; Ritchie and Crouch, 2003; Edgell, 2006; Herremans, 2006); or specific to a tourism product, e.g., eco-tourism (see Cater and Lowman, 1994; Page and Dowling, 2002; Fennell, 2002; Buckley, 2004). There are also a few texts that specifically address environmental management in hospitality (Webster, 2000). By and large, these texts do not seek to investigate the response of government/national tourist organisations to the international sustainability agenda and the related responses/actions of tourism enterprises.

The objective of this contribution to the Advances in Tourism Research Series therefore is to bring together, in one volume, an overview of what is happening in major tourist receiving regions of the world as regards progress towards the objectives of sustainable development. More specifically to explore the application to and response of tourism enterprises to these objectives within the context of a country's attention to the quest for sustainable development in tourism policy and related initiatives in promoting tourism development. The pursuit of this objective required extensive searching to identify and investigate what research has and is being undertaken. This established that in comparison with many other aspects of tourism little actual research has been carried out and published which focuses not only on environmental management systems adopted by tourism enterprises (particularly in categories of supply other than accommodation operations [see Bendell and Font, 2004; Leslie, 2006]) but also, and more broadly, their environmental performance (EP).

As such, this text is not about "sustainable tourism" per se, which is more nostrum than panacea in terms of sustainability given the invariable failure to consider provision for touristic consumption and, all the more so, the travel element. The travel element is fundamental, which is a major reason why, as Porritt argued, ' . . . the industry cannot begin to claim it's even remotely sustainable' (2005: 2), a view which is further supported in an incisive critique of tourism in terms of sustainable development from the United Nations Commission on Sustainable Development (UNCSD, 2005). This critique and the preceding point on travel could equally be applied to this text. Furthermore, what may also be considered as a notable omission is that of attention to tourists—the consumers of tourism. To include diatribes on these two fundamental dimensions would create a weighty tome indeed! Even so, the importance of these key facets of tourism are not to be overlooked as many of the following chapters, though invariably implicit, draw attention to touristic consumption. The travel element, because of the primary focus of this text, gains little overall attention, which for some readers might be considered a weakness. However, its significance is explicitly considered in the introduction (also see Chapters 1 and 2); albeit this is potentially to digress from our primary focus—that of the EP of tourism enterprises and progress towards the objectives of sustainability.

Certainly one can read of the World Travel and Tourism Council's initiatives (see WTTC et al., 1996), find many examples of good practice (notably in the Green Hotelier http://www.greenhotelier.org/pages/about_us.html), and initiatives of the World Tourism Organisation and United Nations Environment Programme. Invariably the policies and practices propounded and exemplified are presented within the broad context of "sustainable tourism." This is not to denigrate such laudable initiatives but rather that they are primarily based on the precept that tourism exploitation continues but, in the process, ideally under best management practices (see Leslie, 2007). Whilst these suggest much progress has and is being made, this is not representative of the majority of enterprises—the myriad small and medium-sized operations—involved in tourism supply in any country/region/destination/locality. Thus, it is this paucity of attention to what is really happening that this text seeks to address through drawing together within these pages active researchers from around the world.

Before we move to the introduction, key questions arise which include Why is such attention important? In considering this question, the fundamental underpinnings to, and background rationale for, this text are established. These underpinnings and the primary themes, though not necessarily always explicit, throughout are:

- the sustainability agenda—sustainable development—Agenda 21 and local agenda 21, global warming and consumerism;
- international developments and responses, e.g., United Nations Commission on Sustainable Development and their Environment Programme, Intergovernment Panel on Climate Change, World Travel and Tourism Council, Tour Operators initiative;
- the global marketplace; as such, "no destination is safe from rash assault";
- national responses to the international environmental agenda and dimensions of tourism policy;

- the three pillars of sustainability and how they are entwined and application to tourism enterprises.

The preceding factors are all germane to the sustainability of tourism enterprises. As such, this text aims to provide an invaluable contribution, of some originality, to this field of enquiry. In effect, a high-quality, informative, comprehensive text which in total provides a substantive 'state of the art' perspective on progress towards the objectives of sustainable development within the tourism sector across the globe by focusing on the environmental performance and adoption of environmental management systems by tourism enterprises.

REFERENCES

Aronsson, L., 2000. *The development of sustainable tourism*. London: Continuum.

Bendell, J. & Font, X., 2004. Which tourism rules? Green standards or GATS. *Annals of Tourism Research*, 31(1), p. 139–56.

Buckley, R. ed., 2004. *Environmental impacts of ecotourism*. Wallingford: CABI.

Cater, E. & Lowman, G., 1994. *Ecotourism: a sustainable option?* Chichester, UK: Wiley.

Edgell, D.L., 2006. *Managing sustainable tourism—a legacy for the future*. Binghampton: Haworth.

Fennell, D.A., 2002. *Ecotourism programme planning*. Wallingford: CABI.

Hall, C.M. & Lew, A.A. eds., 1998. *Sustainable tourism—a geographical perspective*. Harlow: Pearson.

Leslie, D., 2006. Scottish rural tourism enterprises and the sustainability of their communities: a local Agenda 21 approach. In M. Augustyn & R. Thomas eds. *Tourism in the new Europe, perspectives on SME policies and practices*. Advances in Tourism Research Series. Oxford: Elsevier, p.89–108.

Leslie, D. (2007) The missing component in the 'greening' of tourism: the environmental performance of the self-catering accommodation sector. Special issue on self-catering accommodation. *International Journal of Hospitality Management*, 26(2). p.310–22.

McCool, S.F. & Moisey, R.N., 2001. *Tourism, recreation and sustainability—linking culture and the environment*. Oxon: CABI.

Middelton, V.T.C. & Hawkins, R., 1998. *Sustainable tourism: a marketing perspective*. Oxford: Butterworth-Heinneman.

Mowforth, M. & Munt, I., 2003. *Tourism and sustainability—development and new tourism in the third world*. 2nd ed. Oxon: Routledge.

Page, S. & Dowling, R.K., 2002. *Ecotourism*. Harlow: Prentice-Hall.

Ritchie, J.R.B. & Crouch, G.L., 2003. *The competitive destination—a sustainable tourism perspective*. Oxon: CABI.

Swarbrooke, J., 1999. *Sustainable tourism management*. Oxon: CABI.

UNCSD, 2005. *Tourism and sustainable development: a non-governmental organisation perspective*. Background Paper 4. New York. UN: CSD NGO Steering Group, April.

Webster, K., 2000. *Environmental management in the hotel industry*. London: Cassell.

WTTC, 1996. *Agenda 21 and the travel and tourism industry: towards environmentally Sustainable Development*. Oxford: World Travel and Tourism Organisation, World Tourist Organisation and Earth Council.

Acknowledgments

First and foremost this book would not have come to fruition without the encouragement and indeed patience of Stephen Page, Series Editor for "Advances in Tourism Research." Even then, the book would not have developed without the ready responses to my invitation to contribute by the authors herein—a humbling experience given their renown. Furthermore, they have all additionally given of their time in one way or another in contributing to the processes involved in bringing this collection together for your perusal and hopefully enjoyment. As regards such processes I am indebted to my colleagues Debbie Hinds and Ian Baxter of Glasgow Caledonian University for their support and constructive comments.

The book itself, or rather the theme, has its genesis in times past. I grew up in the country and during my early years gained firsthand experience of both the impacts of agricultural practices, heralded by Rachel Carson, and the expansion of tourism in rural areas. It is perhaps not surprising that much later when I found myself lecturing in leisure and tourism, a particular focus became their impacts on the environment. Interest in "green" organisations continued fuelled by the rise of the environment on the international political agenda and the quest for sustainable development—the "Holy Grail" perhaps of the twenty-first century.

But even with such personal commitment and the support and patience of the contributors, this text would still be a "work in progress." That it is now available is testament to Stephen Page and to Benjamin Holtzman and Jennifer Morrow of Routledge for their support and guidance throughout the development and publication of this book.

To one and all my grateful thanks.

David Leslie
Glasgow
United Kingdom

Introduction

The rise in recognition and increasing attention to the environmental agenda, whether global warming/climate change or more broadly sustainable development, has stimulated much debate and activity (see Chapter 2). Latterly we have witnessed progress in the business sector in the recognition of environmental reporting and adoption of environmental auditing, corporate social responsibility and carbon offsetting. Tourism has not been immune from this, though by far the major focus has been the impact of tourism on the destination's physical environment and the emergence of a variety of categories of tourism activity considered 'more environmentally friendly,' e.g., "green," "Eco-tourism," "sustainable tourism." This orientation to 'greener' forms of tourism was primarily catalysed by the significant rise in environmentalism during the 1980s, the United Nations Stockholm Conference of 1987, and the subsequent United Nations World Congress on the Environment and Development held in Rio de Janeiro, the world-renowned Earth Summit of 1992. This led to myriad policy developments and initiatives (for example, see Chapter 3) and as such serves as a particularly apposite starting point for this introduction and discussion. The aim is to highlight and explore the major themes, and specifically draw into contention areas such as air travel, the exploitation of "new" destinations and tour operators, which are not explicitly dealt with in the following chapters, by way of establishing a broader contextual framework for these chapters.

The Earth Summit of 1992 established a set of principles known as the Rio Declaration, which both at the time and since has gained little attention. Perhaps this is because the principles contained therein present substantive challenges to the major economies of the world: for example, the "precautionary approach" should be adopted in those situations where the impact of an activity is not clear or known; the "polluters pay" principle whereby pollution arising from an activity should be included in the product cost or delivery of the service: and—arguably the most difficult to address—"unsustainable patterns of westernised consumption" should be discouraged. In many ways tourism in postmodern societies is a manifestation of conspicuous consumption (Leslie, 1999), which has notably avoided attention in terms of these principles of the Rio Declaration. Principles which were considered to be overarching in the quest for sustainable development and the framework produced to guide such a quest in the twenty-first century—Agenda 21. However, between then and now the accent has changed. Today, the message is climate change and global warming (IPCC, 2007a). This has and continues to dominate the environmental debate and in the process shift the focus from addressing, in business terms, "the triple bottom line"; or in the context of the objectives of sustainable development—achieving a balance between the economy, the environment, and the people, the three pillars of sustainability (see Chapter 2). This shift has narrowed the focus of attention and opened up a whole new area of contention, providing an open field for critics opposing the notion of global warming. Witness the view of the Oregon Institute of Science and Medicine, who argue that there is a lack of substantive scientific evidence that greenhouse gasses are changing the global climate (see: http://www.oism.org/project/). In the light of such a contrary view it is notable that much of the burgeoning volume of writing on climate change is predicated on the outputs of the UN's Intergovernmental Panel on Climate Change (IPCC). The IPCC was a driving force behind the Kyoto Protocol and subsequent developments on emissions. However, the validity of its reports are questioned; witness the article by Booker (2008) aptly titled "The 'consensus' on climate change is a catastrophe in itself." This perspective would find favour with those consumers in the USA participating in what is termed "Carbon footprint stomping" (Spiegelman, 2008); the antithesis of the eco-friendly movement, in that it means explicitly going against green practices by, for example, driving a high-carbon-emitting car and embarking on numerous air journeys with selfish disregard about the consequences. Such a stance further supports Lomberg's (2001) impressively detailed and very comprehensive thesis countering many 'doom and gloom' scenarios whilst adding further weight to the argument that it is all scaremongering, as well articulated by Booker and North (2007). Conversely we have Gore's (2006) *An Inconvenient Truth* (and Warner Brothers' *The 11th Hour*), which have received a remarkable level of attention and acclaim such that the DVD was been promulgated as a part of the school curricula across the UK. A political minefield, of Orwellian doctrination furthered by an emerging political correctness on global warming/climate change, which appears to brook no gainsayers. Are those who either do not accept this and/or offer counterargument (who notably gain little media attention) the heretics of the twenty-first century? Evidently, in the case of global warming and the extensive media coverage there appears to be much truth in the adage "lies, damn lies and statistics."

The attention given to climate change throughout the media over the last few years leads to the premise that people know about climate change through its representation and the discourse that surrounds it. Thus the media play an important role in influencing the views on climate change which is not aided by the finding that newspaper coverage of climate issues contains conflicting messages which vary from tabloid to broadsheet and with the political stance of the publication (such as Futerra 2006; Johns & Leslie, 2008; Holmes et al., 2008). However, it remains unclear how this information is noticed, interpreted, and used by consumers when making choices; in particular what influence, if any, it has on consumer choice when it comes to choosing the mode of transport for touristic activities.

However, the point here is that global warming has subtly shifted the ground away from the basic premise of sustainable development. Currently the flavour is global warming and climate change when what we should be addressing is sustainable development and the fundamental principle that our consumption should balance with our resources—in the long term. This is not a new concept (see Greenwood et al., 2008) and brings into focus the United Nations deliberations on the environment from the early years of the seventies to the Bruntland Report and subsequent Earth Summit, followed ten years later by Rio plus 10 (held in Johannesberg), which gained comparatively little attention. However, their actions and the World Congresses on Environment and Development led the way for a raft of initiatives and protocols, which have engendered today's debates on global warming and climate change. The reality of this only time will tell and therein lies the persuasiveness of Booker and North's argument. But what the promotion of global warming has done is shift the focus and with it attention to nonrenewable resources—of which the most important to the global economy is oil. Increasingly fast consumption is contributing to declining stocks which, according to some commentators (Becken, 2009), have already passed peak production. Yes, there are alternative fuels but the associated opportunity costs of production bring into question their viability as real alternatives to oil. Meanwhile, oil consumption continues apace and, in combination with consumption of other fossil fuels, is a major factor in arguments supporting climate change. Tourism is a major consumer of such fuels through travel and then through the consumption of products and services at destination localities (Gossling et al., 2007; Kelly et al., 2007; Nepal, 2008). In total this use of fossil fuels has now reached a scale of consumption that would be sufficient to contribute to the alteration of biochemical cycles and to global warming (Daggett et al., 2006). Meanwhile, tourism continues to expand, further encouraged through globalisation.

Globalisation is taken as "The flow of capital across the globe, making available vast array of cultural products in one place; the nation state is no longer the only entity that affects peoples life's" (Waters, 2001: 6). As such, no state today is insulated from the effects of the actions of any other state. In much the same way, so is tourism, a factor which has been recognised for some time (Duval, 2004). Furthermore, it has been argued that "There is no way to stop economic globalization because tourism and travel have already created globalization" (McLaren, 1998: 130). Tourism is thus seen both as a vector in and a beneficiary of globalisation, which, according to Waters, " . . . appears to justify the spread of western culture . . . and are forces operating beyond human control that are transforming the world"

(2001, p. 6). Forces which are at one and the same time both enabling and facilitating people who live in the consumer culture of the comparatively "rich world" to satisfy their needs with a variety of products and services, reflecting their "westernised consumption patterns" (see Aronsson, 2000; Mintel, 2007a). These patterns of consumption demonstrate the shift from a production-based society, a by-product of which is tourism (Leslie, 1999), to one of consumption-based, which has generated extensive debate on the negative environmental effects of the consumer society and how 'westernised' lifestyles have influenced consumption patterns. Thus most pressures on the environment across the globe are seen to be outcomes of industrial and postindustrial societies and the associated lifestyles. Many people are now so accustomed to this lifestyle (or aspire to such lifestyles) they would be unwilling to relinquish this perceived standard of living in order to reduce their carbon footprint (Johns & Leslie, 2008). These demands of consumption are considered as immaterial requirements, in particular international travel (Aronsson, 2000), and exacerbate those factors argued to contribute to climate change. Thus not only is tourism affected by a changing climate but it contributes to climate change by the consumption of fossil fuels and hence the production of greenhouse gas emissions. However, this substantive facet of the global expansion and impacts of tourism has hardly gained significant attention (see Gossling, 2002; Gossling & Hall, 2006; Pleumarom, 2007; and Chapter 2). Global impacts which are fuelled as international tourist travel patterns expand temporally and spatially as costs of travel in both time and monetary terms comparatively decrease.

A review of the development of air travel post-1940s shows continued development and expansion fuelled by seemingly endless growth in leisure-based travel. This has been furthered by airline deregulations (first in the USA and then UK/EU) and the emergence of low-cost airlines, which facilitate consumers to enjoy lifestyles now, including jetting off to choice European cities for "hen" and "stag" parties, that they previously could or would not have done, due to the price and frequency of these services. This growth is largely down due to the success of low-cost airlines, whose dramatic reworking of the traditional airline business model has brought substantial economic and social benefits to consumers with their rock-bottom prices and convenient regional departure points along with a frequency of service never seen before. This has been further fuelled by an increase in foreign travel generated by cheaper air fares and no-frills airlines (Calder & Lynas, 2005), which has been increasing at an annual rate of 5 to 6 per cent (Mintel, 2006); BAA Scotland alone reported an approximately 14 per cent rise in passengers for international flights for February 2008 compared with the same month in 2007. Indeed, statistical evidence from the Civil Aviation Authority shows that the increasing numbers of passengers using UK airports shows no sign of slowing down but rather indicates substantial and continued growth. Technological innovations may well reduce emissions per flight, for example, the Airbus A380, and related initiatives such as those by Virgin Atlantic (2008). Such increased efficiency from developments in aircraft technology and air traffic management will not be sufficient to compensate for the projected growth in the commercial aviation industry (see Schipper, 2004), growth which is fuelling the estimated sixteen thousand commercial jet planes in the world responsible for releasing six hundred tonnes of CO_2 per year (Pleumarom, 2007), currently estimated at approximately 5 per cent of total human-generated greenhouse gas emissions (IPCC, 2007b) and given all the indicators it will continue to be so, especially in comparison with other sectors of the economy (Penner, 2004). Airports are also hardly 'environmentally friendly' (see Mintel, 2006; West, 2008) and continue to develop and expand. Heathrow's Terminal 5 was estimated to involve £3.2 billion on the part of the British Airport Authority and spending of a further £3.4 billion on improvements to existing terminals (Friends of the Earth, 2003). Another important factor to consider is that over 90 per cent of the people who go to and from airports prefer to travel by car; estimates for Heathrow's new terminal 5 alone forecast that there would be over forty-six thousand extra car trips every day across London (Friends of the Earth, 2003). Although aviation accounts for substantially more energy use for international tourists, once at the destination, tourists' energy consumption is similar and still transportation accounts for the main use of energy (Becken et al., 2003). A major factor is car use; for example, in the UK domestic tourists' car use has increased by 3.1 per cent since 2002, which now stands at 74.3 per cent (Mintel, 2007a). The problem with this popularity is the effect cars have upon the environment; as Zervas and Lazarou claim: "The road transport sector is one of the main anthropogenic sources of CO_2 emissions in the European Union" (2008, p. 1).

Overall, greater free time, access to credit, the Internet, and low-cost airlines have all combined to produce today's 'wherever–whenever' consumer society; which is greatly facilitated by tour operators. The key point here is that as 'new' destinations emerge and as they become fashionable, demand increases. Witness Antarctica—once a destination for explorers and scientists but now a fashionable tourist destination receiving thousands of visitors per year (Mintel, 2007b). This is despite limitations on the number of visitors landing at any one time and awareness of Antarctica's delicate nature (Spennemann, 2007). According to the International Association of Antarctic Tour Operators (IAATO), an industry group which aims to set the highest possible tourism operating standards in its effort to protect Antarctica (IAATO, 2008), more than thirty-seven thousand tourists visited the continent in 2006—double the number of five years ago; furthermore "A company that runs Arctic and Antarctic tours is doubling its capacity and opening up new routes" (Shipman, 2007: 2). How is this "responsible" tourism? (Heape, 2007). Global warming has led to these polar regions being seen as under threat, and yet it is exactly this threat that is attracting more tourists to the Antarctic, ironically further promoted by the media (see

Davis, 2007; Shipman, 2007). Other places of the world, comparatively all the more accessible today, have gained sobriquets such as the "Coca-Cola Trails" of the Peruvian Andes or the "Toilet Paper Trails" of Nepal (UNEP, 2002: 3; see also Lachapelle & Freimund, 2003, and Pleumarom, Chapter 2.). Meanwhile, the oceans around popular tourist destinations are becoming the playground of cruise ships which generate substantial air pollution and waste (see Johnson, 2002; Friends of the Earth Norway, 2006), considered to contribute to 77 per cent of all marine pollution (Duval, 2004). Again, there is an organisation seeking to promote responsible practices amongst its members, The International Council of Cruise Lines (ICCL), with a clear policy on waste management and attention to supply chain management, but how effective is it in policing these standards to which its members are expected to adhere?

Overall, over the past quarter century we have witnessed dynamic expansion of tourism around the globe with a continuous increase in tourists using high-carbon-emitting vehicles such as the plane (Kelly et al., 2007). As Schivelbusch stated some twenty years ago and all the more germane today: "For the twentieth century tourist, the world has become one large department store of countrysides and cities" (1986: 197, cited in Urry, 2001). The effects of this were heralded ten years later, e.g., "How long can this process continue within limited space? The ecological impact of this growth can already be clearly seen globally. At present the state of the world is a matter of some concern; at the same time the opportunities for positive action have perhaps never been greater" (Worldwatch Institute, 1996, cited in Aronsson, 2000: 13). The transport sector has and is the main facilitator in this, accounting for a large and growing share of emissions in industrialised countries. This was recognised, rather belatedly given the convention on atmospheric pollution agreed at the Earth Summit of 1992 and subsequently developed via the Kyoto Protocol, at the First International Conference on Climate Change and Tourism at Djerba (UNWTO, 2003). The Conference concluded that there was an urgent need for strategies to be implemented to face changing climate conditions and to take preventative actions for future effects, and also to moderate tourism's environmental impacts contributing to climate change (Pleumarom, 2007; see Chapter 1). Worldwide tourism accounts for 60 per cent of air travel; furthermore, it is concentrated in Europe and the United States of America, which account for 70 to 80 per cent of the world's flights (Mintel, 2007c). Thus, according to Gossling et al. (2007), there is an overwhelming need to reduce tourism's carbon footprint arising not only from the oft cited emissions from transportation systems but also from the enterprises themselves. This need is further reinforced in the Stern Review (Stern, 2006), which concluded that without successful mitigation measures climate change will affect the basic elements of life for people around the world.

However, global issues are becoming more and more publicised, which, according to Mintel (2005), is having some effect on the tourist sector;

which is inescapable (see Chapters 1–3). The rise of attention to the environment and tourism, most notably as a result of "Our Common Inheritance" and the Bruntland Report, accounts for the rise in the development and interest in forms of tourism termed "alternative," "responsible," green," "hard," "soft," and, gaining most attention, "sustainable" and "ecotourism" (see Leslie, 1999). The latter is furthered by the production of the WTTC et al.'s (1996) "Agenda 21 for the Travel and Tourism Industry" and countless articles in the academic press. Before we begin to discuss such developments, it is recognised that tourism can be " . . . an important force for sustainability by raising standards in under-developed areas" (WTTC, 2006, p. 3). Further, that tourism: ' . . . has the potential to bring about substantial environmental and socio-economic improvements. . . . ' and ' . . . make significant contribution to the sustainable development of communities. . . . ' (WTTC et al., 1996: 4). Although this argument is justifiable, it is a self-serving one (e.g., to members of the council) and reflects the view that the goal of sustainable tourism is to choose one or more approaches that foster practical, acceptable, and profitable tourism enterprises while preventing damage to the built and natural environment (Edgell, 2006: 6), which reinforces the view that sustainable tourism is essentially nothing other than best practice applied within the destination locality (Leslie, 2008). This rather skates over the fact that for tourism to be a major contributor to an economy requires substantial demand and as such investment, particularly in the infrastructure, as well as invariably a need for the development of westernised-style accommodation and related products and services (see particularly Chapter 2), all of which come with economic leakages; for example, it was estimated that in Thailand 60 per cent of the £4 billion annual tourism revenue leaves the country, or in the case of the Gambian government all-inclusive hotels were banned in the interests of local communities but then the ban was rescinded shortly afterwards due to external pressure form tourism companies (Tearfund, 2002). Furthermore, there are the opportunity costs which may well outweigh the aforesaid benefits in terms of the host country's people (for wider debate on this, see Wahab & Pigram, 1997; Mowforth & Munt, 2003; Smith & Duffy, 2003; and most recently Pluemarom, Chapter 2). Arguably, the second most cited 'new' form of tourism is "ecotourism" (see Fennell, 2002), acclaimed by many commentators as the fastest growing tourism product, yet it is still a niche market (Robinson & Novelli, 2005: 9). Demand is dominated by persons over fifty-five years of age, comparatively affluent and well read (Mintel, 2007d) and who probably do not act in what could be termed environmentally friendly ways or "behaving responsibly towards destination communities" (see Budeanu, 2007). However, it has been promulgated as a form of "green" tourism (though how arriving at an ecotourism destination via cars and planes is considered so green is a good illustration of myopia). This is seen in a positive light but its green credentials are now being more closely questioned, particularly as its oft-cited popularity rises (see Teh & Cabanban, 2007; Spennemann, 2007). Indeed, participation in ecotourism might not even be a function of environmental concern on the part of consumers (Sharpley, 2005) whilst it is nothing other for suppliers than "big business" (see Wheeller, 1994). Such a critique is not aided by the lack of studies that seek to evaluate ecotourism developments with due consideration to and involvement of the community they are expressly promoted to help. Certainly, ecotourism does provide an incentive for conservation, but it also introduces changes within the communities involved which are both positive and negative, and overall may not necessarily be to their benefit (Stronz & Gordillo, 2008). Furthermore, as Font expressed: "Attempts to promoting sustainable tourism and ecotourism as quality products suffer from the lack of methods to ensure these are not just a green wash" (2002: 197). Also, it is argued that even where there are verified accreditation systems, these tend to be based on the operation at the tourist's destination locality and summative, for example, based on indicators for the three pillars of sustainability when a more integrative and adaptive approach would be both more comprehensive and effective (see Ko, 2005; Cawley and Gillmor 2008); and as illustrated, for example, in the Plimsoll Model (Greenwood et al., 2008). Even so, such forms of tourism, for example, ecotourism, encompassed under the umbrella of sustainable tourism, that have developed over the last twenty years should not be dismissed given that they do seek to promote positive environmental practices (see Chapters 4, 5, and 9).

Tour operators play a leading role in the promotion of these 'green' tourism products, and thus pertinent to this context of tourism enterprises are the actions they may have taken to address their environmental performance. To an extent, such actions have been promulgated by the WTTC and also in response to the market; for example, Goodwin and Francis state: "Responsible tourism is emerging as a significant market trend in the UK as wider consumer market trends towards lifestyle marketing and ethical consumption spread to tourism" (2003: 271) Yet there is little substantive evidence of such a trend (see Holmes et al., 2008). Interestingly, success in such niche markets may be even counterproductive to the continuance of a TO's "green label" promotion (Budeanu, 2005). By and large the actions potentially introduced by TOs are encompassed in the Tour Operators' Initiatives (see www.toinitiative.org), which includes attention to supply chain management (see Font & Carey, 2005). For example, First Choice (2006) has developed, with the Federation of Tour Operators (FTO) and a range of stakeholders, the "Travelife" *Supplier Sustainability Handbook* for accommodation suppliers covering environmental management, employee rights, and local sourcing of products. However, just how much commitment there is to the adoption of the advocated practices is questionable (as noted earlier; also see Cole, 2007, and Chapter 3). As with any business, the primary objective of tour operators is to stay in business (see Chapter 1), which " . . . results in reducing economic and socio-economic benefits for the destinations" (Carey et al., 1997: 429). Thus realisation of the objectives of sustainability is limited (see Budeanu, 2005). As regards the environmental performance of these TOs, there is limited evidence of progress in adoption of either EMS or Corporate Social Responsibility (Tepellus, 2005), the latter advocated by the WTTC and promoted in the TOI as sustainability. This finding further affirms Tearfund's conclusion: "With a few notable exceptions, tourism has been one of the slowest industries to adopt corporate social responsibility practices" (2002: 5). Today, there are more enterprises involved but yet again we find it is the comparatively larger companies which also perform better, compared with other categories of supply, in promoting environmental matters to their customers (Wijk & Persoon, 2006). But such promotion is not without pitfalls; for example, Mintel (2007b) found that many people (64 per cent in their survey) believed that such companies were trying to "greenwash" customers (interestingly, greenwash complaints quadrupled in the UK in 2007 [Greenbiz, 2008]). Even so, Goodwin and Francis (2003) identified that 8 per cent of consumers are influenced by promoting a green image, which is not an insignificant market segment. This market can be further refined through establishing past environmentally friendly behaviour of tourists at destinations and then using such knowledge to target more accurately environmentally friendly tourists (Dolnicar & Leisch, 2007).

Whilst these initiatives are all welcome, they are hardly addressing the fundamental need to reduce fossil fuel consumption. Thus other and more comprehensive measures are necessary, particularly given that seeking to change consumer transportation choices has been on the agenda for some time (see OECD, 2002; Defra, 2005). The world focus has therefore moved to post-Kyoto agreements in an effort to establish binding emission-reduction targets and carbon-trading schemes which economists claim will play a pivotal role in driving change. In effect, this is a shift towards the polluter-pays principle, an approach manifest in the proposed introduction of CO_2 caps and carbon trading for airline operators. This would have the effect of raising costs and hence airfares which, coupled with fuel taxes, is seen by the EU as an effective solution to the problem (Mintel, 2006). The potential impact on demand of putting such a "green" tax on tourist flights would not just be restricted to the UK or EU but across the world. Also, the impact on prices will increase disparities between the "haves" and "have-nots" within any one society and between communities across the globe. Challenges would arise from stakeholders based on the potential competitive disparities amongst and between stakeholders (see Chapter 3). The latter might explain why, despite the aims to cut carbon emissions by 60 per cent by 2050, the UK did not impose a tax on air fuel as a step towards reducing carbon emissions. Aviation, which in 2006 accounted for about 15 per cent of these emissions, has been estimated to account for the entire sustainable carbon quota for the UK agreed by the Kyoto protocol (Calder & Lynas, 2005), instead choosing to increase charges for airport duty, green taxes, and the formation of carbon-offsetting schemes (Mintel, 2007d). In effect, a tax on users when what could be more effective in influencing consumer choice is to introduce a reward system for nonusers, thus creating a reverse green tax (Hanlon, 2006; Darling, 2008). Alternatively, users could purchase "carbon credits" through programmes such as Co2Balance and Target Neutral and Climate, the revenues gained funding environment projects. However, despite the benefits voiced by champions of carbon-offsetting schemes, Mintel's (2008) study suggests that such schemes at best will account for but a small reduction in emissions. Their report also stated that even then assessing their effectiveness is problematic; as such, these schemes are seen as little more than a facade in terms of carbon-emission-reducing behaviour for political and commercial agendas, a view which is supported by the little attention given in the travel/holiday press to CO_2 emissions (Johns & Leslie, 2008). Furthermore, questions arise over actual use of revenues; for example, and albeit perhaps overstating the situation, the UK government raised approximately £24.2 billion from "green taxes" in 2007–2008, and the estimated figure for what was actually needed was £4.6 billion (Kirkup, 2008). More basically: "Emissions could be reduced the old-fashioned way by flying less, turning off the air-conditioning or buying a more fuel-efficient car. But that would probably require some sacrifice and perhaps even a change in lifestyle. Instead, carbon-offset programs allow individuals to skip the sacrifice and simply pay for the right to pollute" (DePalma, 2006). This rather echoes Cater and Lowman of over ten years ago, who found that even if tourists are aware they " . . . may rationalise that we have paid and they have taken our money, so we are entitled to enjoy our holidays as we wish" (1994: 32).

Consumers may be becoming more aware of environmental issues that surround their chosen destination, but there is little evidence that this is changing their touristic behaviour (Dolnicar & Leisch, 2007; also see Mintel, 2007b, 2007d; Defra, 2007; Johns & Leslie, 2008); albeit surveys regularly find respondents indicating a willingness to pay more if such additional costs were to go towards supporting environmental initiatives (Goodwin & Francis, 2003). Certainly awareness may be increasing and there are consumers who express they are prepared to adapt; more likely the older generation than those persons under 25 years of age whilst families are less likely given they place more significance on safety and concern for their children (Mintel, 2007e). But indicators of 'willingness' all too often do not translate into responsive action, described as cognitive dissonance theory (Festinger, 1957) whereby individuals do not always behave in accordance with their professed aspirations. For example, consumers may show interest in green holidays but this is not reflected in demand (Manaktola & Jauhari, 2007). Furthermore, Holmes et al. (2008) found that environmental awareness and concern tend to revolve around the home at best and rarely translate into actions in leisure-based behaviour outwith the home environment, which is further supported by the unwillingness on the part of consumers to change to less energy-consuming modes of transport. This is reinforced in the view that tourism demand is based on "irrational factors" (Kamp, 2003: 1)—associated with fashion trends, relaxation, and escapism; people do not want to think about the effects that their trip has caused to the environment. Indeed, Edgell reported a study that found that 75 per cent of American travellers " . . . feel that their visits do not damage the environment" (2006: 7). More recently, surveys have found that few participants would change their holiday plans based on ethical and environmental issues (Mintel, 2007b). Add to this the increase by 22 per cent of those flying due to the availability of low-cost airlines and it can be seen that financial and logistical factors are more important (Mintel, 2007c, 2008; Johns & Leslie, 2008). All of which evidence little change to earlier studies (see Salem, 1995; Bhate, 2001; Leslie, 2001; Font & Tribe, 2001).

Clearly, consumerism is being brought into focus as the clamour to address global warming increases and hence the emphasis on energy production and consumption and ways to reduce this through international protocols such as the Kyoto Agreement. In combination with other policy initiatives, this has catalysed national policies and initiatives designed to promote the three Rs—reduce, reuse, recycle. In this process the consumer is becoming the centre of attention with the accent on behaviour in terms of energy consumption. Consumers are being encouraged, through varied means, to adjust their behaviour and adopt more environmentally friendly practices; to 'go green.' an approach which evidences signs of success in some areas of consumer behaviour but hardly in tourism (see Holmes et al., 2008). At the same time, destinations are encouraged to address tourism's impact on the environment and suppliers of tourism products and services to address their environment behaviour and introduce environmentally friendly management practices (as the following chapters all attest).

Given such exhortations, which are not as recent as some commentators appear to think in terms of tourism's impact on destinations and the comparatively more recent attention to tourism enterprises, the question arises what progress has and is being made across the globe. This is addressed in the following chapters. The broader context, and providing an overarching background, is developed well by Hall and Gossling (Chapter 1). They present a comprehensive, and insightful, analysis of the relationships between tourism and global environmental change, in the process developing key themes of this text. Subsequently, and drawing extensively on their research, they discuss the responses of tourism enterprises to these themes which are manifestly supported by the following chapters. Undercurrents of the globalisation of tourism and the quest for the "tourist dollar" are explored by Pleumarom (Chapter 2). In contrasting and lively style, she substantially develops other thematic issues of this text, noted earlier, particularly the global expansion of tourism and questioning whether the tourism sector per se has progressed in terms of sustainability. In the process, a critical analysis of how tourism is developing in Asian regions through a range of substantive examples is presented. Buckley (Chapter 3) then narrows the scope of enquiry by way of discussing the links between tourism enterprises and sustainable development, thus establishing a more focused context within which the subsequent chapters may be considered, especially those well focused on tourism enterprises and their environmental performance in very different tourist destination countries. But, as noted in the preface, research specifically on this is limited and/or in terms of a specific country would not necessarily be representative. As such, the chapters by Bicker (Chapter 4) and Lara (Chapter 5) are invaluable in contributing to the breadth of this text, whilst serving to exemplify further that there are substantive differences, yet similarities, in the responses of governments to the environmental agenda and tourism development. Additionally, there is the chapter by Warnken and Guilding, which, although a singular case study, brings to attention another substantive influence on the environmental performance of tourism enterprises, namely that of the context of the development and ownership within which enterprises operate.

In combination, these chapters identify a plethora of issues, responses, and reactions to the environmental agenda in the context of tourism development and, more specifically, tourism enterprises. The scope ranges from the politics of global warming to the purchase of local goods. Whilst we can not possibly do full justice to any of these factors within these pages, we trust we have highlighted them sufficiently to engage your attention and stimulate thought and further debate. To achieve such an outcome would make all the contributions herein worthwhile.

REFERENCES

Aronsson, L., 2000. *The development of sustainable tourism*. London: Continuum.

Becken, S., 2009. Developing indicators for managing tourism in the face of peak oil. *Tourism Management*, 29(4), p.695–705.

Becken, S., Simmons, D.G. & Frampton, C., 2003. Energy use associated with different travel uses. *Tourism Management*, 24, p.267–77.

Bhate, S., 2001. One world, one environment, one vision: are we close to achieving this? An exploratory study of consumer environmental behaviour across three countries. *Journal of Consumer Behaviour*(2), p.169–84.

Booker, C., 2008. "The 'consensus' on climate change is a catastrophe in itself. *The Sunday Telegraph*, 31 August p.25.

Booker, C. & North, R., 2007. *Scared to death: from BSE to Global Warming: why scares are costing us the Earth*. London: Continuum.

Budeanu, A., 2005. Impacts and responses for sustainable tourism—a tour operator's perspective. *Journal of Cleaner Production*, 13, p.89/97.

Budeanu, A., 2007. Sustainable tourist behaviour û a discussion of opportunities for change. *International Journal of Consumer Studies*, 31(5), p.499-508.

Calder, S. & Lynas, M., 2005. Feel good travel: cheap flights: a force for good? Or a threat to the planet? *The Independent on Sunday*, 19 June p.2.

Carey, S., Gountas, Y. & Gilbert, D., 1997. Tour operators and destination sustainability. *Tourism Management*, 18(7), p.425–31.

Cater, E. & Lowman, G., 1994. *Ecotourism*. Chichester, John Wiley & Sons Ltd.

Cawley, M. & Gillmor, D.A., 2008. Integrated rural tourism: concepts and practices. *Annals of Tourism Research*, 35(2), p.316–37.

Cole, S., 2007. Implementing and evaluating a code of conduct for visitors. *Tourism Management*, 28(2), p.443–51.

Dagget, D., Hadaller, O., Hendricks, R. & Walther, R., 2006. NASA: alternative fuels for aviation. *Energy Bulletin*, NASA, 3 December.

Darling, A., 2008. *Budget 2008: report*. London: HM Treasury. Available at: www.hm-treasury.gov.uk/budget2008 [accessed 18 March 2008].

Davis, T.H., 2007. *Tourism threatens Antarctica*. Available at: http://travel.timesonline.co.uk/tol/life_and_style/travel/holiday_type/cruises/ [accessed 19 March 2008].

Defra, 2005. 'Green holidaymaking.' Press release. London: Department for Environment, Food and Rural Affairs. July 25.

Defra, 2007. *Survey of public attitudes and behaviours toward the environment*. London: Department for Environment, Food and Rural Affairs. August.

DePalma, A., 2006. Gas guzzlers find price of forgiveness. *New York Times*. Available at: http://www.nytimes.com/2006/04/22/nyregion/22guilt.html? [accessed 16 March 2008].

Dolnicar, S. & Leisch, F., 2007. Selective marketing for environmentally sustainable tourism. *Tourism Management*, 27(1), p.1–9.

Duval, T., 2004. *Tourism in the Caribbean; trends, development, prospects*. London: Routledge.

Edgell, D.L., 2006. *Managing sustainable tourism—a legacy for the future*. Binghampton: Haworth.

Fennell, D.A., 2002. *Ecotourism programme planning*. Oxon: CABI.

Festinger, L., 1957. *A theory of cognitive dissonance*. New York: Row Perterson & Company.

First Choice, 2006. *Environment and people report*. Available at: http://www.fcenvironmentandpeople.com/fcenviro/environment/aviation.html [accessed 20 March 2008].

Font, X., 2002. Environmental certification in tourism and hospitality: progress, process and prospects. *Tourism Management*, 23, p.197–205.

Font, X & Carey, B., 2005. *Marketing sustainable tourism products*. Nairobi: United Nations Environment Programme and Regione Toscana.

Font, X. & Tribe, J., 2001. Promoting green tourism: the future of environmental awards. *International Journal of Tourism Research*, 3. p.9–21.

Friends of the Earth, 2003. *Briefing UK plc*: British Airports Authority, July. Available at: http://www.foe.co.uk/resource/briefings/ [accessed 18 March 2008].

Friends of the Earth Norway, 2006. *Green groups call for cleaner ships and engines*, 15 November. Available at: http://www.naturvern.no/cgi-bin/naturvern/imaker? [accessed 19 March 2008].

Futerra, 2006. *Climate fear v climate hope; are the UK's national newspapers helping tackle climate change?* http://www.futerracom.org/downloads/Climate_Fear_v_Climate_Hope_Sundays_and_Dailys [accessed 12 November 2007].

Goodwin, H. & Francis, J., 2003. Ethical and responsible tourism: consumer trends in UK. *Journal of Vacation Marketing*, 9(3), p.271–84.

Gore, A., 2006. *An inconvenient truth*. London: Bloomsbury.

Gossling, S., 2002. Global environmental consequences of tourism *Global Environmental Change*, 12(4), p.283–302.

Gossling, S. & Hall, C.M. eds., 2006. *Tourism & Global Environmental Change—ecological, social, economic and political interrelationships.* Abingdon: Routledge.

Gossling, S., Broderick, J., Upham, P., Ceron, J-P., Dubois, G., Peeters, P., and Strasdas, W., 2007. Voluntary carbon offsetting schemes for aviation: efficiency, credibility and sustainable tourism. *Journal of Sustainable Tourism,* 15(3), 223–48.

Greenbiz, 2008. U.K. Greenwash compaints quadrupled in 2007. Available at: http://greenbiz.com.news [accessed 5 September 2008].

Greenwood, J., Brothers, G. & Henderson, K., 2008. Don't sink the boat! The Plimsoll model of tourism sustainability. In D. Leslie, guest ed., Leisure, consumerism and sustainable development: "Mission Impossible." *Leisure Studies Newsletter,* 80, p.31–34.

Hanlon, M., 2006. *Green tax will hurt only the poor. This is money.* Available at: http://www.thisismoney.co.uk/news/article.html?in_article_id=414225&in_page_id=2 [accessed 15 March 2008].

Heape, R., 2007. Responsible tourism: is tourism development to Antarctica responsible? *The Tourism Society Journal,* 4(134), p.18.

Holmes, K., Miller, G., Scarles, S. & Tribe, J., 2008. "I just don't think about it." Public attitudes towards sustainable leisure. In D. Leslie, Guest ed., Leisure, consumerism and sustainable development: "Mission Impossible." *Leisure Studies Newsletter,* 80, p.27–31.

IAATO, 2008. *About IAATO.International Association of Antarctica Tour Operators.* Available at: http://www.iaato.org/about.html [accessed 19 March 2008].

IPCC, 2007a. Summary for policymakers. In: "Climate change 2007: the physical science basis" *contribution of Working Group I to the Fourth Assessment Report of the Intergovernmental Panel on Climate Change* [S. Solomon et al. eds.]. Cambridge and New York: Cambridge University Press [online]. Available at: http://www.ipcc.ch/pdf/assessment-report/ [accessed 18 November 2007].

IPCC, 2007b. *About IPCC* [online]. Available at: http://www.ipcc.ch/about/index.htm [accessed 28 November 2007].

Johns, C. & Leslie, D., 2008. Leisure consumers of air miles—the unlikelihood of change. In D. Leslie, guest ed,m Leisure, consumerism and sustainable development: "Mission Impossible." *Leisure Studies Newsletter,* 80, p.35–38.

Johnson, D., 2002. Environmentally sustainable cruise tourism: a reality check. *Marine Policy Studies,* 26, p.261-70.

Kamp, C., 2003. *Influencing consumer behaviour to promote sustainable tourism development.* Available at: http://csdngo.igc.org/tourism/tourdial_cons.htm [accessed 4 March 2008].

Kelly, J., Haider, W. & Williams, P., 2007. A behavioral assessment of tourism transportation options for reducing energy consumption and greenhouse gasses. *Journal of Travel Research,* 45, p.297–310.

Kirkup, J., 2008. Green taxes cost families £800 a year more than necessary. *The Daily Telegraph,* 28 August p.4.

Ko, T.G., 2005. Development of a tourism sustainability assessment procedure: a conceptual approach. *Tourism Management,* 26(3), p.431–45.

Lachapelle, P. & Freimund, W., 2003. Commercial use of Mt. Everest—Sagarmatha National Park, Khumbu, Nepal: How much and who decides? *Studies in protected area management,* Case 2. University of Montana Wildness Institute.

Leslie, D., 1999. 'Sustainable Tourism'—or more a matter of sustainable societies? In M. Foley, D. McGillivray & G. McPherson eds., *Leisure, tourism and environment: sustainability and environmental policies.* Brighton: Leisure Studies Association, P.173–93.

Leslie, D., 2001. *An environmental audit of the tourism industry in the Lake District National Park.* Report for Friends of the Lake District/Council for the Protection of Rural England, Murley Moss, Kendal.

Leslie, D., 2008. Managing sustainable tourism—a legacy for the future by Edgell, D.G. *Tourism Management.* 29 (3), p. 665–66

Lomberg, B., 2001. *The skeptical environmentalist—measuring the real state of the world.* Cambridge: Cambridge University Press.

McLaren, D., 1998. *Rethinking Tourism and ecotravel: The Paving of Paradise and What You can do to Stop it.* Connecticut, Kurarian Press.

Mintel, 2005. *Ethical Holidays.* October htt[://acaemicmintel.com/sinatra/mintel accessed 3 March, 2008.

Mintel, 2006. *International tourism forecasts.* Available at: http://academic.mintel.com.

Mintel, 2007a. *British on Holiday at Home.* Mintel Country Reports. Available at: http://academic.mintel.com. Accessed 18 March, 2008.

Mintel, 2007b. *Holiday lifestyles—responsible tourism.* Available at: http://academic.mintel.com. Accessed 3 March, 2008.

Mintel, 2007c. *Ecoaccommodation.* November. Mintel Country Reports. Available at: http://academic.mintel.com.

Mintel, 2007d. *Green and ethical consumers—UK.* Available at: http://academic.mintel.com. Accessed 15 March 2008.

Mintel, 2008. *Sustainable tourism practices—UK.* Available at: http://academic.mintel.com. Accesed 15 March, 2008.

Mowforth, M. & Munt, I., 2003. *Tourism and sustainability—development and new tourism in the third world.* 2nd ed. Oxon: Routledge.

Nepal, S.K., 2008. Tourism-induced rural energy consumption in the Annapura region of Nepal. *Tourism Management,* 29, p.89–100.

OECD, 2002. *Household tourism travel: trends, environmental impacts and policy responses.* Environment Directorate. Paris: Organisation for Economic Co-operation and Development, April.

Penner, J.E., 2004. IPCC special report on aviation and the global atmosphere in southern Pulau Banggi: An assessment of biophysical conditions and their implications for future tourism development. *Journal Environmental Management,* 85. p.999–1008.

Pleumarom, A., 2007. Tourism feels the heat of global warming. *Tourism Investigation & Monitoring Team,* Banghok October.

Robinson, M. & Novelli, M., 2005. *Niche tourism: an introduction. Niche tourism contemporary issues trends and cases.* London: Elsevier.

Salem, N., 1995. Water rights. *Tourism in Focus,* 17, p.4–5.

Sharpley, R., 2005. *Tourism, tourists and society.* 3rd ed. Cambridgeshire: Elm Publications.

Schipper, Y., 2004. Environmental costs in European aviation. *Transport Policy,* 11, p.141–54.

Shipman, T. 2007. Nature's 'doom' is tourist boom. *The Daily Telegraph,* 23 December p.8.

Smith, M. & Duffy, R., 2003. *The ethics of tourism development.* Oxon: Routledge.

Spennemann, D., 2007. Extreme cultural tourism from Antarctica to the Moon. *Annals of Tourism Research,* 34, p.898-918.

Spiegelman, A., 2008. *Shock jock named king of politically incorrect.* Reuters. Available at: http://ca.reuters.com/article/entertainmentNews [accessed 20 March 2008].

Stern, N., 2006. *Stern review on the economics of climate change.* Cambridge: Cambridge University Press.

Stronz, A. & Gordillo, J., 2008. Community views of ecotourism. *Annals of Tourism Research*, 35(2), p.448–68.

Tearfund, 2002. *Worlds Apart: A call to responsible global tourism*. London: Tearfund.

Teh, L. & Cabanban, A., 2007. Planning for sustainable tourism in southern Pulau Banggi: an assessment of biophysical conditions and their implications for future tourism development. *Journal of Environmental Management*, 85, p.999–1008.

Tepelus, C.M., 2005. Aiming for sustainability in the tour operating business. *Journal of Cleaner Production*, 13, p.99–107.

UNEP, 2002. *Industry as a partner for sustainable development*. Paris: United Nations Environment Programme.

United Nations World Tourism Organisation (UNWTO), 2003. *Djerba Declaration* [online]. Available at: http://www.unwto.org/climate/index.php?=0 [accessed 18 March 2008].

Urry, J., 2001. Transports of delight. *Leisure Studies*, 20, p.237–45.

Virgin Atlantic, 2008. *Just the flight. Virgin Atlantic's green strategy under siege*. Available at:__www.news.cheapflights.co.uk/flights/2006/03/virgin_atlantic. html [accessed 18 March 2008].

Wahab, S. & Pigram, J.J., 1997. *Tourism, development and growth*. Oxon: Routledge.

Waters, M., 2001. *Globalization*. 2nd ed. New York: Routledge.

West, L., 2008. *What are the health effects of airport noise and airport pollution?* [online]. Available at: http://environment.about.com/od/pollution/a/airport_ noise.htm_[accessed 19 March 2008].

Wheeller, B., 1994. Ecotourism: a ruse by any other name. In C.P. Copper & A. Lockwood, eds. *Progress in tourism, recreation and hospitality management*. Vol. 6. Chichester: John Wiley, p.3–11.

Wijk, J. van & Persoon, W., 2006. A long haul destination: sustainability reporting among tour operators. *European Management Journal*, 24(6), p.381–95.

WTTC, WTO and Earth Council, 1996. *Agenda 21 for the travel and tourism industry: towards environmentally sustainable development*. Oxford: World Travel and Tourism Council, WTO and Earth Council Report.

WTTC, 2006. *Corporate social responsibility in the tourism sector*. Oxford: World Travel Tourism Council.

Zervas, E. & Lazarou, C., 2008. Influence of European passenger cars weight to exhaust CO_2 emissions. Energy Policy, 36, p.248–57.

1 Global Environmental Change and Tourism Enterprise

C. Michael Hall and Stefan Gössling

Global environmental change is one of the major challenges facing business in the twenty-first century. Whether it be how they adapt to such change or whether they can conduct business at all. There is hardly a day that goes by when the media do not cover an element of environmental change in their news coverage, whether it be stories surrounding climate change, the increasing costs of fuel, or concern over food security. Tourism, and tourism enterprises, are deeply embedded in change issues both in terms of the contribution that tourism makes to global environmental change and the effects of such changes on tourism and tourism firms.

This chapter seeks to detail some of the relationships between tourism and global environmental change and the implications that this has for tourism enterprises and sustainable development. The chapter addresses a number of issues. First, it outlines some of the dimensions for global environmental change and their relationship to tourism. Second, it provides a framework for examining the relationships between sustainability and tourism enterprises and the research themes that they provide. Third, it then goes on to investigate some of these major themes with respect to empirical analysis drawn from several jurisdictions on what tourism enterprises are actually engaged in with respect to responses to global environmental change. The chapter concludes by stressing that the range of responses of tourism enterprises to global environmental change mirrors the present range of government actions with respect to environmental change in that they are highly variable and often reflect concerns over short-term economic disadvantage and competitiveness.

GLOBAL ENVIRONMENTAL CHANGE AND TOURISM

Although climate change is often a focal point for contemporary environmental concern, including within the tourism industry, it is important to realize that climate change is only one albeit highly significant dimension of global environmental change (Gössling, 2002; Gössling & Hall, 2006a, b). Human impacts on the environment can be described as global in two ways. First, 'global refers to the spatial scale or functioning of a system' (Turner et al., 1990: 15). For example, the climate and the oceans have the characteristic of a global system and both influence and are influenced by the tourism production and consumption that take place anywhere within that system. A second kind of global environmental change exists if a change 'occurs on a worldwide scale, or represents a significant fraction of the total environmental phenomenon or global resource' (Turner et al., 1990: 15–16). Therefore, global environmental change refers to such issues as modifications of global biogeochemical cycles, land alterations, changes in climate, loss of nonrenewable resources, unsustainable uses of renewable resources, species extinctions, and reductions in biodiversity. The environment, whether at a global or a local level, is always changing. However, much of this change occurs so slowly that it has been imperceptible to the human eye. Yet all of these changes have intensified as the size and rate of growth of the world's population, and its accompanying mobility and resource use, have continued to expand, although not uniformly, across time and space (Hall & Lew, 2009). Because tourism and travel-related activities reach almost every corner of the globe and are an important part of the economies of many countries, they are significant for both types of change (Gössling & Hall, 2006a, b).

Although many of the environmental impacts of tourism have long been recognized (e.g., Mathieson & Wall, 1982), there have been few attempts to quantify tourism's contribution to environmental change beyond more than the most local of scales. Gössling (2002) provided the first attempt to overview the global environmental consequences of tourism with respect to five major aspects of the leisure-related alteration of the environment: (1) the change of land cover and land use, (2) the use of energy and its associated impacts, (3) the exchange of biota over geographical barriers and the extinction of wild species, (4) the exchange and dispersion of diseases, and (5) a psychological consequence of travel, including changes in the perception and the understanding of the environment brought about by travel. Of these, the latter is not usually included in assessment of the impacts of tourism on the physical environment (Hall & Lew 2009). Gössling developed various relatively conservative estimates for these factors, some of which are included in Table 1.1, along with estimates of the number of tourists worldwide, and hence their resource use and more recent examinations of tourism's contribution.

As Table 1.1 suggests, the amount of tourism's contribution to global environmental change is difficult to assess and, given the potential political and economic implications of such assessments, can also be highly contentious. For example, in the case of climate change and tourism it is estimated that CO_2 emissions from tourism have grown steadily since the mid-1960s as a result of increased mobility to its 2005 level of 5.0 per cent of all anthropogenic emissions of CO_2 (UNWTO [World Tourism Association] et al., 2008). Although organizations such as IATA (International Air Transport

Table 1.1   Tourism's Contribution to Global Environmental Change

Dimension	2001 estimate	2007 estimate
Number of international tourist arrivals	682,000,000[1]	898,000,000[1]
Number of domestic tourist arrivals	3,580.5[2]	4,714.5[2]
Total number of tourist arrivals	4,262.5[2]	5,612.5[2]
Change of land cover— alteration of biologically productive lands	0.5% contribution[3]	0.66% contribution[4]
Energy consumption	14,080 PJ[3]	18,585.6 PJ[4]
Emissions	1,400 Mt of CO_2-e[3]	1,848 Mt of CO_2-e[4] (1461.6 Mt of CO_2)[5]
Biotic exchange	Difficult to assess[3]	Difficult to assess; however, rate of exchange is increasing[6]
Extinction of wild species	Difficult to assess[3]	Difficult to assess, particularly because of time between initial tourism effects and extinction events as well as differentiation between point and non-point tourism impacts but rate of extinction is increasing[6]
Health	Difficult to assess[3]	Difficult to assess in host populations, but sickness in tourists may be up to 50% in developed countries and 90% in developing. Approximately 8% of travelers to the developing world require medical care during or after travel[7]

Sources: 1. UNWTO figures; 2. Hall and Lew (2009) estimates based on UNWTO data; 3. Gössling (2002) estimate; 4. Hall and Lew (2009) estimates based on Gössling (2002); 5. UNWTO, UNEP and WMO (2007, 2008) data for 2005 extrapolated to 2007 by Hall and Lew (2009); 6. Cliff and Haggett (2004); Hall (2006a, 2006b); Ricciardi (2007); Hall and Lew (2009); 7. Cartwright and Chahed (1997). Ericsson (2003); Steffen et al. (2003); Bowman et al. (2004); Freedman et al. (2006); Hill 2006; also see WHO (2008).

Association) talk positively of their environmental record (e.g., IATA 2008), it is the transport sector that contributes most greenhouse gas (GHG) emissions. It is estimated that transport generates 75 per cent of tourism-related CO_2 emissions, followed by accommodation (2 per cent) and activities (3 per cent). Significantly, a small number of energy-intense trips is responsible for the majority of emissions, i.e., the 17 per cent of air-based trips cause about 40 per cent of all tourism-related CO_2 emissions. Long-haul travel between the five world regions that the UNWTO use for statistical aggregation purposes (Africa, Americas, Asia-Pacific, Europe, and the Middle East) accounts for only 2.7 per cent of all tourist trips, but contributes 17 per cent to global tourist emissions. In contrast, trips by rail and bus/coach account for about 34 per cent of all tourist journeys, but only 13 per cent of all CO_2 emissions. However, in terms of the relative contribution of radiative forcing to climate change, the share of transport is significantly larger and ranges from 82 per cent to 90 per cent, with air transport alone accounting for between 54 per cent and 75 per cent of the total (UNWTO et al., 2008) (This also potentially brings the estimates of emissions much closer to that extrapolated from Gössling [2002] by Hall and Lew [2009]). IATA (2008) argue that aviation accounts for 2 per cent of total anthropocentric CO_2 emissions, and that this could reach 3 per cent by 2050. When factoring in all greenhouse gas emissions, they state that aviation accounts for 3 per cent of the total man-made contribution to climate change and that this could reach 5 per cent by 2050. However, this figure is underestimated as it depends partly on dated research (IPCC, 1999).

The range of potential emissions is important as it highlights the way in which estimates can be used to justify environmental policy positions (Gössling et al., 2009), particularly as industry groups, such as IATA or the World Travel and Tourism Council, tend to use the lower range estimates in commenting on their emissions. For example, the implications of emissions estimates for the development of mitigation strategies are substantial as individual trips can cause emissions with up to a factor difference of 1,000: from close to zero for a holiday by bicycle and tent to more than 10 tons of CO_2 for a return journey to Antarctica from Europe (UNWTO et al., 2008).

Nevertheless, although greenhouse gas emissions and climate change are a major focal point for contemporary concerns with respect to tourism and sustainable development, they are only one dimension of environmental change and may also be related to other aspects of change through the creation of positive and negative feedback relationships (Hall, 2008a; Gössling et al., 2009). For example, tourism-related urbanization in some resort areas can create heat islands that can exacerbate the effects of warmer temperatures as a result of climate change. These in turn can then create further pressure on increasingly scarce water supplies while the process of tourism urbanization can also affect biodiversity and ecosystems that may also help make locations more resilient to sea-level rises and warming effects (Hall, 2006b, c). Such resources pressures can obviously be significant for the business sustainability of tourism enterprises, although the effects of global environmental change are not just resource related but are also closely connected to the regulatory regimes that may be put in place at various scales of governance to combat environmental change (see UNEP [United Nations Environment Programme], UNWTO, & WMO [World Meteorological Organization], 2008). A framework to describe such issues is provided in the next section.

CONNECTING SUSTAINABILITY AND TOURISM ENTERPRISE

Although only mentioned in passing in the landmark World Commission on Environment and Development (1987) report (better known as the Brundtland Report), tourism, like many sectors, has eagerly embraced the concept of sustainable development, although its application and interpretation remain a source of significant dispute (e.g., see Hall & Lew, 1998; Williams & Montanari, 1999; Ceron & Dubois, 2003; Hall, 2008; Gössling et al., 2009). The concern over tourism's environmental impacts clearly predates the rise of the concept of sustainable development, but the positioning of sustainability on the policy agenda is significant as it highlights a shift from local and sometime national concerns with respect to the environment to a global concern. Clearly such shifts also relate to changes in understanding of environmental change, but the key point is that environmental policymaking and regulation began to take on a global flavour, for example, through international agreements on biodiversity, ozone, climate, marine environments (Hall, 2008a), while increasingly consumers have also become interested in environmental issues both in and outside their own country (e.g., Anderson, 1996; Barkin & Shambaugh, 1999; Goodwin & Francis, 2003). Such changes have meant that the business environment in which tourism enterprises operate has expanded substantially in scope and has become multi-scaled as they have become affected by governance in scales ranging from the local to the international as well as being potentially affected by the perception of destination areas by consumers that reside in other political jurisdictions as well as other cultures (Coles & Hall, 2008a; Hall & Coles, 2008).

The range of shifts in the business environments of tourism enterprises as a result of sustainability issues since the early 1980s is also reflected in the various approaches and themes that emerged in studying sustainable development in both the tourism and general business literature (e.g., Welford, 1992; Hart, 1997; Hawken et al., 1999; Russo, 2003; Dean & McMullen, 2007). Figure 1.1 indicates a number of these business elements in terms of demand and supply with respect to sustainability and enterprise. Importantly, the figure stresses the way in which sustainable consumer behaviour and demand and sustainable production are conceptually intertwined, and in the case of tourism services are co-created and produced with consumption and production exchanges providing an ongoing basis for positive and negative feedback through the business system (Hall, 2008a).

However, such a model, while useful for identifying some of the contributing dimensions of sustainable tourism enterprises, fails to provide a dynamic visualization of change over time with respect to the adoption of sustainable practices by firms and organizations as well as changed consumer behaviour. Figure 1.2 therefore provides an alternative presentation of some of the key research themes in sustainability and enterprise by framing the adoption of sustainable behaviours and practices within the lens of

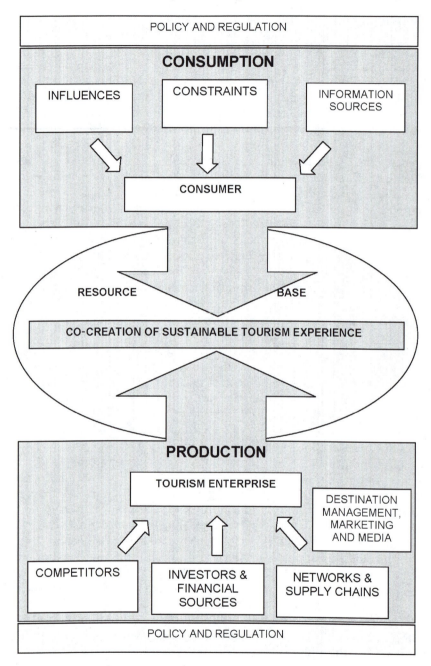

Figure 1.1   Sustainability and enterprise (Hall, 2008b).

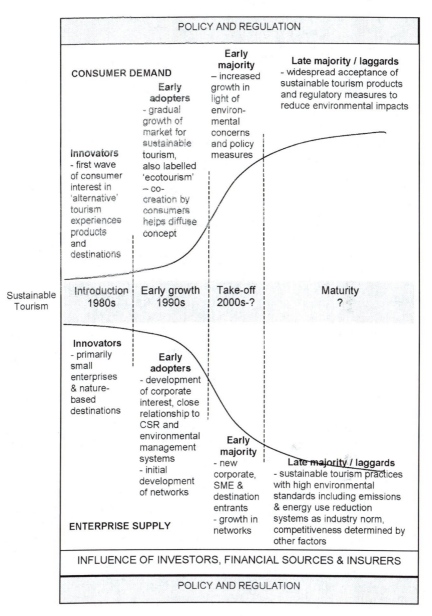

Figure 1.2 Innovation and diffusion of sustainable tourism behaviours and practices (Hall, 2008b).

innovation (Gössling et al., 2009; Hall, 2009). The diffusion of innovation concept (Hägerstrand, 1967; Rogers, 2003) is used as a means to represent the significance of sustainable tourism adoption processes in both consumers and producers of the tourism experience, including enterprises. Public policymaking and regulation is also regarded as a significant factor in innovation and adoption, while for enterprises, financial, investment, and insurance sources are also extremely important because concern over the environmental sustainability of an enterprise is becoming an increasingly important decision for financial institutions (Mills, 2005). Institutional concerns over the financial viability of tourism developments is already a factor in investment and insurance decisions in areas regarded at risk from climate change (Agrawala, 2007). Therefore, this becomes a significant constraint on tourism enterprise decision making.

The attitudes, behaviours, and perceptions of consumers with respect to various dimensions of sustainable tourism and the environment are already a well-established research tradition within tourism studies and will not be discussed any further here.

However, the organisational dimension of sustainability, particularly at the level of the tourism firm, has received substantially less coverage than either consumers or destination-level analyses. For example, Hall (2009) argues that the lack of a well-developed model of tourism firms and the various points of value creation that exist within them have substantially limited the development of sustainable tourism innovations and adoption. Indeed, broader issues of sustainable innovation in tourism have also received only limited coverage in the tourism literature (see Hjalager, 1996, 1997 as significant exceptions).

Such a situation is quite remarkable when considering the extent to which tourist firms in general can be understood as adapting to their business environment and perhaps even more so given the emphasis in studies of sustainable tourism towards mitigation and adaptation of undesirable aspects of tourism development (e.g., Gössling & Hall, 2006a; UNEP, UNWTO, & WMO, 2008). Although, arguably, the notion of adaptation has only come into popular usage in the tourism sphere following recognition of tourism's role in climate change and the subsequent importation of the discourse of climate change studies into tourism (see Gössling et al., 2009). Nevertheless, it should also be noted that there has also been relatively little interplay between the innovation literature and the climate change literature (Hall, 2009). Primarily this can be regarded as a result of climate change research historically focussing on more system-wide adaptations to climate change, as in economic and natural systems, rather than individual firm response, whereas innovation studies have historically focussed on the firm, although more recently there has been much greater attention given to the integration of firms in systems, including tourism systems (Hall & Williams, 2008; Hjalager et al., 2008).

In discussing the relationships between organizations and the systems within which they are located in the context of sustainable tourism, Hall (2009) has argued that, in some situations, firms may be intrinsically unable to develop sustainable business practices because of the way in which they are designed to function within specific cultural-economic systems that do not economically value the long-run nature of sustainable business. This is because with many national economic systems and associated models of management the maximization of shareholder value has emerged as the dominant goal and metric of corporate performance. In such situations shareholder value is operationalised in terms of future cash flows and return on investment within relatively short timespans, whereas sustainability tends to be focused over the longer term. Neoconservative and neoliberal economists justify this lack of attention to social issues by arguing that social welfare is maximized when organizations exclusively pursue profits (e.g., Friedman, 1970). As a result, many management theorists argue that, in order to maximise social welfare via the pursuit of profits, firms must focus on shareholder wealth creation as a single objective function (e.g., Jensen, 2002; Sundaram & Inkpen, 2004). In fact, in many jurisdictions corporations may legally have little choice but to follow such an agenda (Bakan, 2004). For example, writing primarily in the North American context, Bakan (2004: 1–2) commented, 'The corporation's legally defined mandate is to pursue, relentlessly and without exception, its own self-interest, regardless of the often harmful consequences it might cause to others.' Such a perspective stands in contrast to much of the way in which sustainable tourism and sustainable development in general is understood, given its emphasis on equity, collaboration, and understanding the business environment in terms of a more general concept of stakeholders rather than shareholders (e.g., Weaver, 2006; Gössling et al., 2009). However, Hall (2009) argues that the differences between definitions of corporate and public interest provide explanations for the substantial gap that exists between sustainable tourism theory and practice, at least from the perspective of commercial organizations, and the limited progress that has been made with self-regulatory and market-driven approaches towards sustainable business development in the tourism industry.

A major difficulty in assessing the extent to which tourism enterprises have become more sustainable, especially with respect to adaptation and mitigation of global environmental change, is that while there has been a growth in the literature on sustainable tourism, and seemingly endless clichés with respect to 'ecotourism as the fastest growing area of tourism' (along with all the other fastest growing areas!), there is no accurate baseline data with respect to measures of sustainable tourism business enterprise beyond the most local of scales or anecdotal of evidence. Although Figure 1.2 presents assumptions with respect to adoption of sustainable practice, it must be recognized that the empirical evidence is rather weak, especially when it is also extremely hard to recognize whether the adoption of sustainable innovations is growing in relative and/or absolute terms with respect to overall tourism enterprise practice.

In the case of tourism innovation, for example, the vast majority of research is presented with respect to case studies rather than more comprehensive aggregate data (Hall & Williams, 2008; Hjalager et al., 2008). There are limited data on tourism firm survival and innovation rates, a situation that is not helped by the fact that tourism is not a standard industrial classification. Instead, the hotel and restaurant sector often has to serve as a de facto measurement.

TOURISM ENTERPRISE INNOVATION AND SUSTAINABILITY

One of the very few tourism-specific studies of firm survival and mortality was undertaken by Santarelli (1998) in Italy in relation to the survival of hotels, restaurants, and catering firms between 1989 and 1994. Examining new firm survival rates, defined as the share of new firms starting in 1989 that were still in existence at the end of each subsequent year, Santarelli found that one year after start up 68 per cent of firms still operated, dropping to 45 per cent by the sixth year. This was significantly lower than the 59 per cent survival rate identified for Italian manufacturing firms during approximately the same period, but similar to that identified for American manufacturing firms (Hall & Williams, 2008). Significantly, Santarelli found substantial regional variation in the survivability rates of tourism firms with the overall growth rate of tourism visitation being an important factor in survival as it appeared to lessen inter-firm competition. However, Santarelli (1998) did not analyse the contribution of environmental practices to business survivability.

In New Zealand the accommodation, cafés, and restaurant industrial category has the highest proportion of businesses with tourism-related sales (74 per cent), with the next largest being the transport and storage category at approximately 35 per cent (Statistics New Zealand, 2006). In their national surveys of innovation, Statistics New Zealand use the OECD guidelines contained in the third edition of the Oslo Manual (Organisation for Economic Co-operation and Development and Statistical Office of the European Communities, 2005). Under these guidelines, an innovation 'is the implementation of a new or significantly improved product (good or service), or process, a new marketing method, or a new organisational method in business practices, workplace organisation, or external relations' (OECD and Statistical Office of the European Communities, 2005: 46). Four types of innovations are recognized in the Oslo Manual:

- product innovations—new or significantly improved goods or services;
- process innovations—new or significantly improved methods for production or delivery (operational processes);
- organisational innovations—new or significantly improved methods in a firm's business practices, workplace organisation, or external relations (organisational or managerial processes);

- marketing innovations—new or significantly improved marketing methods.

In the 2005 national innovation survey, which includes businesses over a minimum size of five employees, the accommodation, cafés, and restaurant sector's innovation rate of 50 per cent of businesses engaged in innovative activity is just below the overall innovation rate of New Zealand businesses (52 per cent) (Statistics New Zealand, 2007). However, the sector had the lowest continuation rates for enterprises over the period 2001–6 with 33.1 per cent of firms surviving to 2006 (Ministry of Economic Development, 2007). Unfortunately, the 2005 survey used a different survey approach to that of the previous 2003 survey, so it is not yet possible to identify longitudinal trends, although information is available on environmentally related innovations. Table 1.2 indicates that environmentally related innovations are relatively low in the priority of New Zealand tourism businesses, although still occurring at a higher rate than the overall number of enterprises.

The relatively low priority given to environmentally related innovations in the accommodation, cafés, and restaurant sectors is found elsewhere in the New Zealand tourism industry. Hall (2006d) reported on research undertaken between 2002 and 2005 of forty-three rural tourism businesses and entrepreneurs in the Bay of Plenty (North Island) (32) and

Table 1.2 Reasons for Innovating in the New Zealand Accommodation, Cafés, and Restaurant Sector

Reasons for innovating	Accommodation, cafés, and restaurant sector	Overall for businesses with innovation activity
Increase revenue	99%	92%
Improve productivity	83%	81%
Reduce costs	77%	73%
Increase market share	85%	71%
Increase responsiveness of customers	53%	70%
Establish/exploit new market opportunities	52%	61%
Improve work safety standards	20%	46%
Replace goods or services being phased out	18%	26%
Reduce energy consumption	28%	22%
Reduce environmental impact	28%	22%

Derived from Statistics New Zealand (2007).

Otago/Southland (South Island) (11) regions of New Zealand that was part of a study of attitudes and behaviours of entrepreneurs in relation to global environmental change. With respect to climate change, the majority of interviewees did identify it as a potential issue that may affect their business and personal well-being, but importantly climate change ranked well below other more immediate business concerns in terms of changes to entrepreneurial behaviour. Many respondents noted that although they were interested in climate change, it was not an immediate or even main priority as they have more day-to-day concerns with running a business. The five most important issues for respondents being:

1. Costs of operating a business.
2. Regulation by government—in terms of costs and time taken by small businesses to meet regulatory requirements.
3. Competition—in terms of too many operators which may then lead to a loss of market share as well as price-cutting.
4. Quality—concern over the entrance of other operators that provided a poor standard of service which could then be seen as affecting their own business viability.
5. Inappropriate rural development and pollution and its impact on the landscape and personal and visitor amenity.

Climate change was seen by some respondents as a potentially significant business and even personal issue. But in comparison with more immediate issues that were identified as more important in terms of business survival (see preceding), climate change was recognized as a possible medium- to long-term issue (five years). Significantly, such comments were consistent over the research period, meaning that climate change was constantly being seen as a problem in the longer term. The only exception was when a storm, flood, or other high-impact event had occurred that respondents potentially associated with climate change and which was perceived as potentially damaging to the immediate environment on which the business partly relied, including the property of the respondent. Interestingly, those respondents who had directly experienced extreme weather events during the study period were also those who were most likely to have shifted in agreement to the notion that climate change was occurring.

Innovation and adaptation measures were developed by some respondents in relation to environmental change issues with respect to biosecurity and water security concerns but were not necessarily overtly directed to climate change. Indeed, the issue of adapting or changing business practices of enterprise to deal with potential climate change was a fraught subject. Despite the recognition of a number of respondents of the potential longer term effects of climate change and the need for 'government to do something,' increased regulation or taxes were opposed if it added to business costs as they believed that regulatory and compliance costs were already too high. Nearly all respondents felt that they could have little direct influence on government policies through business or tourism associations, although they felt far more positive with respect to influencing local decision making. Should regulatory and compliance costs, for whatever reason, be perceived as unacceptable, then the primary means for response was seen as the ballot box. This attitude was consistent even with the substantial proportion of respondents who had not registered a business for tax purposes and who were, in effect, operating in a grey economy by taking much of their income in cash and not declaring it. This situation reflected the prime focus on respondents on managing day-to-day immediate business risk rather than what was seen as something in the future. Responses of businesses whether at the personal or a national level therefore focused on adaptation rather than mitigation. Indeed, concerns were expressed over the potential of 'green' or 'carbon taxes' to increase the cost of aviation or car travel and therefore affect the travel market to the regions in which respondents were located.

The results of the New Zealand study were similar to that of a Finnish survey of winter tourism entrepreneurs (Saarinen & Tervo, 2006). The Finnish entrepreneurs were aware of the issue of global climate change, although half of the interviewees did not believe that the phenomenon actually existed and would influence tourism in their destinations in the future. As in New Zealand, the issue of climate change was seen only as a minor threat by Finnish tourism operators, if a threat at all, particularly relative to other factors that impact the industry or their enterprise. The Finnish operators were able to rationalize why they had not, or why they were not even considering, plans for adaptation strategies and measures to face projected climate change. According to respondents, the most important reason was the slow pace of change. As Saarinen and Tervo (2006: 224) comment, 'A tourism entrepreneur hardly ever plans his future more than five years in advance; in some cases, one year's forethought is sufficient . . . Although the tourism business is often based on taking risks, entrepreneurs were not willing to rush into implementing uncertain actions if they do not know if the climate in the future is going to be warmer, colder, or more unstable in their region, and how it will actually affect their operations.' The scepticism towards climate change may also help explain why there were almost no adaptation strategies developed by the respondents. Nevertheless, the lack of adaptation strategies does not necessary imply that the Finnish winter tourism industry could not cope with a changing climate in the future. As many of the Finnish operators argued, they have been working and also struggling with climatic variability and extreme weather events with moderate or good success during the existence of their business career.

The work of Hall (2006d) and Saarinen and Tervo (2006) highlights the tensions that exist between awareness of climate change and other forms of environmental change and actions to adapt and mitigate such change. Such relationships have also been examined in the Swedish context by Gössling and Hall (2009), who sought to identify how key actors in Swedish tourism considered emissions and climate change in information available on their Web sites. Web sites were searched for information relating to climate change or other aspects of the environment, including annual reports, environmental and sustainability reports, environmental and sustainability policies, and related documents. Whenever such documents were found, these were analysed based on criteria, related to the position taken with regard to climate change and action taken to address the problem. Based on the results of the evaluation, tourism actors were then ranked with regard to two parameters, i) awareness versus ignorance of climate change as represented by the extent and nature information available on the Web site and ii) responsibility versus irresponsibility with respect to climate change as indicated by offering opportunities to customers to reduce their travel impact, for example, by making carbon offsets availability or by utilising accredited sustainable business programmes (Figure 1.3). Gössling and Hall (2009) argue that there is now wide awareness of climate change in Sweden as a result of extensive coverage of the topic by international and national media as well as coverage of the Swedish government's own initiatives to curb emissions and therefore there were no reasons why tourism organizations should display ignorance of climate change and other environmental issues.

Gössling and Hall (2009) reported substantial variability between Swedish tourism actors, whether public or private, with respect to their

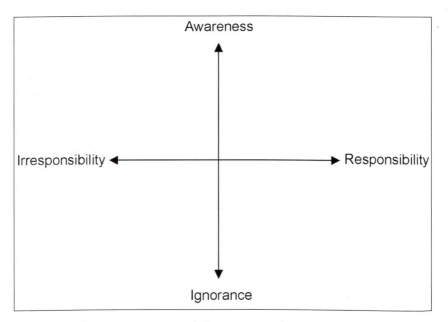

Figure 1.3   The awareness-responsibility spectrum of tourism actors.

reporting on emissions and other aspects of environmental sustainability related to climate change. Very few enterprises or public organisations stated what their contribution is to emissions. In many cases, of course, they may not have even sought to measure it. However, such a situation is problematic as consumers are unable to find relevant environmental information or, if they wish to, seek to offset or reduce their emissions. Moreover, it raises substantial questions about how possible will it be to actually reduce the emissions contribution of the tourism sector and achieve government policy unless such studies are conducted and then made publicly available. Gössling and Hall (2009) did find that many Swedish tourism industry actors are aware and working with sustainability. However, only two could be identified who reported absolute reductions in emissions in their operations: Scandic Hotels, a chain that has put down considerable effort into environmental management and is regarded as one of the leading sustainable tourism businesses in the Nordic region, and SJ (Swedish Railways), a company that has taken a very proactive stance on climate change with respect to energy, recycling, environmental management systems, and customer information with respect to emissions. For most key actors in Swedish tourism, the business reality is that there is a focus on volume growth with relative improvements in emission levels. Consequently, while efficiency (and relative sustainability) may improve, overall emissions continue to grow (as in the case of Scandinavian Airlines), thereby creating considerable challenges for the Swedish government to meet future emissions targets. It is also important to note that there is a range of actors who appeared from the information available as uninterested in sustainable tourism, supporting growth of highly energy-intense forms of tourism, and/ or not acknowledging the emissions implications of the markets they seek to develop. This included Sweden's national tourism marketing agency Visit Sweden's, which maintain an emphasis on long-distance markets.

ENVIRONMENTAL CHANGE AND THE SUSTAINABLE TOURISM ENTERPRISE: CONCLUSIONS

Tourism enterprises have a vital role to play in the development of sustainable tourism practices and in adapting and mitigating global environmental change. The notion of adaptation as a form of tourism enterprise innovation has not been well articulated, but it remains an essential component of understanding the capacities of firms, communities, and destinations to adapt and respond to the challenges of environmental change. Especially as the capacity of businesses to survive and grow is a measure of individual resilience as well as a potential indicator of system resilience at a destination level (Hall, 2009).

Much of the focus of adaptation to climatic and environmental change is on technical responses to climate change. Yet, the development and transfer of improved emissions or energy technologies are only a small element of what constitutes innovative tourism business practice. Indeed, research on innovation in tourism and similar service firms indicate that there is a range of other measures that firms can adopt to respond to external stimuli and stresses, such as those brought about directly and indirectly by climate change, in order to survive and, ideally, maintain or even increase margins (Hall & Williams, 2008). However, in the absence of mandatory environmental requirements, unless tourist firms of all sizes can be persuaded that adaptation will positively influence their survival and returns, they will not act in the short term in response to the threats of climate and environmental change no matter how concerned they may also be about climate change in the longer term. Some enterprises and entrepreneurs have undoubtedly made significant changes in business practice with respect to the environment and sustainability without government intervention. Yet these organizations, often featured in case study literature and accounts of sustainable tourism programmes and certification systems, are the exception rather than the rule. The reality is that the majority of tourism enterprises are not sustainable in an environmental sense.

Tourism enterprises and the systems within which they are embedded co-evolve in response to externally induced change, including climate and environmental change. But the lesson of many years of natural hazard research is that, while some people develop new responses to problems, others carry on doing the same thing—when allowed people still build in floodplains. The reality of environmental change is that in the absence of standard policy and regulatory regimes, different tourism enterprises will respond to change pressures in different ways.

Sustainable enterprises are extremely important with respect to the resilience and hence sustainability of destinations, although this observation is not the same as Friedmann's notion that the social responsibility of business is to increase profits (Friedman, 1970). Nevertheless, sustainable enterprises should be understood in terms of survivability and profit, as clearly they are not sustainable if they cease to exist. However, the notion of survivability also suggests that the conceptualisation of enterprise behaviour needs to be extended beyond that of being solely responsible to shareholders with respect to the provision of immediate returns and instead indicates that return needs to be understood over extended time periods, in a sense approximating to the concept of sustained yield. Furthermore, the incorporation of survivability of the firm as an indicator of sustainability may also provide support for the development of concepts of managerial responsibility from being beholden to shareholders to one that is more stakeholder oriented and based in the public good. Interestingly, many smaller tourism enterprises do appear based on a much broader set of business goals in comparison with larger corporations. Therefore, the role of institutional and enterprise structures and cultures is likely to be an important future area for research on sustainable tourism and seeking to explain enterprise responses to change. But without significant government intervention or a major environmental catastrophe, it is unlikely that rates of business change towards sustainability will continue to be anything else but incremental.

REFERENCES

Agrawala, S., 2007. *Climate change in the European Alps: adapting winter tourism and natural hazard management.* Paris: OECD.

Anderson, K., 1996. The intrusion of environmental and labor standards into trade policy. In W. Martin & L.A. Winters eds., *The Uruguay round and the developing countries.* Cambridge: Cambridge University Press, p.435–62.

Bakan, J., 2004. *The corporation: the pathological pursuit of profit and power.* New York: Free Press.

Barkin, J.S. & Shambaugh, G.E. eds., 1999. *Anarchy and the environment: the international relations of common pool resources.* Albany: State University of New York Press.

Bowman, C.L, Finley, R.L., Chandran, A.U. & Isaacs, S., 2004. An assessment for the development of a national surveillance system for travel-acquired enteric disease. *Canada Communicable Disease Report* 30–08; Available at: http://www.phac-aspc.gc.ca/publicat/ccdr-rmtc/04vol30/dr3008ea.html. Accessed 1 April, 2008.

Cartwright. R.Y. & Chahed, M., 1997. Foodborne diseases in travellers. *World Health Statistics Quarterly,* 50: p.102–10.

Ceron, J.-P. & Dubois, G., 2003. Tourism and sustainable development indicators: the gap between theoretical demands and practical achievements. *Current Issues in Tourism,* 6(1), p.54–75.

Cliff, A. & Haggett, P., 2004. Time, travel and infection. *British Medical Bulletin,* 69, p.87–99.

Coles, T.E. & Hall, C.M. eds., 2008. *International business and tourism: global issues, contemporary interactions.* London: Routledge.

Dean, T.J. & McMullen, J.S., 2007. Toward a theory of sustainable entrepreneurship: reducing environmental degradation through entrepreneurial action. *Journal of Business Venturing,* 22(1), p.50–76.

Ericsson, C.D., 2003. Travellers' diarrhoea. *International Journal of Antimicrobial Agents,* 21, p.116–24.

Freedman, D.O. et al., 2006. Spectrum of disease and relation to place of exposure among ill returned travelers. *New England Journal of Medicine,* 354, p.119–130.

Friedman, M., 1970. The social responsibility of business is to increase its profits. *New York Times Magazine,* 13 Sep. p.32–33, 122, 124, 126.

Goodwin, H. & Francis, J., 2003. Ethical and responsible tourism: consumer trends in the UK. *Journal of Vacation Marketing,* 9(3), p.271–84.

Gössling, S., 2002. Global environmental consequences of tourism. *Global Environmental Change,* 12, p.283–302.

Gössling, S. & Hall, C.M. eds., 2006a. *Tourism and global environmental change. Ecological, social, economic and political interrelationships.* London: Routledge.

Gössling, S. & Hall, C.M., 2006b. An introduction to tourism and global environmental change. In S. Gössling & C.M. Hall eds., *Tourism and global environmental change. Ecological, social, economic and political interrelationships.* London: Routledge, p.1–34.

Gössling, S. & Hall, C.M., 2009. Climate change responses of Swedish tourism actors: an analysis of actor websites. In C.M .Hall, D. Müller, & J. Saarinen eds., *Nordic tourism: issues and cases.* Clevedon: Channelview.

Gössling, S., Hall, C.M. & Weaver, D. eds., 2009. *Sustainable tourism futures: perspectives on systems, restructuring and innovations*. New York: Routledge.
Hägerstrand, T., 1967. *Innovation diffusion as a spatial process*. Translated by A. Pred. Chicago: University of Chicago Press.
Hall, C.M., 2006a. Tourism, disease and global environmental change: the fourth transition. In S. Gössling & C.M. Hall eds., *Tourism and global environmental change. Ecological, social, economic and political interrelationships*. London: Routledge, p.159–79.
Hall, C.M., 2006b. Tourism, biodiversity and global environmental change. In S. Gössling & C.M. Hall eds., *Tourism and global environmental change. Ecological, social, economic and political interrelationships*. London: Routledge, p.211–25.
Hall, C.M., 2006c. Tourism urbanisation and global environmental change. In S. Gössling & C.M. Hall eds., *Tourism and global environmental change. Ecological, social, economic and political interrelationships*. London: Routledge, p.142–56.
Hall, C. M., 2006d. New Zealand tourism entrepreneur attitudes and behaviours with respect to climate change adaptation and mitigation. *International Journal of Innovation and Sustainable Development*, 1(3), p.229–37.
Hall, C.M., 2008a. *Tourism planning*. Harlow: Pearson Education.
Hall, C.M., 2008b. *Innovation value creation points in the tourism firm*. Paper prepared for the 4th Creative Lapland Seminar 2008, Rovaneimi, Finland, 17 April.
Hall, C.M., 2009. Tourism firm innovation and sustainability. In S. Gössling, C.M. Hall, & D. Weaver eds., *Sustainable tourism futures: perspectives on systems, restructuring and innovations*. New York: Routledge.
Hall, C.M. & Coles, T.E., 2008. Introduction: tourism and international business—tourism as international business. In T.E. Coles & C.M. Hall eds., *International business and tourism: global issues, contemporary interactions*. London: Routledge, p.1–26.
Hall, C.M. & Lew, A.A. eds., 1998. *Sustainable tourism development: geographical perspectives*. Harlow: Addison Wesley Longman.
Hall, C.M. & Lew, A., 2009. *Understanding and managing tourism impacts: an integrated approach*. London: Routledge.
Hall, C.M. & Williams, A., 2008. *Tourism and innovation*. London: Routledge.
Hart, S., 1997. Beyond greening: strategies for a sustainable world. *Harvard Business Review*, 75(1), p.66–76.
Hawken, P., Lovins, A. & Lovins, L.H., 1999. *Natural capitalism: creating the next industrial revolution*. Boston: Little, Brown.
Hill, D.R., 2006. The burden of illness in international travelers. *New England Journal of Medicine*, 354, p.115–17.
Hjalager, A.-M., 1996. Tourism and the environment: the innovation connection. *Journal of Sustainable Tourism*, 4(4), p.201–18.
Hjalager, A.-M., 1997. Innovation patterns in sustainable tourism: an analytical typology. *Tourism Management*, 18(1), p.35–41.
Hjalager, A-M et al., 2008. *Innovation systems in Nordic tourism*. Oslo: Nordic Innovation Centre.
International Air Transport Association (IATA), 2008. *Building a greener future*. 2nd ed. Geneva: IATA.
IPCC, 1999. *Special report on aviation and the global atmosphere*. Geneva, IPCC.
Jensen, M.C. , 2002. Value maximization, stake-holder theory, and the corporate objective function. *Business Ethics Quarterly*, 12, p.235–56.

Mathieson, A. & Wall, G., 1982. *Tourism: economic, physical and social impacts.* Harlow: Longman Scientific and Technical.

Mills, E., 2005. Insurance in a climate of change. *Science,* 309(5737), p.1040–44.

Ministry of Economic Development, 2007. *SMEs in New Zealand: structure and dynamics.* Wellington: Ministry of Economic Development.

Organisation for Economic Co-operation and Development and Statistical Office of the European Communities, 2005. *Oslo manual: guidelines for collecting and interpreting innovation data.* 3rd ed. Paris: OECD.

Ricciardi, A., 2007. Are modern biological invasions an unprecedented form of global change? *Conservation Biology,* 21(2), p.329–36.

Rogers, E.M., 2003. *Diffusion of innovations,* 5th ed. New York: Free Press.

Russo, M.V., 2003. The emergence of sustainable industries: building on natural capital. *Academy of Management Journal,* 40(3), p.534–59.

Saarinen, J. & Tervo, K., 2006. Perceptions and adaptation strategies of the tourism industry to climate change: the case of Finnish nature-based tourism entrepreneurs. *International Journal of Innovation and Sustainable Development,* 1(3), p.214–28.

Santarelli, E., 1998. Start-up size and post-entry performance: the case of tourism services in Italy. *Applied Economics,* 30(2), p.157–63.

Statistics New Zealand, 2006. *Business operations survey.* Wellington: Statistics New Zealand.

Statistics New Zealand, 2007. *Innovation in New Zealand.* Wellington: Statistics New Zealand.

Steffen, R., de Bernardis, C. & Banos, A., 2003. Travel epidemiology—a global perspective. *International Journal of Antimicrobial Agents,* 21, p.89–95.

Sundaram, A.K. & Inkpen, A.C., 2004. The corporate objective revisited. *Organization Science,* 15(3), p.350–63.

Turner, B.L., et al. eds., 1990. *The Earth as transformed by human action.* Cambridge: Cambridge University Press.

UNWTO, UNEP & WMO, 2007. *Climate change and tourism: responding to global challenges: summary* (prepared by D. Scott et al.). Madrid and Paris: UNTWO & UNEP.

UNWTO, UNEP & WMO, 2008. *Climate change and tourism: responding to global challenges, technical report (draft)* (prepared by D. Scott et al.). Madrid and Paris: UNTWO & UNEP.

UNEP, UNWTO and WMO, 2008. *Climate change adaptation and mitigation in the tourism sector: frameworks, tools and practice.* M. Simpson et al. eds. Paris: UNEP; University of Oxford, UNWTO, WMO.

Weaver, D., 2006. *Sustainable tourism: theory and practice.* Oxford: Butterworth-Heinemann.

Welford, R., 1992. Linking quality and the environment: a strategy for the implementation of environmental management systems. *Business Strategy and the Environment,* 1(1), p.25–34.

Williams, A.M. & Montanari, A., 1999. Sustainability and self-regulation: critical perspectives. *Tourism Geographies,* 1(1), p.26–40.

World Commission on Environment and Development (WCED) (the Brundtland Report), 1987. *Our common future.* Oxford: Oxford University Press.

World Health Organization, 2008. *International travel and health.* Geneva: WHO.

2 Asian Tourism
Green and Responsible?

Anita Pleumarom

Since the United Nations Rio Earth Summit in 1992, national and supranational government organizations, businesses, local communities, and civil society initiatives have made significant efforts to steer the tourism industry towards more social and environmental sustainability. The outcome is a host of agreements and action programmes including the WTTC/WTO Agenda 21 for the Travel and Tourism Industry (1996), the WTO Manila Declaration on the Social Impact of Tourism (1997); the UN CSD Working Programme for Sustainable Tourism (1999); the WTO Global Code of Ethics for Tourism (1999); the Quebec Declaration on Ecotourism (UN International Year of Ecotourism, 2002); the CBD's Guidelines on Biodiversity and Tourism Development (COP7, 2004), the UNWTO Djerba Declaration (2003), and Davos Declaration (2007) on Climate Change and Tourism (UNWTO, UNEP, CBD web sites).

However, as more and more people are jetting across the globe for leisure, exploration, and entertainment, social, cultural, and environmental problems are inevitably mounting and an increasing number of destinations are facing degradation. According to the UNWTO (2008), the Asia-Pacific region—including the giant nations China and India—has been a major driving force behind the global tourism growth. International travellers here grew by 10 per cent in 2007, reaching a new record figure of 185 million, compared to almost 900 million worldwide.

The purpose of this chapter is to explore whether the many initiatives aimed at laying the foundations for a more benign tourism have translated into fruitful action. Rather than discussing the response and performance of individual tourism enterprises, the aim is to shed some analytical light on the question whether the industry as a whole has moved to become a viable contributor to sustainable development in destinations. To illustrate this approach, three case studies will be presented: Island tourism drawing on the experience of Koh Samui, Thailand; Himalaya tourism with a focus on India and China; and tourism redevelopment in tsunami-affected destinations in Southern Thailand.

ISLAND PARADISE LOST

Rapid tourism development has hit many Asian islands unprepared. Given that islands are particularly vulnerable in both environmental and social terms, the WTO/UNEP 2000 Hainan Conference on 'Sustainable Tourism in the Islands of the Asia-Pacific Regions' agreed that tourism needs to be carefully developed and managed if it is to sustain tourism-based economic development in the long term. Importantly, the conference recognized local communities as "primary stakeholders" in tourism development, emphasising that " . . . one of the failures of tourism planning in the past has been the lack of attention given to local populations who are not consulted regarding decisions which have long term direct impacts on their lives and futures" (WTO, 2000: 2). It therefore called for " . . . ongoing community participation and educational programmes at all levels that explain the role of tourism vis-à-vis the environment and the economy" (ibid.).

Like countless other small islands in the region, Samui Island in the Gulf of Thailand was a secret backpacker haven three decades ago, with pristine beaches, a few huts, and only basic facilities. Over recent years, however, official and private sector tourism promoters have spent much money and effort on promoting Samui as a 'world-class destination.' In 1999, the WTTC tried to encourage Samui to become Thailand's first tourism destination to receive the ISO certificate for international environmental standards in line with the Green Globe programme. Criteria for certification included: waste minimization, reuse and recycling; energy efficiency, conservation, and management; wastewater management; environmentally sensitive purchasing policy; and community partnerships.

The Thai government approved the plan and instructed the Tourism Authority of Thailand (TAT) to hold up Samui as an environmental model for other tourist areas in the country. A major argument for joining the Green Globe programme was that in the long term it was a lucrative business proposition. Accredited local enterprises would benefit as they were allowed to use the Green Globe logo in their promotional materials, and that was an effective way of informing overseas tour operators—and ultimately consumers—of their good environmental habits (TTG, 1999). But it turned out that Samui's tourism lobby was more interested in short-term profits, and Green Globe eventually withdrew altogether due to lack of local support.

Meanwhile, the island's infrastructure has fallen far behind the aggressive tourism expansion. Samui is receiving more than one million tourists annually. But the island's official population is forty thousand and, according to estimates, it additionally accommodates one hundred thousand non-registered residents, mostly migrant workers from northeastern Thailand and Burma (Srimalee, 2008; Assavanonda, 2006).

Today, Samui's most popular beaches, Chaweng and Lamai, are decaying due to unregulated construction, traffic congestion, air and noise pollution, and the dumping of waste and untreated sewage. "Gone are its serenity and lush green surroundings, the credentials that made the island much sought-after by holidaymakers, both local and foreign," wrote Assavanonda in a *Bangkok Post* feature story with the alarming title 'The Rape of Koh Samui' (2006). The following comments by a native islander are noteworthy: "Samui never had a development plan. We never thought the growth would be so fast and extreme, and local people were never prepared for the changes when tourism was being promoted. They never learned to manage their own resources. In the end, the power of money won, and we've seen the islanders lose their land to foreigners" (Assavanonda, 2006). Notably, there is no citizens group on Samui that would take on the task to lobby decision makers for a more responsible tourism approach. But that does not mean that natives of Samui are all happy about the uncontrolled tourism boom. In fact, islanders do complain about problems such as high commodity prices, lack of public services, and increasing social problems such as prostitution, drug and alcohol addiction, crime, and corruption. Given the deteriorating quality of life, many locals have sold their land and moved to other nearby provinces or Bangkok. It is evident that ordinary people in Samui just do not have enough power to stand up against influential politicians and businesspeople who tend to form alliances in the race for tourist dollars.

Today, tourism's insatiable water demand is proving the toughest challenge on the resort island. The mushrooming of hotels, spa resorts, pool villas, and golfing facilities is the prime cause for frequent water shortages. In 2002, Samui's main sources of municipal tap water ran dry for five months due to scant rainfall. The local waterworks authority had to ration tap water on a schedule. Tourists, however, were not affected because most hotels had dug their own ground wells and arranged for shipments of freshwater from the mainland. There were also no public information campaigns aimed to reduce water consumption, partly out of fear that if the problem was known it could affect tourism (*New Frontiers*, 2002: 6). The crisis prompted the local administration to build two new water reservoirs. But it turned out that they were simply too small to hold enough water to supply the entire island. According to the local waterworks office, water consumption in 2006 had jumped to about 15,000 cubic metres a day, compared to 13,000 cu/m/day in 2003 (Wongruang, 2006). Other options to ensure a stable and sufficient freshwater supply have been discussed for years, for example, the construction of an underwater pipeline from the mainland or a desalination plant. But so far it has not been possible to persuade the central government in Bangkok to cover the costs for such expensive projects (Samui Community, 2003).

Even as new investment plans are being revealed for Samui on a regular basis, including projects by major international hotel chains such as Accor, Hyatt, Avasorn, and Four Seasons, warnings of permanent water shortages continue to fall on deaf ears. According to a survey by the Tourist

Association of Samui, the number of hotel and resort rooms on the island will grow from 14,405 at the end of 2007 to 15,500 by the end of 2008 (Srimalee, 2008). That Samui is ripe for an environmental catastrophe was clearly signalled in November 2007. Affected by severe floods after heavy rains, the island had to be officially declared a disaster zone for the first time in history. The news of cars floating down Samui's main tourist strips and holidaymakers ensconced in their hotel rooms alarmed the international business community. The *Asia Property Report*, for example, ran an unusually critical article about Samui's environmental degradation and the authorities' failure to upgrade infrastructure (APR, 2007) .

There has not been a lack of discussion and concrete proposals in order to improve Samui's environmental management. In 2005, the Thai consultancy firm Environmental Engineering Consultants Co Ltd (EEC), with support of the European Commission-ASEAN Energy Facility (EAEF), initiated the 'Feasibility study for the sustainable development of Samui Island' (EEC, 2008). The project aims to identify the most suitable management solutions for the island's energy supply, solid waste, wastewater, and water supply. It also addresses other crucial issues such as land encroachments, uncontrolled land use of commercial developments including hotels and resorts, congestion, and pollution. The advantage of the project is that it is not restricted to the tourism sector but takes a comprehensive approach to work towards sustainable development island-wide. Among other objectives it proposes to implement a 'Green and Clean Environment Programme' based on the reduce/reuse/reclaim/recycle/renewable concept, and to launch educational campaigns to save water and energy (EEC, 2008).

In conclusion, technical solutions are available. Environmental and construction laws as well as zoning and anti-pollution regulations also exist in Thailand. But unless the government and the private sector can be persuaded to act more responsibly and decisively, Samui's environment—and ultimately its tourism industry—may soon be completely ruined.

SAVE HIMALAYA!

The 2,500-km-long Himalayan mountain chain has served for thousands of years as a rich reserve of biological resources and a centre of culture, tradition, and recreation. The International Year of Mountains (IYM) 2002 initiated by the United Nations was a major event to promote the protection of the mountains in the face of the rapid pace of globalization, urbanization, and mass tourism that increasingly affect communities and the natural resources they depend on (Sharma, 2002).

The impacts of Himalayan tourism have been a cause of concern for many years. At a conference in Kathmandu, hosted by the Austrian NGO Oeko-Himal to discuss " . . . responsible tourist perspectives to lead Himalayan tourism onto the sustainable trail" (East et al., 1998: 1), Sunderlal

Bahuguna, an Indian spiritual leader and coordinator of the 'Save Himalaya' citizens movement, called for a holistic approach towards an environmentally sound future: "The Himalaya has already started groaning under the burden of luxury tourism. . . . In a world full of dust, noise, smoke and tension, humankind will need more and more places with peace and tranquility. The Himalaya and other mountains, if visited with the right attitude and manner, can provide that much needed peace and tranquility. Thus the Himalaya should be protected from the onslaught of materialism. Instead of bringing to this holy land the marketplace with all its luxuries, austerity and restraint should be observed during Himalayan travels" (Bahuguna, 1998: 22).

Sadly, such voices of wisdom are being ignored. In the Himalayan foothills of India's Himachal Pradesh, for example, American millionaire Alfred Ford, great-grandson of the pioneer carmaker Henry Ford, announced in 2005 the ambitious plan for a US$500 million ultra-luxury Himalayan Ski Village project. If completed, this would be to date the largest single foreign investment in the tourism sector in India (Lisolet, 2005). The project, in the old mountain resort of Minali in Kullu Valley, includes 15 luxury hotels, 300 villas, 150 condos, shops, restaurants, spas, entertainment facilities, gondolas, and ropeways on an area of more than 130 acres reaching up to 14,000 feet above sea level. Moreover, the ski resort will consume over 6,000 acres of land in high altitudes for skiing, trekking, and adventure activities (Asher, 2008). Designed to rival the famous winter sports destinations in Europe and America, several international hotel chains have shown interest to invest in the project (Lisolet, 2005). However, the mega-project has encountered strong opposition from the community and environmental groups. Locals launched an awareness-raising campaign at the national level and prepared to file a public interest litigation against the project in the High Court because they fear the ski village project will destroy the pristine mountain landscape and pollute watercourses. Oracles of over a hundred local deities who gathered in Kullu Valley in February 2006 also unanimously rejected Ford's project as culturally and environmentally unsound (Chauhan, 2006; Asher, 2008).

In this case, there is not only a clear conflict of interests between tourism developers and the local community, but it also shows the vast difference in perceptions on what sustainable or responsible tourism is all about. In response to mounting protests, the project managing director, John Sims, tried to portray the ski village project as a frontrunner of altruistic 'ecotourism': "Alfred did not come here to exploit India. This is not his interest. He came here because he wanted to show a better way forward in environmentally responsible tourism" (quoted in Lisolet, 2005).

Undoubtedly, Himalayan tourism is an important source of revenue to governments. But rarely, the hill peoples are the major beneficiaries of this rapidly growing industry. It is primarily outsiders who run big hotels using cheap local or migrant labour, and a large proportion of tourism income is not reinvested in the area to support the local economy and to safeguard local people's natural and cultural heritage (Sharma, 2002).

The comments by Nepalese journalist Kanak Mani Dixit made ten years ago are still valid: "Tourism is an industry with enormous present and potential value for Nepal . . . The primary role of monitoring and regulating the tourism sector is the government's, but for various reasons the political leadership and the bureaucracy have not been able to be fully effective. Meanwhile neither has the private sector achieved the level of professionalism and awareness to be a self-regulator and setter of standards in tourism. Till now, the trend has been for the travel business to squeeze any tourism possibility dry, through overuse and undercutting, without giving any thought to sustainable exploitation" (Dixit ,1998: 147).

Massive tourism developments are now reported from the Himalayan region of China, a country that has been experiencing an unprecedented travel revolution over the last decade. In order to stimulate tourism and consumption, the Chinese government in 1999 decreed citizens should enjoy three mandatory vacations a year—the 'Golden Weeks.' The Chinese New Year holidays (late January or early in February), the Labour Day holidays beginning May 1, and the autumn holidays in October became an extraordinary economic success with the Chinese spending more and more each year on holiday tours across the country. In October 2007, *Asia News* reported that no less than 370 million people were on the move during the autumn holidays. Following increasing criticism of the Golden Weeks for creating a lot of problems like the huge movements of people, poor services, traffic congestions, and environmental constraints, the government recently decided to readjust its public holidays in order to relieve the heavy burden placed on popular tourist attractions (*China Daily*, 2007).

Northwestern Yunnan at the eastern end of the Himalaya has become one of China's major tourist hotspots. Due to improved transport systems, tourists are arriving in great numbers in the once remote town of Lijiang inhabited by Naxi and Tibetan people. In 1999, there were 2.6 million visitors, up from only 100,000 in 1990—an increase of 2,600 per cent! (McKhann, 2001: 149). In 2005, tourist numbers had further jumped to four million.

Despite UNESCO's listing of Lijiang as a World Heritage site in 1997 in order to protect its unique architecture and culture, tourism has changed the once scenic ethnic town almost beyond recognition. American anthropologist McKhann described Lijiang's development from a quiet and green place with wooden-fronted houses and narrow streets for bicycles, carts, and horses to a modern bustling town with glass and steel high-rises, hotels, shops and entertainment places, and widened, high-speed boulevards full of tour buses and taxis (2001: 147f). Farmland around the town is disappearing and water sources are increasingly polluted (*East Day*, 2005).

The highly competitive tourism business has led to serious conflicts within the community as well as with business newcomers, most of whom are Han

Chinese. Approximately one-third of the residents have only recently moved to Lijiang due to the new economic opportunities. "The rapidly growing 'outsider' population is causing considerable discontent among locals, many of whom complain openly about 'losing' their town" (McKhann, 2001: 159). In the old times, indigenous knowledge and traditions in Yunnan's ethnic communities were led by a sense of harmony with the natural environment, ensuring the careful and sustainable use of natural resources. The mountains and lakes were considered deeply sacred by Tibetans and Naxi. When a deadly earthquake occurred in the area of Lijiang in 1996, Naxi people attributed the disaster to the Mountain God Saddo, who, according to their belief, was angry about the excessive tourism development that was going on. " . . . a chairlift had been installed to take visitors up to Cloud Mountain Meadow on the flank of the mountain. Further south, at dry Lake Basin, a resort was built, and there were plans for a three-mile-long gondola (completed after the earthquake in 1996) to take thrill-seeking tourists high on the mountains glaciers. Over on the west side, there were plans to cut a highway through the gorge (completed in 1999), so that buses carrying less hearty travellers could make the trip. All that poking and prodding, cutting and gouging, strangers tromping around: Saddo was kicked off, and he let the people know it" (McKhann, 2001: 149).

But regardless of traditional beliefs and practices, official and private tourism promoters organized in August 2002 China's first outdoor rock festival on the slopes of Lijiang's Jade Dragon Snow Mountain in order to boost tourism. Thousands of music fans came from as far away as Beijing, Shanghai, Guangyhou, and Kunming to enjoy what was dubbed the 'Chinese Woodstock,' and the local people's sacred mountains echoed to the sounds of pop, punk, heavy metal, and Beijing opera-based rock (Agence France Press, 2002).

Further north in Di Qing Tibetan Autonomous Prefecture, Chinese authorities held an extravagant ceremony in 2002 to rename the small community Zhongdian into 'Shangri-La.' Inspired by James Hilton's 1933 novel *Lost Horizon* about a mystic place in the Himalaya, they had decided to put Shangri-La—made-in-China—onto the world's tourism map. Following the opening of an airport here in 2003, arrivals surged to 2.6 million in 2005, and a tripling of visitors is expected over the next fifteen years (Watts, 2006).

However, Chinese government's top-down policy to boost mass tourism has sparked considerable debate countrywide and internationally. The creation of a Himalayan Disneyland " . . . is part of a new phase of China's economic expansion, which is taking the modernization drive into some of the most remote places on earth, reducing poverty but ruining the environment," wrote Watts for *The Guardian* (2006).

At the 2006 World Heritage Conference held in Suzhou, China, environmentalists warned that unchecked tourism development along with dam-building would cause irreparable damage to the culturally and naturally sensitive area. Di Qing was in 2005 listed by UNESCO as a World Natural Heritage site, called the 'Three-River-in-Parallel' because three great Asian rivers—the Yangtze River, the Salween River, and the Mekong River—run in parallel within just about sixty kilometres in this area. Although counting for only 0.4 per cent of the Chinese territory, Di Qing, with climates ranging from subtropical to alpine, is extraordinarily rich in biodiversity, sustaining 20 per cent of animal species and 25 per cent of plant species of the country. To highlight its biological significance and vulnerability, the U.S.-based NGO Conservation International has recognized the area as 'World Biodiversity Hotspot.' Moreover, Di Qing is culturally unique as it is the home of more than twenty-five ethnic groups, including Tibetans, Han Chinese, Yi, Naxi, and Bai (Liu Ke, 2006: 3).

Due to the frenzied construction of tourism facilities, environmental problems abound, including deforestation, destruction of grass- and wetlands, and soil erosion. The large amount of trash left behind by tourists has led to the degradation of pastures, causing hardship for local communities around tourist resorts (Buckley, 2006). In Sicun community near Shudu Lake, for example, herdsmen had to move their yaks far away because the pastures near the village were so polluted with plastic bags that they were no longer safe for raising livestock (Liu Ke, 2006: 5).

Sidle pointed out the disastrous impacts of road construction around Shangri-La. He estimated that 80 to 95 per cent of the direct sediment contributions into the headwaters of the 'Three-Rivers-in-Parallel' area are presently attributable to road erosion and landslides. "The Chinese are simply blasting roads into unstable hillsides with virtually no attention paid to road location, construction practices or erosion control. Their objective appears to focus only on building the shortest possible route between locations of interest at the lowest cost with little or no regard for environmental consequences" (Sidle, 2007).

In 2006, it was reported that a real estate company based in the provincial capital Kunming planned to establish a huge tourist theme park in Jisha village at the foot of the Haba snow mountain. For several years, the local government had tried to persuade the Tibetan villagers that they would reap the economic benefits from the development. But many locals resisted because of the potential environmental impact on their sacred mountains (Lin Gu, 2006).

Chinese civil society groups have only recently begun to raise awareness about tourism impacts in their country and to discuss the concepts of 'eco' or 'sustainable tourism,' which have emerged as offshoots of Western environmentalism. In 2007, Shen Xiaohui of the Beijing-based NGO Friends of Nature said in an article, "No to luxury and artificialization" in tourism as it destroys the authenticity and integrity of natural destinations. "The current tourism in China is flooded with slogans for 'packaging heritage sites,' 'forging rivers and mountains,' and 'creating' a certain brand. It is often ignored that the ecological systems of nature reserves are unique and irreplaceable—they cannot be artificially 'packaged,' 'forged,' or 'created.' 'Packaging' will only make nature unnatural. 'Forging' will damage nature beyond recognition. This type of 'creating' is preventing our natural culture from being passed to the next generation. These are blind behaviours driven by commercial benefits. . . . Today, transportation networks are extending in all directions in reserves. Outdoor travel looks increasingly like fast food—done in a few minutes. With the arrangement of travel agencies, tourists seem to be sent on a conveyor belt that can be neither stopped nor reversed" (Xiaohui, 2007).

Recent calls for more sustainable development have in fact translated into policies and decrees towards a better regulation of China's tourism industry. In the 'Master Plan for the Development of Western Provinces' that includes Himalayan destinations, the Chinese government emphasizes that all development should be put onto a "new and sustainable track" (Liu Ke, 2006: 9). Accordingly, local governments have introduced some new regulations aimed to tackle tourism-related environmental and social problems. Di Qing, where Shangri-La is located, is the first prefecture in Yunnan that has banned the use of plastic packages and installed a wastewater treatment plant (Liu Ke, 2006: 10). Authorities have also made some changes in the annual inspection of tour agencies—for instance, by adding 'criteria points' for safety, environmental impact, and engagement in local communities, such as schools, scholarships, and trainings (Buckley, 2006).

Nevertheless, as Liu Ke argues, environmental sustainability in tourism can not be simply achieved through administrative measures and improved environmental techniques. In order to explain the root causes of tourism-related problems, a better understanding is needed about the political perspectives that drive tourism development as well as the power relations among different stakeholders. Di Qing's " . . . local communities may be those with less power compared to government" because any utilization of land and resources needs the permission of government. Meanwhile, "other stakeholders including tourists, tour operators, as well as conservation NGOs in Di Qing may enjoy larger scale of power than local communities" (Liu Ke, 2006: 11).

Dong, who studied tourism and environmental governance in Yunnan province, gives an explanation for the increasing conflicts over the ownership of local resources between ethnic communities and the government as a result of tourism development (Dong, 2004). Since the land is seen by Yunnan's ethnic peoples as their ancestral domains, they expect the government to respect their customary rights over the natural assets that attract tourists and to provide sufficient financial support for environmental protection. However, according to the provincial legal system, all natural assets belong to the state. Realizing that tourism is the most lucrative economic sector, the provincial government wants to keep its grip on the natural resource base and encourages external—foreign and domestic—tourism-related investments to accelerate economic growth, which often results in negative environmental impacts and disputes with ethnic communities (Dong, 2004: 195) .

In conclusion, pressure on Himalayan peoples, cultures, and ecosystems is increasing dramatically, as governments seem to be intent to turn every corner of the mountains into a tourist site. Since the world's highest railway between Beijing and Tibet's capital Lhasa was inaugurated in 2006, the entire Tibetan Plateau is also no longer safe from a mass tourism onslaught. Highways are already crisscrossing the plateau, and a bumpy road to Mount Everest base camp has recently been improved so the bearers of the Olympic torch can announce the 2008 Beijing Games from the roof of the world (Spano, 2007). Here we have another clear case to argue that existing policies and action programmes to curb harmful tourism growth are either utterly inadequate or simply ignored.

POST-TSUNAMI TOURISM—MISSED OPPORTUNITY

Thailand was among the nations worst hit by the Asian tsunami of 26 December 2004, which cost more than two hundred thousand lives. According to official statistics, 5,395 people were killed, 8,457 were injured, and 2,932 persons went missing when the giant waves hit Thailand's Andaman coast, and many of the victims were tourists (TEC, 2006: 6).

Thai commentators such as Mukdawan Sakboon suggested the tsunami should serve as a wake-up call: "We have been mercilessly exploiting nature and the environment in the name of tourism development for far too long. Local administrations have allowed hotel and resort developers to squeeze every inch of the country's once-pristine beaches in their hunger for tourist dollars. As a result, numerous hotels and resorts were built too close to beaches, something that is prohibited in many other countries. Perhaps this is one of the reasons why so many people died when the tsunami struck beach resorts in six provinces in the South." (quoted in Pleumarom, 2007: 4).

As part of the post-tsunami reconstruction efforts in southern Thailand, academics, environmental organizations, and international development agencies, including the United Nations, worked hard to present plans to bring about more environmental sustainability in tourism. A UNEP study recommended that tsunami-hit countries should establish natural buffer zones, particularly mangroves forests, and to rebuild in areas less prone to natural calamities. Referring to Thailand's inadequate land use and coastal management planning system, UNEP said: "There is a risk that a fast track recovery of the tourism industry may lead to a rapid rebuilding of the infrastructure that existed before the disaster. Such an approach would pre-empt an integrated coastal zone management plan which is now absolutely essential to reduce human vulnerability to natural disasters and ensure long-term sustainability" (UNEP 2005: 53).

However, advocates of 'sustainable tourism' were soon disillusioned because the Thai government's efforts were mainly directed towards restoring tourists' confidence in Andaman destinations after the disaster. While a hefty budget was allocated for rebuilding Phuket's most popular beach resort Patong in order to showcase successful tourism recovery, financial assistance for environmentally sound reconstruction of other tsunami-ravaged destinations was lacking and the needs of small- and medium-scale tourism businesses were often disregarded.

Residents and small tourism traders in Phuket frequently protested against the government's hastily drawn-up post-tsunami zoning plans that would no longer allow people to do business on the beach, for the sake of 'safety' in case of future tsunamis and 'beautification.' In some resort areas, big hotels took advantage of the disaster to privatize beaches and to take over the business from local food vendors, masseurs, and people renting out chairs and umbrellas (*New Frontiers*, 2005).

Following the Thai government's call on foreign investors to help rebuild tsunami-hit coastal areas, land developers flocked in from the United States, the Middle East, Hong Kong, Singapore, and Russia, pumping millions of dollars into Phuket, Phang Nga, and Krabi. The new economic boom is no longer driven only by tourism but by the real estate industry. Construction in Phuket is pursuing as if there were hardly any provisions for environmental protection and safety. Hotels, resorts, restaurants, and shops are built on beaches close to the sea as before and in even greater numbers, and on top of that hill slopes are now being cleared and bulldozed to pave the way for holiday villas and condominiums. More catastrophes may occur, not caused by tsunamis but due to slope destabilization, landslides, and flash floods resulting from the indiscriminate construction on the hills.

In the climate of increased economic deregulation and globalization, local communities find themselves in an increasingly powerless situation. Disputes over land and natural resources emerged as a key issue in the tsunami aftermath. The land status of most of the tsunami-hit communities has proven very difficult because many villagers never had legal rights to the plot of land they used to live on. By the end of 2007, more than 35,000 families in 160 villages in the disaster-affected provinces were still having legal problems as investors had filed lawsuits demanding villagers' eviction from seaside plots earmarked for the construction of resorts and hotels (Pongrai, 2007).

The government's policy to develop 'quality tourism' to attract high-spending visitors has favoured foreign tourism developers to take over pristine beaches for the creation of exclusive luxury hideaways. Khao Lak in Phang Nga province, one of the most devastated tourist sites with about 90 per cent of all accommodation destroyed by the tsunami, has experienced a significant shift of ownership in tourism. A survey by this researcher found that in contrast to pre-tsunami times, Khao Lak is now almost completely controlled by urban-based or foreign entrepreneurs, and rather than employing locals, these new businesses increasingly rely on migrant workers from Burma and Nepal.

Unfortunately, various international donors and consultants involved in post-tsunami redevelopment projects have tended to impose their concepts and projects onto local communities without a thorough examination of existing tourism realities and an understanding of the broader developmental context.

In June 2007, for example, the UNWTO and Thailand's Ministry of Tourism and Sports (MTS) agreed on a high-profile 'sustainable tourism and biodiversity' project in two tsunami-affected areas in Phang Nga. The project was introduced as a follow-up of the UNWTO's 2005 Phuket Action Plan and an effort to implement the United Nations' 'Guidelines on Biodiversity and Tourism Development of the Convention on Biological Diversity' (CBD) (UNWTO, 2007).

The CBD tourism guidelines, adopted by signatories to the CBD at the 2004 7th Conference of Parties (COP7) in Kuala Lumpur, are designed " . . . for activities related to sustainable tourism development in vulnerable terrestrial, marine and coastal ecosystems and habitats of major importance for biological diversity and protected areas, including fragile riparian and mountain ecosystems" (CBD, 2004: 5). While the critiques of the UN International Year of Ecotourism 2002 received considerable media attention, little is known about the tourism-related controversy at the CBD (Johnston, 2007; Tourism Investigation and Monitoring Team, 2001/2). The development of the guidelines began at COP4 in Bratislava in 1998 with a German government proposal and pursued with little meaningful discussion in public. Critical civil society organizations working in the CBD process insisted that any process for international guidelines on sustainable tourism should be more transparent and accountable and show respect for the rights of local communities and particularly indigenous peoples. The fast-growing ecotourism industry was increasingly seen as harmful as it opened up new areas to forest encroachment, logging, mining, and exploitation of biological resources, including 'biopiracy' by unscrupulous individual and corporate collectors (IIFB [International Indigenous Forum on Biodiversity], 2004).

The present guidelines are voluntary and can be easily bypassed or abused for commercial purposes, especially in countries where law enforcement and monitoring systems are weak. Yet, high expectations have been raised. In the foreword of a recently published 'user's manual,' the CBD executive secretary, Ahmed Djoghlaf, states, "The User's Manual is a tool for Parties and other stakeholders to apply the Guidelines, and to make tourism more biodiversity-friendly, considering the three objectives of the Convention—the conservation and sustainable use of biodiversity, and the fair and equitable sharing of the benefits arising from the use of biological resources. More than a toolbox, it should also be a guide that can bring about a novel paradigm in the tourism sector; that of the emergence of new consumption patterns driven by respect for life on Earth" (CBD, 2006: 5).

To manage the post-tsunami project in Phang Nga, a UNWTO Consulting Unit on Biodiversity and Tourism was established in Bonn with funding provided by the German government (UNWTO, 2007). As goal of the three-year project, officially called 'Biodiversity and Sustainable Tourism Development at Kho Khao Island and in the Lam Kaen Community/ Thai Muang National Park, Phang Nga province, Thailand,' is stated the development of two selected sites into 'sustainable tourism' attractions. The MTS appointed a committee composed of stakeholders from the public and private sectors which according to the UNWTO Consulting Unit has taken on the task to establish sustainable tourism development plans for the two model sites by May 2008. The expected outcome of the project will also include the construction of a mangrove natural walkway on Kho Khao Island and a forest study trail at Thai Muang National Park, capacity building for stakeholders on several tourism-related subjects as well as marketing and promotional activities (UNWTO, 2008).

Although one of the project requirements is "to allow for local community involvement and participatory processes" (UNWTO, 2007), this researcher found that as of April 2008 the villagers were not even properly informed about the UNWTO project that is to be completed by September 2009. Apart from the concerned community leaders, only a handful of locals have been involved in the discussions, and a real consultative process in concerned communities has yet to start, according to the project consultant on community development (personal communication with Tanu Nabnien, 13 April 2008).

A key player in the implementation of the UNWTO project is the Kenan Institute Asia (KIA), an offshoot of the U.S. Kenan Institute of Private Enterprise (KIPE) based at the University of Northern Carolina. KIA's mission is to boost economic competitiveness and entrepreneurship, and one of its projects in Thailand is the Community-based Tsunami Recovery Action Initiative (CB-TRAI) that focuses on tourism development in tsunami-affected communities.

The list of partners and funding agencies in KIA's post-tsunami initiative is impressive: Apart from the U.S. Kenan organizations and the UNWTO, it includes USAID, the Bush-Clinton Tsunami Relief Fund, the European Union, the Microsoft Corporation and the pharmaceutical giant Merck (TRAI, 2007: 3). Given this high degree of official and corporate involvement in the UNWTO/KIA project, the question arises: Is there a special reason for the interest of these omnipotent global players in biodiversity and tourism in Phang Nga? Perhaps the issue is not just about nature conservation and livelihood-building in poor tsunami-struck communities.

Southern Thailand is geopolitically an extremely significant region between the Indian and Pacific Oceans, where America and China are struggling for control. Plans to build a canal near the Isthmus of Kra to connect the Indian Ocean with the Gulf of Thailand have been pondered for decades. More recently, the Thai government considered to establish a

'Land bridge' included the building of highways linking Phang Nga and Surat Thani provinces and a deep sea harbour on the Andaman coast. China showed interest to develop the port, with Thap Lamu in Phang Nga's Lam Kaen district (one of the UNWTO's project sites!) mentioned as a possible location, but the Chinese withdrew from the project after the tsunami. However, there are plans for a so-called 'Southern Seaboard' scheme that targets several southern provinces for large-scale industrialization including petrochemical complexes, even though the government has not yet revealed details.

Meanwhile, the United States has advocated to turn Phuket into a Special Economic Zone (SEZ) and to develop the coastal strip in Phang Nga and Ranong for leisure and tourism. After the tsunami, the tourism lobby has been in the driving seat, but the future remains very uncertain. With Thai governments frequently changing, political and development policies are changing too. And following the bombings in Bali and the outbreak of armed conflicts in Thailand's southernmost provinces largely inhabited by Muslims, there have also been great worries that Andaman tourist destinations may be drawn into terrorist and anti-terrorist wars, in which local communities are just a pawn in the game. In view of this, 'community-based' tourism projects in southern Thailand such as the one initiated by the UNWTO are operating on a shaky ground. Local people feel insecure not only because they fear natural and human-made disasters but because they do not understand the complex political economy issues that determine their lives. They tend to accept what is being offered to them from various sides. There may be the strategy to make local people believe that tourism works for them as long as it is projected as 'community-based.' The UNWTO project may bring about a new brand of local entrepreneurship, but only few of small tourism providers may be able to grow given the increasing influx of urban and foreign-based tourism businesses.

As a result of the post-tsunami tourism and real estate boom, illegal takeovers of beaches and forests have become so rampant that Phang Nga Governor Vichai Praisangob warned in February 2008 he would get tough with land grabbers and take disciplinary action against local politicians collaborating with influential businessmen believed to be masterminding the illegal encroachments (*Bangkok Post*, 2008). The local community specialist for the UNWTO tourism initiative confirmed that illegal land takeovers, corruption, and other irregularities are occurring in the project areas, sometimes with the involvement of local administration bodies (personal communication with Tanu Nabnien, 13 April 2008). But there is no indication that the UNWTO project managers are addressing fundamental questions of ethics, equitability, and justice in relation to stakeholders involved in their initiative.

After the tsunami left many tourist spots severely damaged, priority should have been given to the reconstruction and rehabilitation of affected areas in an environmentally sound way. But instead of assisting in redevelopment on Phuket's beaches or in Khao Lak to protect the coastal ecosystems from the impacts of mass tourism, the UNWTO project selected two relatively small biodiversity-rich areas including fishing communities that had hardly accommodated visitors before the tsunami hit.

In fact, the project involves new risks. For instance, foreign research tourists and pharmaceutical corporations may be interested to exploit Phang Nga's biodiversity. 'Ecotourism' provides easy access to biological and genetic resources as well as to villagers' traditional knowledge on how to use plant and animal species.

Despite the UNWTO's emphasis on biodiversity conservation, the local project management appears to be ill-equipped to engage in environmental activities. To this point, only one part-time staff has been hired by KIA to work on biodiversity issues in the project. And given that one of the project sites, Laem Kaen community, is located in a national park, the lack of participation by Thai government agencies and NGOs specifically concerned with nature conservation is conspicuous. It is not even clear if the responsible National Park, Wildlife and Plant Conservation Department and Ministry of Natural Resources and the Environment are involved in this project at all. Under these circumstances, can we expect that a viable model can be created that combines sustainable tourism development and biodiversity?

QUESTIONING GREEN AND RESPONSIBLE TOURISM

Glossy tourism brochures and postcard images do not reveal the often alarming state of the environment in Asian destinations. Although there will be a number of individual tourism enterprises and projects that have embraced environmentally and socially viable actions, the rhetoric of a paradigm shift towards green and responsible tourism does not match the harsh realities on the ground. Rather than safeguarding public interest, governments of Asian countries usually give in to wealthy and influential vested-interest groups who are pushing for privatization, deregulation, and liberalization in order to maximize their profits. In this age of globalization, 'people's participation' and 'community involvement' in tourism development have become buzzwords—or even marketing gimmicks—with little meaning. In tourism—even if projected as 'eco,' sustainable, responsible, or fair—the old exploitative relations between colonizers and the colonized are often replicated as the industry continues to disregard, disempower, disown, and displace local people. These conclusions can be easily drawn from the aforementioned three case studies as well as from other experiences from around the world (tim-team, 2001/2; Pleumarom, 2001; Mowforth & Munt, 2003; Johnston, 2007; TWR, 2007).

Samui Island's tourism model is badly flawed, with government agencies showing an abysmal record in handling infrastructure and environmental problems. Good governance and willpower by all parties are indispensable to counter over- commercialization and to restore the values of equitability, social responsibility, and ecological justice in community development. The case of Samui illustrates well that voluntary industry initiatives are not the key to control tourism's excesses. It is the government's responsibility to establish strong legal and regulatory frameworks and to ensure the enforcement of these rules and regulations on the industry that is known to operate in a predatory and sometimes illegal way.

The study of Himalayan tourism shows how tourism mercilessly devours naturally and culturally unique places and threatens ethnic mountain peoples' ancestral rights and ways of life. The distinctive local customary laws, socio-cultural practices, and environmental management systems should be valued and form the base for any tourism project in indigenous peoples' territories because they offer genuine alternatives to purely market-driven development schemes.

Finally, post-tsunami tourism in Southern Thailand represents a typical example of 'lessons not learned.' Conventional mass tourism has been restored in popular destinations, clearly revealing the old-fashioned 'more tourists–more cash' mentality with scant regard for environmental and developmental concerns. In the meantime, a project such as the one overseen by the UNWTO to implement the CBD guidelines for sustainable tourism development and biodiversity protection is an obvious example of misplaced priority. All efforts should have focussed on environmentally sustainable redevelopment of Andaman tourism hotspots. This would have also been in line with the CBD guidelines that are designed to "cover all forms and activities of tourism," including conventional mass tourism (CBD, 2004: 5). However, while failing to address the multi-dimensional problems in tsunami-affected tourism areas, the UNWTO initiative provides in the typical top-down manner for the expansion of industrial tourism into socially weakened communities and biodiversity-rich areas.

The global tourism industry has arrived at the crossroads, and its leaders can no longer afford to just pay lip service and resort to 'greenwash' practices. The worsening climate crisis, to which tourism itself has contributed significantly, is ticking like a time bomb for the industry as many tourist areas may be irreversibly destroyed by the impacts of global warming. It certainly needs more public awareness raising and action by all parties, including affected local people, civil society groups, independent researchers, and media representatives, to turn tourism into a more sustainable activity for the benefit of this and future generations.

REFERENCES

Agence France Presse (AFP), 2002. China's 'Woodstock' rocks on, 19 August.
Asher, Manshi, 2008. *Dream destination for world class tourists . . . nightmare for the Himalayas! Impacts of the proposed Himalayan ski-village project in Kullu, Himachal Pradesh.* A preliminary fact-finding report prepared by the

Him Niti Campaign, Himachal Pradesh Jan Jagran Evam Vikas Samiti (JJVS), Kullu District/HP and Equations, Bangalore, March.

Asia News, 2007. Some 370 million people on the move during Golden Week, 9 October.

Asia Property Report, 2007. Samui floods highlight infrastructure shortfalls, December. Available at: http://www.property-report.com/. Accessed 22 March, 2008.

Assavanonda, Anjira, 2006. The rape of Koh Samui, *Bangkok Post*, 12 August.

Bahuguna, Sunderlal, 1998. Save Himalaya!. In P. East, K. Luger, & K. Inmann eds., *Sustainability in mountain tourism—perspectives for the Himalayan countries*. Delhi: Book Faith India & Innsbruck/Vienna: Studienverlag, p.15–25.

Bangkok Post, 2008. Phangnga governor warns local politicians—helping bail out forest encroachers intolerable. 25 February.

Buckley, L., 2006. *New models needed for sustainable development of Western China*. Beijing: Global Environmental Institute Beijing, 14 December Available at: http://www.worldwatch.org/node/4773. Accessed 21 December, 2006.

Chauhan, Baldev S., 2006. Deities oppose Ford's ski village. *New Kerala*, 17 February.

China Daily, 2007. China to readjust holidays to ease tourism burden. 8 October.

Convention on Biological Diversity (CBD), 2004. *CBD guidelines on biodiversity and tourism development*. Available at: http://www.cbd.int/doc/publications/tou-gdl-en.pdf. Accessed 2 April, 2008.

Convention on Biological Diversity (CBD), 2006. *User's manual on the CBD Guidelines on Biodiversity and tourism development*. Available at: http://tourism.cbd.int/manual.shtml.

Dixit, K. M., 1998. Tourism and development. In P. East, K. Luger, & K. Inmann eds., *Sustainability in mountain tourism—perspectives for the Himalayan countries*. Delhi: Book Faith India & Innsbruck/Vienna: Studienverlag, p.147–56.

Dong, E., 2004. Tourism and environmental governance in Yunnan province. Department of Recreation, Park and Tourism Management, Pennsylvania State University, *Proceedings of the 2004 Northeastern Recreation Research Symposium (GTR-NE-326)*, p.192–99. Available at: http://www.fs.fed.us/ne/newtown_square/publications/technical_reports/pdfs/2005/326papers/dong326.pdf. Accessed 28 March, 2008.

East Day, 2005. Lijiang at the crossroads. 5 December. Available at: http://english.eastday.com/eastday/englishedition/features/userobject1ai1696444.html. Accessed 28 March, 2008.

Environmental Engineering Consultants Co, Ltd (EEC), 2008. *Feasibility study for the sustainable development of Samui Island, Executive Summary*, Available at: http://www.samui-sd.net/Asset/PDF/ExecutiveSum_Mix.pdf [accessed 22 March 2008].

International Indigenous Forum on Biodiversity (IIFB), 2004. *Statement on tourism*, Working Group 1, Agenda Item 19.7, COP7 to the CBD, Kuala Lumpur, 9–20 February.

Johnston, Alison M., 2007. *Is the sacred for sale? Tourism and indigenous peoples*. 2nd ed. London: Earthscan.

Lin Gu, 2006. Modernizing Shangri-la. *The Seoul Times*. Available at: http://theseoultimes.com/ST/?url=/ST/db/read.php?idx=862 [accessed 20 Aug. 2006].

Liu Ke, 2006. *Tourism, environment and politics in Di Qing Tibetan Autonomous Prefecture* (unpublished paper). Beijing.

Lisolet, Qiwi Lin, 2005. The valley of gold? Ford's plan to turbocharge Himalayan tourism. *The Escape Artist*, December. Available at: http://www.escapeartist.com/efam/76/In_The_Himalayas_Of_India.html [accessed 1 Sept. 2008].

McKhann, C.F., 2001. The good, the bad, and the ugly—reflections on tourism development, in Lijiang, China. In Cheung Tan Chee-Beng, C.H. Sidney C.H., & Hui Yang Hui eds., *Tourism, anthropology and China*, Studies in Asian Tourism No.1. Bangkok: White Lotus Press, p.147–66.

Mowforth, M. & Munt, I., 2003. *Tourism and sustainability: development and new tourism in the Third World*. 2nd ed. London/New York: Routledge.

New Frontiers, 2002. Koh Samui: unprecedented water crisis. Vol. 8, No. 4, July–August, p.6. Available at: http://www.twnside.org.sg/tour.htm. Accessed 22 March, 2008.

New Frontiers, 2005. The politics of post-tsunami tourism in Thailand. Series in Vol. 11, No.1–6. Available at: http://www.twnside.org.sg/tour.htm. Accessed 22 March, 2008.

Pleumarom, A., 2001. *Mekong tourism—model or mockery?: A case study on 'sustainable tourism.'* Third World Network, Environment & Development Series No.3, Penang.

Pleumarom, A., 2007. CEOs and the deep blue sea. Tsunami Response Watch ed., *Miles to go—tsunami, rehabilitation, future*. Available at: http://www.tsunamiresponsewatch.org/2007/01/01/ceos-and-the-deep-blue-sea/. Accessed 28 March, 2008.

Pongrai, J., 2007. Developers taking over beachfront, say activists. *The Nation*, 26 December.

Samui Community Online Magazine, 2003. A drop in the ocean—Samui's chronic water supply problems. 5 April. Available at: http://www.samuicommunity.com/index.php?option=com_content&task=view&id=559&Itemid=67 [accessed 1 April 2008].

Sharma, G., 2002. The distress call of mountains. *The Tribune* (India), 19 May.

Sidle, R., 2007. Dark clouds over Shangri-La. *The Japan Times*, 15 March.

Spano, S., 2007. Tibet's transformation: a new age for Lhasa. *Los Angeles Times*, 17 August.

Srimalee, S., 2008. Big money pouring into Koh Samui. *The Nation*, 22 February.

Third World Resurgence, 2007. Rethinking tourism: an engine for Third World Tourism development? No. 207–208, November-December. Available at: http://www.twnside.org.sg/title2/resurgence/twr207–208.htm. Accessed 2 April, 2008.

Tourism Investigation & Monitoring Team, 2001/2. *Clearinghouse for reviewing ecotourism*, 24 issues. Available at: http://www.twnside.org.sg/title/iye.htm. Accessed 28 March, 2008.

Travel Trade Gazette Asia, 1999. Tourism council wants a green Samui, No.1204, 16–22 April.

Tsunami Evaluation Coalition (TEC), 2006. The International Community's Funding of Emergency and Relief: Local response—Thailand. June. Available at: http://www.tsunami-evaluation.org/NR/rdonlyres/D10D0883–3A33–47E2-A3EA-C3F702A1C734/0/local_response_thailand.pdf. Accessed 2 April, 2008.

Tsunami Recovery Action Initiative (TRAI), 2007. Launch of biodiversity and sustainable tourism development project. *Revival*, Newsletter of the Kenan Institiue Asia, Vol. 2, No. 4, August–November, p.1–3.

United Nations Environment Programme (UNEP), *About sustainable tourism: tourism's three main impact areas*. Available at: http://www.uneptie.org/pc/tourism/sust-tourism/env-3main.htm [accessed 22 March 2008].

UNEP, 2008. *After the tsunami—Rapid Environmental Assessment*. February. Available at: http://www.unep.org/tsunami/reports/TSUNAMI_THAILAND_LAYOUT.pdf [accessed 1 Sept. 2008].

United Nations World Tourism Organization (UNWTO) Web site, 2008. Available at: http://www.unwto.org [accessed 22 March 2008].

UNWTO, 2007. *World Tourism Organization project on sustainable tourism development for tsunami affected area in Thailand.* Press release 27 June. Available at: http://www.unwto.de/press.html [accessed 22 March 2008].

UNWTO, 2008. Biodiversity and sustainable tourism development at Kho Khao Island and in the Lam Kaen Community/Thai Muang National Park, Phang Nga province, Thailand. Available at: http://www.unwto.de/thailand.html [accessed 1 Sept. 2008].

Wongruang, P., 2006. Island running dry. *Bangkok Post*, 15 August.

Watts, J., 2006. Welcome to Shangri-la—by order of the state council of the Chinese government. *The Guardian* (UK), 1 June.

World Tourism Organization, 2000. *Hainan declaration on 'sustainable tourism in the islands of the Asia-Pacific regions.'* WTO/UNEP International Conference, Hainan, P.R. China, 8 December 2000. Available at: http://www.world-tourism.org/sustainable/doc/Hainan%20Declaration-Dec%202000.pdf [accessed 1 Sept. 2008].

Xiaohui, Shen, 2007. No to luxury and artificialization! *Friends of Nature Newsletter (Beijing)*, Spring issue.

3 Large-Scale Links between Tourism Enterprises and Sustainable Development

Ralf Buckley

INTRODUCTION

The tourism sector is embedded within the global economy, human society, and natural environment, and large-scale links outside the sector itself are as significant for sustainable development as small-scale environmental management practices within the industry. Sustainable development is still a somewhat contested term in the theoretical literature, but its practical interpretation by national governments and multinational corporations may be deduced from topics covered at the 1992 Earth Summit and the 2002 Rio World Summit on Sustainable Development ("Rio +10") in Johannesburg. Agenda 21, the top-level policy product from the Earth Summit, did not include tourism in its sectoral studies, and a separate Tourism Agenda 21 was produced subsequently by the industry itself. Rio +10 did indeed include tourism, and a number of previous meetings such as the World Ecotourism Summit in Quebec produced internationally agreed documents which were delivered at Rio +10. In addition to inputs from the tourism industry itself, tourism received a significant mention in contemporaneous inputs from the conservation sector, such as the *Benefits Beyond Boundaries* statement from the 2003 World Parks Congress. More recently, as governments worldwide have begun to grapple with policies related to climate change, the tourism sector produced a report and a declaration on this topic at Davos in 2007 (UNWTO et al., 2007).

To assess the significance of tourism enterprises for sustainable development with any degree of thoroughness, e.g., for comparison with other industry sectors, we need a reasonably comprehensive and systematic triple-bottom-line analytic framework, not merely a collection of anecdotes. Triple-bottom-line accounting has a number of theoretical deficiencies, practical difficulties, and data shortages, but does provide a good starting point (Buckley, 2003a).

At a global scale, the tourism industry is commonly estimated to account for about one-tenth of global GNP and employment. Aggregate financial figures from the World Travel and Tourism Council, the peak industry association, are several times higher than those from the UN

World Tourism Organisation, the peak multilateral government organisation, but both estimates are in the trillions of U.S. dollars. The outdoor tourism sector, particularly significant for sustainability because it
involves regional communities and operates in areas of high conservation value, comprises around one-fifth of the entire tourism sector. At a
national scale, many countries now maintain tourism satellite accounts
as part of their GDP statistics, and some have also estimated the scale of
nature-based and adventure tourism, amounting to hundreds of billions
of U.S. dollars in some countries. As with other industry sectors, some
tourism enterprises are large multinational corporations, whereas others
are small businesses run by a single proprietor. Some are commercially
successful and others less so, for much the same reasons as businesses
in other industry sectors. Tourism enterprises, like any other, compile
and report detailed information on financial income, expenditures, and
assets. Very few enterprises compile corresponding information on social
or environmental costs and contributions. This chapter therefore focuses
principally on those aspects.

There are several different reasons why tourism enterprises may adopt
measures to reduce their negative social and environmental impacts, or
commence positive contributions to communities or conservation. For the
global leaders in this field, the main driving force seems to be the personal
convictions of company founders and current senior management. The
opportunity to increase income by attracting environmentally concerned
customers is often quoted, and for some leading enterprises this is indeed
an integral part of the product and marketing strategy. For most enterprises, however, this message forms part of their political strategy rather
than their operational budget. The opportunity to cut costs is also widely
claimed, but the actual reductions are too small to drive significant change
in most enterprises. Rather, these claims form one component of applications for awards, which can confer significant marketing gains. For the
vast majority of tourism enterprises, therefore, as in other industry sectors,
the only real driver of social and environmental management measures is
government regulation.

It is entirely normal that most companies and citizens do no more than
comply with applicable law. One of the functions of government social and
environmental legislation is to require people and corporations to act for
the public good even if unprofitable. Since social and environmental regulations are applied across an entire industry sector simultaneously, the
costs of compliance do not greatly affect their relative competitive positions
within the country concerned. They may do so internationally, and this is
a significant issue in international negotiations on trade and environment
(Buckley, 1993). In examining the links between tourism enterprises and
sustainable development, therefore, government policy forms a critical context for the actions of individual enterprises.

IMPACTS

The operations of tourism enterprises commonly create a range of social, environmental, and economic impacts, some positive and some negative. Positive economic contributions include: income for shareholders and suppliers; employment and entrepreneurial opportunities for staff and contractors; taxes and rates paid to national and local governments; and a range of smaller-scale fees such as those paid to use national parks.

Economic costs include increased demands on publicly funded infrastructure, and consequent increased operational and maintenance costs including staff and salaries. Local government authorities in popular tourist towns express concern that costs for water supply, sewage treatment, garbage collection, litter cleanup, and public-space maintenance are greatly increased to cater for large numbers of tourists. In addition, these costs are met by resident ratepayers, whereas the benefits accrue to private tourism enterprises. Similarly, national parks agencies express concern that an increasing proportion of their operational expenditure is for visitor management and infrastructure, with correspondingly less available for primary conservation management (Buckley, 2002).

Some of the social benefits of tourism are a simple consequence of employment opportunities. Particularly in communities which might otherwise have high unemployment with associated social costs and consequences, tourism generates benefits simply by providing jobs. In some developing nations, tourism provides the only significant local source of cash income, and hence the only opportunity to purchase manufactured goods from elsewhere. Tourism can also provide social benefits through engendering a revival of tradition, history, and community cohesion, as local residents take pride in their own place and culture because of the impression it leaves with tourists. This effect has been reported, for example, for a number of indigenous and first nations communities in developed nations, as well as in developing countries.

Social costs may include, e.g.: increased crime; breakdown of traditional community structures; commodification of traditional culture and practices; and increasing financial inequities between residents involved in tourism enterprises and those who are not. These issues apply in both developed and developing nations. In more impoverished areas, disparities in wealth between tourists and local residents, or between local entrepreneurs with a cash income from tourism and those without, can lead to increases in theft. In richer areas, tourism destinations may become centres for the sale of drugs and stolen goods, sometimes in association with large-scale international organised crime. In developing nations, ceremonial dances and artefacts of religious or other cultural significance may be commodified and copied specifically for sale to tourists. In developed nations, religious buildings such as the great cathedrals of Europe, or more recent cultural traditions such as the mystique of America's Wild West or Australia's outback, have also been converted to commodified tourism attractions. There are enclave resorts in remote Pacific islands where locals can enter only as employees; but the same applies to some of the members-only clubs in developed nations, accessible only to particularly wealthy foreigners.

All forms of tourism produce environmental impacts of various types, some minimal but others severe. All forms of motorised transport consume fuel and produce noise, greenhouse gases, and other atmospheric emissions, together with water pollution in some cases. They also need infrastructure ranging from roads and tracks to airports and marinas; or else they create impacts through wheel damage to soil and vegetation, and to boat launching and anchoring sites. Tourist accommodation consumes energy, water, and a variety of raw materials and manufactured goods. Directly or indirectly, it also produces wastes such as: fly ash and carbon dioxide from electricity generation, sludges from water treatment; a wide variety of garbage and solid wastes; sewage and human wastes; and sullage or grey water from washing and cleaning. Nutrient-rich discharges of treated sewage produce eutrophication and algal blooms. .

Tourist activities and associated infrastructure such as ski fields, golf courses, marinas, racing circuits and riding courses, and so on all generate their own particular impacts. Ski resorts consume water for snowmaking and create a variety of ecological impacts through noise, snow compaction, and snow grooming. Golf courses use large quantities of irrigation water, fertilizers, and pesticides, with damaging consequences for local watercourses and for grass-feeding birds. Coastal and estuarine ecosystems such as mangrove swamps and other wetlands are often cleared for the construction of marinas. In national parks and other conservation areas, some types of recreational activity and associated commercial tourism enterprises can be carried on successfully without causing significant conservation impacts, but some cause considerable impacts through a wide range of mechanisms (Liddle, 1997; Buckley, 2004a). High impacts are commonly created by tourism operations which involve: fixed accommodation or infrastructure development within a protected area; motorised equipment or transport; livestock; and competitive or social events involving large numbers of people who treat the park only as a playground, racetrack, or background.

There are several mechanisms by which tourism can contribute to conservation, but the number of enterprises with a net positive contribution is rather small. The potential economic benefits from new tourism opportunities are often invoked by conservation interests lobbying in favour of new protected areas; but with one or two notable exceptions, it is rare for individual tourism enterprises, tourism industry associations, or government tourism portfolios to lend an active voice to such efforts. In countries and jurisdictions which charge entrance and activity fees for visitors to national parks and similar areas, commercial tourism enterprises must generally also pay such fees on behalf of their clients. In some cases these fees may be either higher or lower than those charged for private individual visitors; but in any event, they do not generally recoup the full pro rata or even marginal cost to the conservation agency of providing facilities for commercial tourism (Buckley, 2003b; Lockwood et al., 2006). Parks fees are thus a positive contribution, but not a net positive contribution.

Net positive contributions to conservation are indeed provided by a small number of commercial tourism enterprises, most commonly through the purchase or lease of private or community land, restoration and if necessary restocking for conservation, and the funding of continued conservation management costs through commercial tourism operations. In addition, there are particular international nature-tour operators who preferentially take their clients to these private reserves. Their preferences are commonly due to the high quality of accommodation and service, and the opportunity to see rare or charismatic wildlife, or particularly spectacular trees or scenery, at close range. That is, these tours and lodges design their products to appeal to a commercial tourism market; but in the process they do make positive net contributions to conservation of the local natural environment (Buckley, 2003c, 2006: 352–79). There is also a key social component in this process, as these tourism enterprises gain local community support for conservation by providing local employment. Whether the net global contributions are still positive after factoring in the impacts of long-haul travel on climate change (Folke et al., 2006) is a much more difficult accounting exercise which has yet to be addressed.

INDUSTRY MEASURES

Many of the operational and political practices of tourism enterprises have consequences for sustainable development. On the positive side, many private tourism enterprises, in all subsectors, have now adopted a range of practical environmental management measures and social responsibility schemes to reduce their immediate impacts; and tourism industry associations and government agencies have attempted to recognise and reward good environmental practice and performance through a variety of awards, ecolabels, and ecocertification programmes. On the negative side, however, many tourism enterprises continue to lobby for extended development and access rights in protected areas, with associated consequences for conservation; and continue to construct large-scale and socially damaging new developments, often with extensive economic leakage away from the local communities and even countries concerned. Across the tourism industry as a whole, lip service to sustainable development is still a great deal more common than best practice.

Practical environmental management measures necessarily differ between different types of tourism enterprise, and also between regions with different terrain and climate. For long-haul air travel the key issue is to maximise fuel efficiency and so minimise atmospheric emissions, through improved design of aircraft engines and fuselages, and improved freight and passenger scheduling. For local light aircraft and helicopter flights, however, noise disturbance to wildlife may be of greater ecological significance, so key concerns may be to choose quieter aircraft and fly well away from critical animal populations. On the water, hull configuration and engine capacity are critical in controlling noise, engine exhausts, and water pollution. Mooring and anchoring practices, toilet design and sewage treatment, and types of antifouling paint are also highly significant, as well as the behaviour of individual boat skippers in approaching marine wildlife and seabirds.

A number of environmental management guidelines and codes of practice have been produced in attempts to disseminate good environmental practice throughout the boat-based tourism industry, with particular reference to diving on coral reefs and to watching whales and other large marine creatures (Rainbow et al., 2000a, b; Buckley et al., 2000; Garrod & Fennell, 2004). Compliance with these codes, however, seems to be highly problematic (Scarpaci & Dayanthi, 2003; Byrnes & Warnken, 2003). Guidelines are also available to encourage drivers of off-road vehicles to minimise their impacts on soil, vegetation, and watercourses (Buckley, 2000). Currently, there are enormous variations between nature-based tours which use off-road vehicles solely for access to remote areas; and excitement-based off-road tours which deliberately promote high-impact vehicle handling.

In the tourist accommodation sector, a variety of energy, water, and resource conservation and recycling measures are available, depending on the scale and location of the facilities concerned. The degree to which such measures are actually adopted is somewhat sporadic and often rather small-scale. The most widespread measure, for example, is simply a small sign telling guests that if they hang towels back on the rack, the hotel will save laundry water by not washing them. At the other extreme, some isolated ecolodges have a comprehensive and integrated set of measures to minimise both the consumption of resources and the production of waste. A number of case studies are described by Buckley (2003c).

Tourism ecocertification schemes are now legion (Font & Buckley, 2001; Honey, 2002; Black & Crabtree, 2007). Most of these purport to improve environmental management amongst their members, but there is rather little evidence that they have actually done so. The market penetration of most such schemes is quite limited, and provisions for audit and enforcement equally so. Certification can provide commercial advantages to tourism enterprises principally by improving their relationship with relevant government agencies. Protected-area management agencies throughout Australia, for example, grant longer multiyear operating permits to tourism enterprises with ecocertification than to those without it.

Recognition of these schemes and labels by individual tourists at retail level appears to be very low, except for two high-level global environmental award schemes. The World Travel and Tourism Council's "Tourism for

Tomorrow" Awards and the *Condé Nast Traveler* "World Savers" Awards are both promoted heavily by their parent organisations. Any tourism enterprise which wins either of these awards is guaranteed global publicity, which is of significant financial value whether or not the customers it attracts are environmentally concerned. Even for the short-listed applications to these top-tier awards, however, many still seem to focus much more on form than substance.

Overall, whilst the various types of tourism ecolabel now available have had a significant role in promoting the range of social responsibility schemes and environmental management measures available, it is not clear that they have led to measurable improvements in the social and environmental bottom lines for the tourism industry as a whole, or perhaps even for the individual tourism enterprises concerned. Tourism enterprises which can justly claim to be global leaders in these regards commonly seem to have adopted their particular philosophies and practices either because of personal convictions or because of local laws and politics, with applications for awards very much as an afterthought.

In some countries particularly, there have been long-term associations between the commercial tourism industry and the protected-area estate. In North America, for example, such associations were established during the early phases of European colonisation. In recent years, however, there has been increasing pressure from the commercial tourism industry for public protected-area management agencies to grant new access and development rights for quite large-scale tourism enterprises. Such lobbying efforts are commonly couched in the language of partnerships, and there are indeed particular circumstances under which such arrangements seem to have yielded benefits for the parks agency as well as the tourism enterprise.

In Australia, for example, there are cases where parks agencies have leased heritage buildings to tour operators so as to avoid high maintenance costs; and others where they have granted development and access rights in remote areas of larger parks so as to improve dispersion of tourists away from gateway areas (see Chapter 7). There are also examples where parks agencies have granted rights to private tourism operators to provide specialised and expensive infrastructure for particular activities, such as diving pontoons, canopy walks, wildlife watching hides, and infrared or underwater cameras (Buckley, 2004b). More commonly, however, it seems that parks agencies and tourism enterprises have rather different ideas of what constitutes a successful partnership (Buckley, 2004c).

CONCLUSIONS

Tourism is a large global industry, and many individual tourism enterprises are large multinational corporations. Whilst smaller specialist enterprises may lead the industry's contribution to sustainable development through the ecotourism subsector, this has rather little significance at global scale unless these principles and practices are also adopted subsequently by mainstream tourism operations. Governments which promote small-scale ecocertification programmes as a marketing measure, whilst at the same time granting development approvals for very large-scale new resorts with major social and environmental impacts, can hardly claim to contribute to sustainable development in the tourism sector.

As in any industry sector, there is a relatively small number of tourism enterprises which already have a high standard of environmental performance and social responsibility, and a very much larger number of enterprises with far lower standards. Any improvement which is adopted across the industry as a whole therefore has a much greater aggregate effect than an improvement of similar scale which is adopted only by enterprises which are already leaders. International airlines and hotel chains need economies of scale, and will no doubt continue to pursue growth and profit to the best of their ability. Most of this activity is essentially urban, and any improvements in its triple bottom line are likely to be driven principally by compliance with changing government regulation. Much of this regulation applies to residential and industrial buildings more generally, not only to the tourism sector. The first key to sustainable development of tourism enterprises is hence through government policy.

Smaller-scale tourism enterprises may sometimes have a disproportionate effect on sustainable development, however, if they operate in areas of high conservation value. Practices and progress in the outdoor tourism subsector, and in particular the management of commercial tourism operations within protected areas, is hence a key component of sustainable development. As human impacts continue to expand over the rest of the world's surface, the protected-area estate is more and more important to the environmental bottom line for the world as a whole, and thus to sustainable development more generally. Because the tourism industry is one of the few sectors permitted in the protected-area estate, it can generate negative effects on the environmental bottom line disproportionate to its economic scale.

On the other hand, the tourism industry harnesses human desires to enjoy and appreciate natural and cultural heritage, from wilderness parks to city cathedrals. It therefore does have the potential to make significant positive contributions to the social and environmental as well as the economic bottom line in global sustainable development. Despite the many impacts which tourism undeniably does produce, these are still generally less than those produced by other industry sectors such as agriculture, forestry and fisheries, mining and manufacturing, or indeed residential settlement.

There is no particular reason, however, why private tourism enterprises should see themselves as agents of sustainable development. From their own perspective, they are simply profit-making businesses like any other. If tourism is to become a significant agent in global sustainable development, it will be up to governments to put in place the necessary legal frameworks. Industry measures alone are unlikely to be effective.

REFERENCES

Black, R. & Crabtree, A., 2007. *Quality control and certification in ecotourism.* Wallingford: CAB International.

Buckley, R.C., 1993. International trade, investment and environment: an environmental management perspective. *Journal of World Trade,* 27(4), p.102–48.

Buckley, R.C., 2000. *Green guide for 4WD tours.* Gold Coast, Australia: Griffith University.

Buckley, R.C., 2002. Managing tourism in parks: research priorities of industry associations and protected area agencies in Australia. *Journal of Ecotourism,* 1, p.162–72.

Buckley, R.C., 2003a. Environmental inputs and outputs in ecotourism: geotourism with a positive triple bottom line? *Journal of Ecotourism,* 2, p.76–82.

Buckley, R.C., 2003b. Pay to play in parks: an Australian policy perspective on visitor fees in public protected areas. *Journal of Sustainable Tourism,* 11, p.56–73.

Buckley, R.C., 2003c. *Case studies in ecotourism.* Oxford: CAB International, 264pp.

Buckley, R.C. ed., 2004a. Environmental impacts of ecotourism. Oxford: CABI, 389pp.

Buckley, R.C., 2004b. A natural partnership, vol. 2. Innovative funding mechanisms for visitor infrastructure in protected areas. Sydney: TTF Australia.

Buckley, R.C., 2004c. Partnerships in ecotourism: Australian political frameworks. *International Journal of Tourism Research,* 6, p.75–83.

Buckley, R.C., 2006. *Adventure tourism.* Oxford: CAB International, p.352–79.

Buckley, R.C., Rainbow, J., & Lawrance, K., 2000. *Green guide to whale watching.* Gold Coast, Australia: Griffith University.

Byrnes, T. & Warnken, J., 2003. Small recreational and tourist vessels in inshore coastal areas: a characterization of types of impacts. In R. Buckley, C. Pickering, & D.B. Weaver eds., *Nature-based tourism, environment and land management,* p.101–10.

Folke, J., Ostrup, J.H. & Gössling, S., 2006. Ecotourist choices of transport modes. In S. Gössling & J. Hultman eds., *Ecotourism in Scandinavia: lessons in theory and practice.* Oxford: CAB International, p.154–65.

Font, X. & Buckley, R.C. eds., 2001. *Tourism ecolabelling.* Oxford: CAB International, 359pp.

Garrod, B. & Fennell, D.A., 2004. An analysis of whalewatching codes of conduct. *Annals of Tourism Research,* 31, p.334–52.

Honey, M. ed., 2002. *Ecotourism and certification: setting standards in practice.* Washington, DC: Island Press, 407pp.

Liddle, M.J., 1997. *Recreation ecology.* Dordrecht, Netherlands: Kluwer.

Lockwood, M., Worboys, G. & Kothari, A., 2006. *Managing protected areas.* London: Oxford.

Rainbow, J., Warnken, J. & Buckley, R.C., 2000a. *Green guide to SCUBA diving.* Gold Coast, Australia: Griffith University.

Rainbow, J., Buckley, R.C., Byrnes, T. & Warnken, J., 2000b. *Green guide to blue seas.* Gold Coast, Australia: Griffith University.

Scarpaci, C. & Dayanthi, N., 2003. Compliance with regulations by swim-with-dolphins: operations in Port Phillip Bay, Victoria, Australia. *Environmental Management,* 31, p.342–47.

UN World Tourism Organisation, UN Environment Program and World Meteorological Organisation, 2007. *Climate change and tourism: responding to global challenge.* UNTWO, UNEP and WMO.

4 Sustainable Tourism Development in the United States of America

An Intricate Balance from Policy to Practice

Kelly S. Bricker

The United States of America (USA) represents a substantial land mass of diverse geography. A country which, in the context of this field of enquiry, is all the more complex given it encompasses such a diverse range of states and given its political structures and overall governance. Thus, to address the environmental performance of tourism enterprises within the United States potentially is beyond the constraints of any one chapter. The objective herein is therefore to provide an overview of the progress that is being made, the steps that have and are being taken, to encourage the protection of the environment per se, on which tourism is so dependent, and to encourage tourism enterprises to address their environmental performance. In pursuance of this objective, first a brief outline of the United States is presented within which the primacy of federal agencies as the guardians of the environment is identified. National tourism policy is then considered before moving on to discuss the role of federal and regional agencies and then key examples of nongovernmental organisations and professional tourism organisations and their contribution to promoting progress towards sustainability in the tourism sector.

Clearly, not all programmes can be discussed and, undoubtedly, there are others in the process of development. Thus, given the overall scope of inquiry, the aim is to highlight some of the efforts of significance to the environmental performance of tourism in the United States; in particular those relevant to tourism management on public lands, memorandums of understanding, and partnerships for a sustainable future.

BACKGROUND

The United States of America (U.S.) has a population of nearly three hundred million people living in an area encompassing three million square miles.

Geographically, the United States is one of the most diverse countries in the world. In its fifty states, which include Alaska and Hawaii, there are coastlines along the Atlantic and Pacific oceans; the Great Lakes; the world's fourth longest river system (i.e., Mississippi-Missouri River); the flat and fertile Great Plains; vast deserts such as the Mojave; and expansive mountain ranges such as the Appalachians, Rocky Mountains, and the Sierra Nevada. Over six hundred million acres (approximately 242 hectares) or one-third of the lands in the United States are public and managed by federal agencies such as the Department of Interior's Bureau of Land Management (BLM), the National Park Service (NPS), and the United States Department of Agriculture's Forest Service (USFS). The environmental and social policies that guide development and other activities on public lands were generated through the National Environmental Policy Act (NEPA) of 1970. For example, within the NEPA, there is a Declaration of National Environmental Policy (Title I) which " . . . requires the federal government to use all practicable means to create and maintain conditions under which man and nature can exist in productive harmony" (USEPA, 2008a: 1). Thus, federal agencies (e.g., the National Park Service, the U.S. Forest Service, the Bureau of Land Management) must employ a systematic interdisciplinary approach to

> Prepar[ing] detailed statements assessing the environmental impact of and alternatives to major Federal actions significantly affecting the environment. These statements are commonly referred to as environmental impact statements (EISs). Section 102 also requires federal agencies to lend appropriate support to initiatives and programs designed to anticipate and prevent a decline in the quality of mankind's world environment. (USEPA, 2008a: 1)

NATIONAL TOURISM POLICY

The National Tourism Policy Act of 1981 elevated the importance of tourism policy in the United States (Edgell et al., 2008) and the United States Travel and Tourism Administration (USTTA) as well as an undersecretary of commerce to " . . . implement broad tourism policy initiatives [and] to develop travel to the United States from abroad as a stimulus to economic stability and the growth of travel in the USA" (Edgell et al., 2008: 48). Despite the critical importance of this act, in 1996 the U.S. Congress abolished the USTTA. The United States also resigned its membership of the World Tourism Organization (WTO), relinquishing any forward momentum on tourism (Edgell et al., 2008). A retrograde step, given that this act and USTTA could have been the impetus for launching a national sustainable tourism strategy because the act not only addressed the overall economic importance of tourism and travel, but offered guidance towards resource, historic, and heritage sustainability. For example, Section 101 specifically addressed the responsibility of the USTTA in: preserving the historical and cultural foundations of the nation as a living part of community life and development; ensuring future generations an opportunity to appreciate and enjoy the rich heritage of the nation; and addressing the compatibility of tourism and recreation with other national interests in energy development and conservation, environmental protection, and the judicious use of natural resources (Edgell, 1999).

Today, the Office of Travel and Tourism Industries (OTTI), formerly USTTA, is housed within the U.S. Department of Commerce and is expected to " . . . [expand] travel and tourism business opportunities for employment and economic growth" (OTTI, 2008: 1). The OTTI's responsibilities include collecting and publishing comprehensive international travel and tourism statistics and marketing information, facilitating the reduction of barriers to travel, providing representation for the United States to foreign governments, maintaining U.S. participation in international trade shows, and developing and implementing a comprehensive tourism policy and plan (OTTI, 2008). Further, the OTTI serves as secretariat for the Tourism Policy Council (TPC), which is " . . . an interagency committee established by law for the purpose of ensuring that the nation's tourism interests are considered in Federal decision-making" (TPC, 2008: 1) Its primary functions are to " . . . coordinate national policies and programs relating to international travel and tourism, recreation, and national heritage resources that involve Federal agencies . . ." (TPC, 2008: 1). Interestingly, several individuals (e.g., the secretary of Interior, the commissioner of the U.S. Customs Service) who sit on the TPC are integral not only to tourism promotion and travel administration services, but also land management. However, from an operational perspective tourism efforts within the United States are " . . . scattered amongst nearly 50 Federal agencies, with much of the power transferred to individual states" (Brewton & Witham, 1998: 59)

Environmental Protection

The United States Environmental Protection Agency (USEPA) was established in 1970 to "protect human health and the environment" (USEPA, 2008b: 1) and is responsible for the Clean Water and Air Acts passed by Congress in the 1970s and oversight of superfund sites, which are linked to hazardous waste and environmental accident prevention. In addition, the agency has established environmental standards and introduced concepts of sustainability into their programmes, which are varied and abundant. For example, USEPA promotes environmental stewardship in partnership with other governmental agencies, businesses, communities, and nongovernmental organizations (USEPA, 2008c). It also promotes concepts of sustainability, such as waste reduction and energy conservation, to over three hundred million Americans at the household level designed to stimulate activities that encourage a more sustainable future and improve the bottom line through stewardship programmes (USEPA, 2005a). For example, within the Environmentally

Preferable Purchasing Programme criteria are included for purchasing low-impact products with high recycled content. A number of programmes have been subsequently developed to incorporate industry sectors, including a programme for waste reduction in hotels and casinos in Indian country which has potential impact on over four hundred hotels, motels, and resorts, and over two hundred casinos (USEPA, 2000). The Energy Star programme is also designed to help consumers and businesses " . . . identify energy efficient products and solutions" (USEPA, 2008d: 1). This programme has had enormous impact on the creation of energy-efficient products. In 2005, USEPA established the Energy Star Challenge. Over twenty states, groups, and businesses, notably including the American Hotel and Lodging Association (AH&LA), joined in the challenge to assess energy use and reach a goal of 10 per cent or more efficient use of energy resources. In addition, USEPA's Green Power Partnership programme supports organisations that purchase or plan to purchase green power. They provide expert advice; tools and resources (e.g., promotional materials); credibility; and publicity and recognition (USEPA Green Power Partner, 2008e: 1). Every quarter, profiles of the top twenty-five Green Power Partners are published; in the first quarter of 2008, one tourism organisation was listed—Vail Resorts, Inc.[1] USEPA also publishes the "100% Green Power Purchaser" list, which in 2008 included thirty travel and leisure-based organisations. In total, "the combined green power purchases of these organizations amounts to more than 4 billion kilowatt-hours of green power annually, which is the equivalent amount of electricity needed to power more than 325,000 average American households each year" (USEPA, 2008f: 1). Another partnership that has evolved through USEPA is the Climate Leadership Programme. This industry-government partnership is focused on developing a comprehensive greenhouse gas emissions reduction management system. Complementing this effort is USEPA's National Environmental Performance Track Programme, which recognises top environmental performance among private and public facilities that go beyond compliance with regulatory requirements. Over five hundred strong, thirty-three members are in the "Arts, Recreation, and Entertainment" sector, and will remain there for three years, as long as they continue to meet program criteria.[2]

USEPA has an established environmental management system (EMS), notably modified for small business,[3] which includes the following criteria:

- *Sustained Compliance*—Members must have a sustained record of compliance with environmental laws.
- *Continuous Improvement*—Applicants must demonstrate past environmental achievements during the current and preceding year. Applicants also must commit to four quantitative goals for improving their environmental performance.
- *Public Outreach*—Applicants must commit to staying involved and active in their community, sharing their accomplishments with the

public, and addressing any community concerns. They also must complete an Annual Performance Report each year of their membership.

Other USEPA programmes of note include the Carpet America Recovery Effort (an initiative that seeks to create recycling alternatives for carpet disposal); the Golf Courses Nitrogen Management Challenge–Region 2 (a partnership between golf courses, the USEPA, the United States Golf Association [USGA], Cornell University, local governments, and citizens with the goal of minimizing loss of surface nitrogen to groundwater); the Green Buildings Workgroup (a programme which brings together many programs within the USEPA that work with building and development sectors to improve their environmental performance); and the Clean Marinas programme, a voluntary, incentive-based program that encourages boaters and marine operators to assist in the protection of water quality through engagement in environmentally sound operations. Over the last decade, the USEPA has encouraged environmental stewardship through voluntary programmes and partnerships, and provided a fairly comprehensive definition for environmental stewardship:

> Environmental stewardship is the responsibility for environmental quality shared by all those whose actions affect the environment, reflected as both a value and a practice by individuals, companies, communities, and government organizations. Positive stewardship behavior demonstrates acceptance of this responsibility through the continuous improvement of environmental performance to achieve measurable results and sustainable outcomes. Further . . . that all parts of society actively take responsibility to improve environmental quality and to achieve sustainable outcomes. (USEPA, 2005a: 8)

Through its leadership role in environmental protection and stewardship, USEPA has enhanced government-private sector efforts to increase recognition and positively encourage sustainable best practices within the travel and leisure sector, which covers a range of business and operational challenges. Despite the lack of a coordinated sustainable tourism policy at the federal level, from an environmental perspective USEPA has advanced voluntary sustainable approaches to business and operations management.

However, there continues to be a major challenge, however, with respect to tourism. For example, tourism is categorised differently depending on the type of programme being referenced. This lack of clarity has led to difficulties in presenting statistics on the growth of sustainable tourism in the United States. In 2005, an evaluation of USEPA's stewardship and voluntary programs was undertaken. Results indicated that USEPA needs to: identify motivators and barriers to participation; continue to incorporate stakeholder feedback into the planning, design, and implementation of stewardship programmes; plan, coordinate, and manage its voluntary programs; and develop a process for assessing these programmes. In July of 2008, USEPA and the Green Meeting Industry Council (GMIC) agreed to work with the Convention Industry Council's Accepted Practices Exchange (APEX) and the American Society for Testing and Materials International (ASTM International[4]) to develop a uniform measurement of environmental performance, and to define what is "green" according to the meetings and events industry. The result will be an accredited standard to be utilised by the federal government's purchasing program. According to Lewis of USEPA's Pollution Prevention Division, " . . . the Government is one of the largest consumers of meeting services in the country and intends to adopt the standards as a measuring stick in making their spending decisions" (Bicker, 2008).

Undoubtedly USEPA is taking a leading role in environmental protection and will continue to provide information and tools for assessing sustainability within their own departments and encourage partnerships and voluntary programs. The agency also will continue dialogue with industry to identify best practice management.

THE ROLE OF PUBLIC LAND AND WATER AGENCIES

While tourism enterprises in the United States are predominantly privately owned and operated, the federal government plays an important role in the provision of natural and cultural attractions and the sustainability of public lands and waters. There are several agencies involved in tourism, which are taking a role in promoting sustainable tourism development through public-private initiatives and active involvement in destination management.

National Park Service (NPS)

The mission of the NPS is "To conserve the scenery and the natural and historic objects and the wildlife therein and to provide for the enjoyment of the same in such manner and by such means as will leave them unimpaired for the enjoyment of future generations" (http://www.nps.gov/aboutus/mission.htm). To help the NPS meet its mission, the 1965 Concession Policy Act was reformed in 1998 to the effect that "The NPS will provide, through concession contracts, commercial visitor services within the parks that are necessary and appropriate for visitor use and enjoyment" (NPS, 2006: 1). There are now over 570 concessionaires who in turn offer a range of services and activities (e.g., food, lodging, guide services, retail shops), which gross in excess of over $800 million (NPS, 2006: 1). The majority of these contracts fall into Category III, meaning that the concession has no facilities located within park boundaries (e.g., guides and outfitters) (Geiger, 2008). In 1999, the NPS established the Concession Environmental Management Program (CoEMP) to address environmental management and compliance of visitor services because " . . . concessionaires operate in or near our country's most treasured resources—the NPS would be neglecting its founding mission if it did not proactively try to minimize concessionaire environmental impacts" (NPS, 2006: 1). CoEMP is active in the concession contract development and selection process. For example, CoEMP provides oversight and guidance for improvement of concession contracts. In 2006, of over 380 contracts issued, sixty-one included environmental management system requirements and all contracts encouraged best management practices implementation (NPS, 2006). In addition, it provides oversight for concession operations. Environmental audits are conducted for all facilities operated in national parks. For those facilities specifically operated by concessionaires, the Concession Environmental Audit System (CEAS), which is the direct means for consulting on environmental issues, has been established. Unfortunately, to date CEAS has not included comprehensive environmental standards and criteria (NPS, 2006: 4). However, CoEMP is developing concession-specific criteria and standards which it envisions will serve as a tool for parks to utilise in addressing the environmental management performance and evaluation of concessionaires, including lodging, food, marina, and retail services. CoEMP also provides outreach education to promote the continual improvement of daily operations, supported by the *Greenline Newsletter*, a CD, and a Web site, which highlight examples of best management practices and concession accomplishments; additionally there a number of guidance documents to support efforts towards more sustainable operational practices. CoEMP also works with other federal agencies on concession management. For example, CoEMP and the USEPA work closely under a memorandum of understanding to assist small businesses in identifying business-specific best management practices.

To date, several concessions have developed environmental management systems and have been recognised for their achievements. For example, Xanterra Parks and Resorts, the largest state and national park concessionaire in the United States, created an EMS called "Ecologix" for its operation in Zion National Park, leading to " . . . a reduction in water consumption by 40%, in solid waste by 59%, and in electricity use by 25%" (NPS, 2005: 1). Xanterra is also making a difference by minimizing solid waste, developing ecologically sound hotel rooms, recycling grease for use as biodiesel, utilizing renewable wind energy to power a portion of their system, and so on.[5]

Bureau of Land Management (BLM)

BLM is primarily involved with ecotourism and heritage tourism initiatives on public lands. Managing over 40 per cent of all public lands in the United States, it is one of the original partners in establishing the National Watchable Wildlife Programme, which now has nearly three hundred designated wildlife viewing areas, spanning the country from Alaska to Florida. BLM has identified tourism as one of the top three industries within all western BLM states (BLM, 2008b). The organisation has worked closely with programmes that minimise environmental impacts, for example, "Leave No Trace" (see http://www.lnt.org/), and is actively promoting heritage-based tourism (i.e., "travelling to experience the places and activities that authentically represent the stories and people of the past and present. . . ." (National Trust for Historic Preservation, 2008: 1) on public lands. As part of its commitment to heritage tourism, it sponsors regional workshops on heritage tourism and has engaged in memorandum of understanding agreements with nonprofit programmes such as "Sustainable Slopes." Somewhat contrary to the initiatives described previously, BLM also manages a range of controversial activities. They administer gas and oil leases under its multiple-use mandate, which are opposed, for example by the National Audubon Society and the Wilderness Society. With increased pressure for oil and gas exploration within the United States, BLM will continue to face scrutiny from a range of environmental organisations.

U.S. Fish and Wildlife Service (FWS)

The mission of the FWS is to work " . . . with others to conserve, protect and enhance fish, wildlife, and plants and their habitats for the continuing benefit of the American people" (http://www.fws.gov/partnerships/mission.html). As with many federal land and water agencies, the FWS partners with a range of entities for sustainable tourism initiatives, including, but not limited to, the EPA, the Forest Service, and the NOAA. It manages more than 540 wildlife refuge areas and 36,000 fee and easement waterfowl production areas, which provide habitat to more than 250 threatened or endangered plants and animals including manatees, bald eagles, and the California jewelflower. All of which attract ecotourism enthusiasts from around the country.

Forest Service (FS)

The FS is one of the largest land-managing agencies in the United States, with approximately eighty hectares of national forests and wilderness areas. The FS has recognised that partnering with the tourism sector is good business, especially in light of its service mission:

> Our policy is to work with our interagency federal tourism partners, state tourism offices and the Departments of Commerce (DOC) and Transportation to promote sustainable natural areas development and visitor use through agreements such as: Federal DOC Tourism Policy Council; Western States Tourism Policy Council and Southeast Tourism Policy Council. Our agency is also a member of Travel Industry of America (TIA) to assist coordination with industry-wide sustainable "best practices" initiatives. (U.S. Forest Service, 2008: 1)

The agency has been active in promoting and enhancing sustainable tourism development across the country; for example, supporting ongoing initiatives to bring sustainable tourism to federal agencies. It also works on tourism efforts at the state and local levels. Further, it holds symposia and workshops with other agencies on sustainable tourism and concessionaires on public lands, including guidelines for outfitters and guides managing nature-based tourism businesses on their managed lands. The agency works with over six thousand private tourism guides on federal lands and sets policy for 60 per cent of the ski slopes in the country. Some of the most significant examples of the agency's contribution to promoting more sustainable practices in tourism are as follows.

- Produced the *Built Environment Image Guide* using sustainability concepts to shape the design and construction of facilities.
- Participated in grassroots projects in the Ozark Mountains, upper Michigan Peninsula, Tennessee, and elsewhere to foster ecotourism experiences.
- Developed heritage tourism partnerships with rural communities and tribal governments including the Castleland Resource Conservation and Development partnership with seventy-five communities and four counties in southern Utah; a joint visitor centre with Jemez Indian Pueblo in Santa Fe National Forest; and cooperation with the Michigan Great Outdoors Cultural Tour with the State Historical Society.
- Was a signatory to the Bar Harbour Declaration on Ecotourism in the United States. This declaration stemmed from the first national ecotourism conference in the United States.

These and other initiatives are helping to develop further the adoption of best management practices in the development of tourism in the United States. Not only are these efforts coordinated by the FS; they are a part of a larger effort by several land and water agencies, private sector and non-governmental organisations.

National Oceanic and Atmospheric Administration (NOAA)

The NOAA is a federal agency located in the Department of Commerce, whose mission is "To understand and predict changes in Earth's environment and conserve and manage coastal and marine resources to meet our Nation's economic, social, and environmental needs" (NOAA, 2008: 1) Among the five departments in NOAA, the National Ocean Service (NOS) is primarily responsible for the nation's coastal and marine resources. "NOS employees work to preserve and enhance the nation's coastal resources and ecosystems along 95,000 miles of shoreline and 3.5 million square miles of coastal ocean" (NOS, 2008: 1) Specifically, the NOS (2008):

- provides products, services, and data, such as nautical charts, a framework for consistent geographic reference, and tidal and water-level monitoring;
- manages thirteen national marine sanctuaries and one national monument and provides funding to coastal states to manage twenty-seven national estuarine research reserves;
- participates in immediate response to hazardous spill events, damage assessment, and restoration activities; and
- supports states in protecting resources and guiding economic development in coastal areas.

NOS also supports training for state coastal managers participating in the programme; assesses, monitors, and predicts the consequences of natural and human-induced environmental hazards such as hurricanes, erosion, and sea-level rise; and promotes the Clean Marina Initiative (CMI) programme in conjunction with the USEPA. The CMI is a voluntary, incentive-based program that provides information, guidance, and technical assistance to marina operators, local governments, and recreational boaters on best management practices that are used to prevent or reduce pollution. NOAA's scientific research, educational outreach, and coastal and marine initiatives provide critical information for sustainable tourism development and coastal zone management. The nation's ocean resources create "natural-capital" sought by tourists from around the globe. Through coral reef conservation, marine protected areas, national marine sanctuary, coastal zone management and decision-making tools, and many other NOS programmes, U.S. coasts, oceans, lakes, and waterways are integrated into a nationwide conservation system.

NONGOVERNMENTAL REGIONAL ORGANISATIONS

The promotion of sustainability and best practices in tourism development is also coordinated at regional levels. Two regions, discussed following, are particularly well organised and have established several initiatives with respect to sustainable tourism development.

Western States Tourism Policy Council (WSTPC)

An excellent example of regional cooperation and integration of federal agencies is this consortium of thirteen Western state tourism offices, including: Alaska, Arizona, California, Colorado, Idaho, Hawaii, Montana, Nevada, New Mexico, Oregon, Utah, Washington, and Wyoming. The mission of the council is "To advance understanding and increase support for public policies that enhance the positive impact of travel and tourism on the economies and environments of the states and communities in the

West" (WSTPC, 2008: 1). In 1997 and later in 2001, the WSTPC signed a memorandum of understanding (MOU) which now includes eleven federal agencies, including and in addition to those noted previously, the Bureau of Reclamation, the Bureau of Indian Affairs, the U.S. Army Corp of Engineers, the Federal Highway Administration, the Department of Commerce Office of Travel and Tourism Industries, and the USDA National Resources Conservation Service. The outcomes of the MOU included a pledge to " . . . share information and provide mutual support and cooperation on common programs and projects" (WSTPC, 2008: 1). To date, there have been eight regional conferences held with themes ranging from tourism and public lands, to transportation, to cultural tourism, to gateway communities. According to the WSTPC, the conferences have had a significant impact on tourism; successes include the establishment of the Gateway Communities Cooperation Act and the National Alliance of Gateway Communities—the nation's first national association dedicated to the interests of gateway communities (WSTPC, 2008).

With respect to transportation in the West, another outcome of one of the WSTPC's regional conferences was the formation of the National Travel, Tourism, and Recreation Coalition for Surface Transportation. This coalition is the only national tourism organisation working to "alert and mobilize" the sector about the importance of highway reauthorization to all of travel and tourism (WSTPC, 2008: 4). More recently, there has been an increased effort to support adequate funding for federal land-managing agencies programmes and activities that are beneficial to tourism and recreation in the West. Also, the WSTPC has increased coordination and planning between state tourism offices and federal land-management agencies. Federal agencies such as the USFS and NPS acknowledge the importance of collaborative efforts, all of which are now included as part of both the NPS and USFS management plans, with policies directing NPS management staff to "work closely and cooperatively with Gateway communities" (WSTPC, 2008: 2).

WSTPC also played a key role in the National Park Centennial Initiative (NPCI), helping to ensure that the programme " . . . accept marketing projects on the national parks and that state tourism offices could help sponsor and administer these projects" (WSTPC, 2008: 3) The NPCI focuses on the following themed issues: Stewardship, Environmental Leadership, Recreation Experience, Education, and Professional Excellence. Each theme carries its own set of specific performance goals. For example, Stewardship has the goal of " . . . restoration of native habitats and rehabilitation of historic buildings," whereas Environmental Leadership focuses on " . . . showcasing exemplary environmental practices and reducing environmental impacts of park operations on air and water quality" (Kempthorne, 2007: 9, 10). These examples of specific performance goals reach beyond the parks' borders and into the surrounding communities. They set the bar rather high in improving not only services to visitors within the national park system but improving and sustaining the quality of the environments and cultural history people are attracted to in the first place. The NCPI has the potential to revitalise visitation and sustain the quality of parks the way our forefathers had envisioned.

Southeast Tourism Policy Council (STPC)

The STPC is the advocacy voice for the Southeast Tourism Society, which includes eleven member states, and is located in Atlanta, Georgia. Their mission is "To provide leadership that insures broad representation of tourism interests in the southeast, encourage partnerships between public and private sectors of tourism and advocate for sustainable economic growth in an environmentally responsible way" (STPC, 2008: 1). Primarily interests focus on federal funding to market the United States as a destination for international travellers; federal highway funding; informational surveys of international visitors whose results can be used to guide individual states' marketing efforts; and a long-term fee demonstration programme for all federal land agencies. These interests were showcased at the State-Federal Tourism Summit in 2002. Shortly following the summit, the STPC formed an MOU with the Departments of Interior, Agriculture, Commerce, Army, and Transportation, as well as USEPA and the Advisory Council on Historic Preservation.

Regional organizations such as the STPC and the WSTCP provide a framework for sustainable tourism development on a regional basis, creating a strong voice and organised platform for addressing issues and challenges facing the tourism sector. Further, these regional organisations have embraced the concept of partnering with agencies at the federal level, which has helped with sustainable tourism initiatives at the federal level.

Voluntary Sustainable Tourism Certification Programmes

From California to Vermont and Pennsylvania to Florida, "green" certification programmes for tourism enterprises are blooming, which all have similar structures, goals, and are voluntary. In most cases, they involve the state level department of environment and oftentimes the tourism marketing arm for the state government, which helps to bring recognition and promotion to the tourism enterprises opting to participate. In other instances, states have aligned with Green Seal's Lodging Standard and Certification, which has been in operation for nineteen years. Table 4.1 provides a summary of state programmes and how they are organised whilst Table 4.2 is a summary of other types of certification programmes utilised in the United States.

Table 4.1   State Focused Sustainable Tourism Certification Programmes

State/Title	Partners/Audits?	General Criteria	Type/Sector
California Green Lodging Program	California Integrated Waste Management Board (State Government) Audits? Yes Participants: 100	• Reduce energy • Conserve water • Minimize waste • Use environmentally preferable cleaners • Educate the public and their customers on reducing environmental impact • Food waste management	Developed to facilitate green lodging and travel by state employees.
Florida Green Lodging Certification Programme	Florida Department of the Environment Audits? Yes Participants: 25, 46 in process	Three Palm (rating) system: • Reduce energy • Conserve water • Minimize waste • Use environmentally preferable cleaners • Educate the public and their customers on reducing environmental impact	Lodging only
Georgia	Partnered with Green Seal to certify facilities	(see Green Seal below)	5 hotels listed to date
Maine Green Lodging	Department of Environment, supported by the Maine Tourism Association; Maine Office of Tourism Audits? Random audits Participants: 52	• Reduce energy • Conserve water • Minimize waste • Use environmentally preferable cleaners • Educate the public and their customers on r educing environmental impact	Focus on lodging

Program	Details	Participation	Focus
Green Lodging Michigan	Joint program through Michigan's Energy Office and the Department of Environmental Quality Audits? Yes, highest two levels, not for entry level Participants: 8, 7 in process	Three levels of participation: • Reduce energy • Conserve water • Minimize waste • Educate the public and their customers on reducing environmental impact	Hospitality Industry
New Hampshire Sustainable Lodging & Restaurant Program	Public Service of New Hampshire (utility company) Audits? Highest level only Participants: 30	Three levels of participation: • Reduce energy • Conserve water • Minimize waste • Use environmentally preferable cleaners • Educate the public and their customers on reducing environmental impact • Reducing hazardous waste	Focus on lodges and restaurants
North Carolina Green Plan for Hotels	Division of Pollution Prevention and Environmental Assistance Audits? No Participants: Unknown	Resources but no certification, list serve, and information.	Focus on lodging
Pennsylvania	Department of Environmental Protection Audits? Through Green Seal Participants: 22 hotels	Partnership with Green Seal to certify facilities; voluntary	Focus on lodging

(continued)

Table 4.1(continued)

State/Title	Partners/Audits?	General Criteria	Type/Sector
Rhode Island	Rhode Island Hospitality & Tourism Association in partnership with the Department of Environment Audits? Certification self-evaluation and technical evaluation; Audits? Unannounced on-site verification. Participants: 17 hotels, 13 restaurants, 3 other type business (i.e., convention centre)	Certification self-evaluation and technical evaluation; potential for unannounced on-site verification.	Focus on lodging, restaurants, and related (i.e., convention center)
Travel Green Wisconsin	Wisconsin Department of Tourism; Wisconsin Environmental Initiative Audits? No Participants: 44	• Reduce energy • Conserve water • Minimize waste • Use environmentally preferable cleaners • Educate the public and their customers on reducing environmental impact	Wide range of tourism businesses and programs.
Vermont Green Hotels	Vermont Business Environmental Partnership Audits? No Participants: 57	• Reduce energy • Conserve water • Minimize waste • Use environmentally preferable cleaners • Environmental management	Lodging
Virginia Green	Department of Environmental Quality Audits? No. Participants: 15,	• Reduce energy • Conserve water • Minimize waste • Green meeting planning	All sectors eventually. Lodging program is established

Table 4.2 Other Types of Certification Programs in the U.S.

Program	Organization / Audit	Description	Sector
Energy Star for Hospitality Label	United States Environmental Protection Agency Audits? Stamped by Engineer Participants: 169	• Guidelines for energy management • No fees to USEPA	All sectors in tourism and hospitality with buildings
Green Seal Certification for Lodging	Green Seal Audits? Yes	• Environmental management with range of solutions possible. • Green product purchasing • Fees determined based on the amount of rooms • Participants in California, District of Columbia, Georgia, Maryland, Pennsylvania, Virginia, City of Chicago, and City of Portland	Lodging
LEED Certification	U.S. Green Building Council Audit? Yes Participants: unknown	Tiered rating process: • Design • Construction • Operation • Sustainable site development • Water savings • Energy efficiency • Materials and indoor environmental quality	Buildings
Audubon Green Leaf Ecorating Program	Terra Choice Environmental Marketing and Audubon International Audit? Yes Participants: 11, with 10 introductory level members	Rating program, not certification. • Environmental management and efficiency	Hotels
Green Globe 21	World Travel and Tourism Council Audit? Yes Participants in the USA: 1	Based on Agenda 21, gradual benchmarking • Environmental management	25 sectors in the Tourism Industry
Sustainable Tourism Ecocertification Program	Sustainable Tourism International Audit? Yes, optional for lower levels, mandatory at professional level Participants: Not listed	• Greenhouse gas emissions Management and reduction • Solid waste management, reduction, reuse and recycling • Freshwater consumption reduction • Wastewater management • Energy efficiency, conservation, and management • Ecosystem and biodiversity conservation • Air quality protection and noise reduction	Multi-sector

PROFESSIONAL TOURISM ORGANISATIONS

There are many associations making contributions to sustainable development in the United States, including a range of wildlife and conservation organisations, and "Friends of . . ." organisations that support land and water initiatives, parks and protected areas, and species, all of which are important to tourism. However, it is the work of those nongovernmental organisations which represents industry-wide as well as niche-based tourism interests, which generate some semblance of a unified tourism sector. Here, given the constraints of space, we can consider just some of the leading tourism organisations within the United States which have a bearing on influencing sustainable tourism development.

Tourism Industry of America (TIA)

The TIA, which is seen as the only national organisation considered to represent all categories of tourism supply, has the primary purpose of promoting travel to and within the United States. Members from the private sector include hotels, travel agencies, airlines, and tour operators whilst there are also members from the public sector who represent a range of local and state organisations including, but not limited to, convention and visitors bureaus, universities, and state and local government travel offices (Brewton & Witham, 1998; TIA, 2008). The TIA provides a forum for industry leaders, holds educational events, undertakes industry-based research, assists with targeted marketing, conducts advocacy campaigns, and assists in all aspects of professional development (see http://www.tia.org/Member-Services/benefits.html).

The International Ecotourism Society (TIES)

TIES, established in 1990, is the largest ecotourism association in the world, serving nearly one thousand members in over ninety countries. The society is committed to promoting the principles of ecotourism and responsible travel and is dedicated to the goal of uniting conservation, communities, and sustainable travel (see ecotourism.org). It organised the first North American Ecotourism conference in 2005. Two important initiatives resulted from the conference. First, the Bar Harbour Declaration on Ecotourism in the United States, which called on the U.S. government at federal and local levels (as appropriate) to support ecotourism and sustainable tourism development. Among the key statements in the declaration was a call to encourage collaborative initiatives with the private sector in an effort to educate tourists about ecotourism practices; encourage sustainable design and low environmental impacts of tourism operations; support clean energy, transportation, and infrastructure; and to develop a green certification program. Second, an impetus for active engagement with federal agencies (as demonstrated earlier by the Forest Service and NPS) was introduced. It set the stage for an adoption of subsequent North American ecotourism and sustainable tourism annual conferences.

TIES is also host to a range of programmes for tourism enterprises, educational institutions, and travellers. For example, it is conducting advocacy campaigns such as "Your Travel Choice Makes A Difference" and "Traveling with Climate in Mind." It also provides a range of online resources relative to ecotourism and sustainable travel initiatives. In addition, TIES is engaged in collaboration with the University of Eberswalde (Germany) and the Center on Ecotourism and Sustainable Development at Stanford University, which resulted in the Sustainable Transportation Guidelines for Nature-based Tour Operators. Recently, the organisation promoted the University Consortium Field Certificate, which aims to bridge communication and experiences between tourism enterprises and students entering the profession. Through its collaborative efforts at international and domestic levels and North American conferences and membership. TIES contributes to an increased level of awareness of both ecotourism and sustainable tourism initiatives in North America. Further, it has facilitated the introduction of certification programmes to North America through a proposed global accreditation programme called the Sustainable Tourism Stewardship Council (see http://www.rainforest-alliance.org/tourism.cfm?id=council).

American Hotel & Lodging Association (AH&LA)

The AH&LA, headquartered in Washington, DC, represents the lodging industry in the United States. It is the " . . . sole national association representing all sectors and stakeholders in the lodging industry, including individual hotel property members, hotel companies, student and faculty members, and industry suppliers" (AH&LA, 2008: 1). In its strategic plan for 2008–2010, the AH&LA outlined sustainability strategies to meet its overall objectives. For example, in an effort to meet its core objective of " . . . capitalise[ing] on [the] AH&LA brand value as the voice of the industry," the organisation suggested "incorporat[ing] AH&LA sustainability/green initiatives into an industry-wide program that hotel owners and operators can use to develop environmentally-friendly properties" (AH&LA, 2008: 1). Additionally, to " . . . strengthen and promote the industry's multicultural and diversity opportunities," the AH&LA suggested " . . . highlight[ing] the industry's diversity accomplishments as AH&LA develops sustainable initiatives to demonstrate the industry's overall outreach and establish permanent industry resources" (AH&LA, 2008: 2). The AH&LA joined the Sustainable Tourism Criteria Global Partnership in September 2008 to emphasise their commitment to developing and implementing global baseline criteria for sustainable tourism development and operations.

U.S. Green Building Council

The U.S. Green Building Council (USGBC) is " . . . committed to expanding sustainable building practices" (USGBC, 2008a: 1). Its mission is "To transform the way buildings and communities are designed, built and operated, enabling an environmentally and socially responsible, healthy, and prosperous environment that improves the quality of life" (USGBC, 2008: 1). One of its most notable initiatives is the Leadership in Energy and Environmental Design (LEED) Green Building Rating System™: " . . . a voluntary, consensus-based national rating system for developing high-performance, sustainable buildings" (USGBC, 2008b: 1).

Sustainable Travel International

The STI is was founded in 2002, with the mission "To promote sustainable development and responsible travel by providing programs that enable consumers, businesses and travel-related organizations to contribute to the environmental, socio-cultural and economic values of the places they visit, and the planet at large" (STI, 2008: 1). Its priorities include the provision of educational resources; to develop, adopt, and market sustainable tourism standards and practices through their Sustainable Tourism Eco-Certification Program™ (STEP); carbon offsets; and protect and positively impact cultures (STI, 2008).

Green Hotels Association (GHA)

The GHA aims to " . . . bring together hotels interested in environmental issues" (GHA, 2008: 1) and promotes research into environmentally friendly products relative to water conservation, solid waste reduction, and energy savings. It produces towel rack hangers and sheet changing cards for the hospitality industry, and publishes "The Green Catalogue," which is host to a range of environmentally friendly products. Members receive bimonthly newsletters with practical ideas and information on greening the hospitality industry.

National Ski Area Association Environmental Charter for Ski Areas

The ski industry adopted an environmental charter called "Sustainable Slopes" in 2000 as a framework for sustainability in their operations. In 2005, Sustainable Slopes was revised to address environmental performance in the ski industry. Several partnering organisations supported the development of the principles within the charter and committed to working with the industry. For example, USEPA, FS, Department of Energy, and the NPS Concession Programme have endorsed the charter in part because its goals are congruent with their own initiatives. For example, they engage in voluntary compliance, exceed compliance where environmentally sound and economically feasible, improve environmental performance, and demonstrate an industry-based collective initiative and commitment to environmental responsibility (Sustainable Slopes, 2005). The charter includes several principles germane to conservation as well as environmental and social responsibility (e.g., use water resources; energy conservation and clean energy waste management; product reuse and recycling). Further the charter also includes an environmental code for ski slopes and a list of recommendations on what skiers and snowboarders can do to help address climate change. According to NSAA, 70 per cent of all ski areas in the United States (nearly 160 resorts and areas) have endorsed the Sustainable Slopes Environmental Charter.

Leave No Trace (LNT)

"The Leave No Trace Center for Outdoor Ethics is an educational, non-profit organisation dedicated to the responsible enjoyment and active stewardship of the outdoors by all people, worldwide" (http://www.lnt.org/programs/index.php). It is orientated to promoting education and ethical considerations rather than prescribing a "set of rules and regulations." It has partnered with federal land-managing agencies to promote the low-impact message to all individuals who play in forests, lakes, rivers, oceans, and deserts. In addition, low-impact techniques and information about them are provided for a range of ecosystems.

The California Roundtable

The California Roundtable on Recreation, Parks and Tourism was founded in 1998 to " . . . encourage cooperation between public and private entities involved and interested in outdoor recreation, public lands, and tourism in California" (CA Roundtable, 2008: 1). The roundtable's goals are to promote and coordinate cooperative efforts between members, improve communication with publics, increase understanding of and support for outdoor recreation, address issues of importance to the future of outdoor recreation, and seek innovative and lasting sources of funding for operations, maintenance, capital outlay, and acquisitions. It is innovative and very effective, as it brings diverse and much focused stakeholders together to address successes, challenges, and partnerships relative to outdoor recreation, education, and tourism in the state of California. Since its inception, the California Round Table has accomplished a great deal. For example, it has sponsored a printed guide to public and private outdoor activities titled "Outdoor California"; produced a series of roadside rest map panels which highlight regional recreation destinations; sponsored a study of the travel patterns and economic impacts of campers in California; produced the California Children's Bill of Rights (see http://calroundtable.org/cobor.htm); and, most recently, sponsored the "Get Healthier Outdoor Symposium."

Boston Green Tourism

Boston Green Tourism is another example of coordination and collaboration at a local level. This initiative is led by tourism champions who are dedicated to encouraging enterprises to "green" their operations. To support this mission, they offer educational seminars; a Web site with up-to-date information on best management practices in the hospitality industry; and a wealth of information on green products and services. They encourage collaboration between members and provide links to various organisations. Members also promote Greater Boston as a green destination—with an emphasis on green meeting planning and conventions. Acting almost as an "accreditation organisation," Boston Green Tourism acknowledges the "green worthiness" of a hotel property by whether or not it has been certified by one of five independent bodies, i.e., Green Seal's Certification for Lodging Properties, USEPA, U.S. Green Building Council's LEED Certification, Audubon Green-Leaf Rating Program, or Green Globe 21 Certification. This organisation demonstrates how the tourism sector in one destination can advocate and support the promotion and adoption of best environmental management practice on the part of tourism enterprises.

The Partnership for Global Sustainable Tourism Criteria (GSTC Partnership)

While not solely a U.S. initiative, several tourism entities in the country are involved in the GSTC Partnership. In a global effort to address what sustainable tourism means and " . . . how can it be measured and credibly demonstrated to build consumer confidence, promote efficiency, and fight greenwashing . . ."; and to come to a " . . . common understanding of sustainable tourism" (GSTC Partnership, 2008: 1), the GSTC developed baseline criteria, some thirty-eight in total, organised around the pillars of sustainable tourism. These were launched in October 2008 at the International Union for Conservation Nature (IUCN) World Conservation Congress in Barcelona, Spain. They include effective sustainability planning; maximizing social and economic benefits to the local community; and reducing negative impacts to cultural and environmental heritage. The partnership is now focused on engaging all tourism stakeholders—from purchasers to suppliers to consumers—to adopt these criteria. To facilitate this, they will develop educational materials and technical tools to guide hotels and tour operators through the process of implementing sustainable tourism best practices. Some of the expected uses of the criteria include the following:

- Serve as basic guidelines for enterprises of all sizes to become more sustainable, and help businesses choose sustainable tourism programmes that fulfil these global criteria.
- Serve as guidance for travel agencies in choosing suppliers and sustainable tourism programmes.

- Help consumers identify sound sustainable tourism programmes and businesses.
- Serve as a common denominator for media to recognise sustainable tourism providers.
- Help certification and other voluntary programmes ensure that their standards meet a broadly accepted baseline.
- Offer governmental, nongovernmental, and private-sector programmes a starting point for developing sustainable tourism requirements.
- Serve as baseline guidelines for education and training bodies such as hotel schools and universities (GSTC Partnership, 2008: 1).

The GSTC will also be used by the Sustainable Tourism Stewardship Council (STSC), a proposed global accreditation body for sustainable tourism and ecotourism certification programmes. In effect, this is not a new certification system, rather a global accreditation system that aims to lend credibility to all existing and future certification systems that meet minimum criteria, based on the GSTC. The STSC is a multi-stakeholder NGO, with representation from environmental and social groups and the tourism sector, and technical advice from UNEP and UNWTO. The STSC will be governed by a balanced international board of directors elected by a full assembly of stakeholders (see sustainabletourism@ra.org). It is likely that the efforts of the GSTC Partnership and the STSC will have substantial impact on tourism development in the United States given that of the thirty plus members of the GSTC Steering Committee there are representatives of major tourism organisations in the United States, many of which have international status. Several large organizations influence the travel and tourism industry significantly.

CONCLUSIONS

The foregoing discussion has sought to highlight a range of the ongoing programmes and initiatives that have developed in the United States with particular emphasis on the overarching role of federal agencies in promoting environmental protection. Furthermore, attention has been drawn to activities at regional and state levels and by professional tourism associations to establish a comprehensive view of the efforts being made towards improving the environmental performance of tourism enterprises through addressing progress towards sustainable tourism development, progress which has and is being hindered by the lack of federal tourism policy. Due to lack of support at the federal level and limited national policy on sustainable tourism, initiatives are taking a foothold through coordinated partnerships and programmes at the federal, state, and regional levels involving the key agencies and through regional state initiatives and the private sector.

The focus of many programmes and partnerships is on environmental management, which primarily addresses various levels of energy efficiency, waste management, water-use efficiency, the purchase of environmentally friendly products, the minimization of products with toxic characteristics, and the education of guests and staff. With global climate-change issues facing decision makers, and fuel and energy prices soaring, action towards best practice management in all sectors of the tourism supply must be taken. As the Travel Industry Association recently acknowledged in a brief on "Climate Change and the Travel Community," the traveller is seeking further definition of sustainability; soaring fuel costs are pulling more companies into looking at ways to become more energy efficient; and going green in the travel industry has the potential to impress consumers as well as sustain the "natural capital" and attractiveness of the places people like to visit (TIA, 2008). Further evidence of growing interest in responsible environmental management is also manifest. In June of 2008, a "Think Tank on Sustainable Tourism" brought together a range of tourism industry partners and media to address how the industry in the United States can get on board with sustainability. The event was sponsored by Tauck World Discovery, American Express, and Northstar Travel Media. As noted by several of the participants, it was one of the first times all industry stakeholders were "in the room" to discuss sustainable tourism development.

Despite the fact that the United States is without a national tourism policy and there is a lack of awareness regarding the importance of tourism at the federal level, there are several initiatives underway to address sustainable tourism development. First, increased participation by state-level departments in creating certification or, at the very least, sustainable tourism awareness programmes is gaining momentum. Partnering these initiatives with promotional efforts of tourism offices appears to be an attractive combination, as demonstrated by Travel Green Wisconsin. Second, policies affecting tourism (such as those of the USEPA and state-level departments of environment) may have far greater impact on sustainability than tourism-specific policies, which in the case of the United States are market-orientated (for further discussion on this area see Hall, 2008) Further, public-private partnerships are increasing, especially with land-managing agencies such as the USFS.

Based on what we have learned of tourism development in the United States (i.e., multi-sector, complex supply systems, seasonality, and distribution of regulation from federal to state, public land-managing entities within states, and local laws and ordinances), there are huge difficulties in managing sustainable tourism within a federal context. However, through agencies such as the USEPA, there are public-private partnerships that can "green" the tourism industry overall. To some extent, these are influenced by the procurement and purchasing power of federal government (e.g., green meetings) as well as the proliferation of public-private partnerships with Public Land Managing Agencies (PLMAs), NGOs, and a range of private businesses.

These partnerships, along with efforts such as the Global Partnership for Sustainable Tourism Criteria and the Sustainable Tourism Stewardship Council, are bringing all sectors of the tourism industry in the United States "to the table," ultimately establishing a clearer and more applied definition of sustainable tourism. There are also many sectors involved in tourism supply which are adopting programmes to increase their environmental management practices and actively promote the sector as a leader in sustainability. Whether intended for the environment, or the bottom line, these programmes are moving towards a larger coordinated effort in the United States.

However, with a range of ecological pressures, much of the sustainable equation is focused on environmental management. Limited attention has been focused on social and cultural aspects of tourism development. Thus, increased attention to culture, heritage, and indigenous tourism by travel and tourism entities, including public-private partnerships; increased visibility of indigenous people's needs; and regional and state level initiatives are warranted.

ACKNOWLEDGMENTS

The author would like to express a special "thank-you" to Deb Kerstetter for her artful editing of the manuscript on which this chapter is based.

NOTES

1. For more information and a comprehensive list of partnering members, see http://www.epa.gov/greenpower/join/index.htm.
2. See http://www.epa.gov/performancetrack/ program/index.htm for details.
3. See http://www.epa.gov/performancetrack/program/sm-bus.htm.
4. ASTM International is one of the largest voluntary standards development organizations in the world—a trusted source for technical standards for materials, products, systems, and services.
5. For more information on Xanterra's environmental performance, see their Web site at http://www.xanterra.com/environmental-program-highlights-372.html.

REFERENCES

American Hotel & Lodging Association (AH&LA), 2008. *AH&LA 2008–2010 Strategic Plan.* Available at: http://www.ahla.com/pdf/2008-Strategic-Plan.pdf [accessed 1 May 2008].

Bicker, K., 2008. Personal communication, September 19.

Brewton, C. & Witham, G., 1998. United States tourism policy: Alive but not well. *Cornell Hotel and Restaurant Administration Quarterly*, 39(1), p.50–59.

Bureau of Land Management, 2008a. About the BLM. Available at: http://www.blm.gov/wo/st/en/info/About_BLM.2.html [accessed 15 September 2008].

Bureau of Land Management, 2008b. Tourism and Community Services Program. http://.blm.gov/wo/st/en/prog/Recreation/recreation_national/tourism_community.print.h.tml. Accessed 15 September 2008

California Roundtable, 2008. Available at: http://calroundtable.org/who_we_are. htm [accessed 15 April 2008]

Edgell, David L., 1999. *Tourism policy: the next millennium*. Champaign, IL: Sagamore Publishing.

Edgell, David L., et al., 2008. *Tourism policy and planning: yesterday, today, and tomorrow*. Oxford: Elsevier.

Geiger, J., 2008. Personal communication with the WASO Concession Program, National Park Service, June 3.

GSTC, 2008. Global Sustainable Tourism Criteria Fact Sheet. Available at: http://www.sustainabletourismcriteria.org/ [accessed 25 September 2008].

Green Hotel Association, 2008. Available at: http://www.greenhotels.com/whatare.htm [accessed 22 April 2008].

Kempthorne, D., 2007. *The future of America's national parks: A report to the president of the United States by the secretary of the Interior, May 2007*. Available at: http://www.nps.gov/2016/assets/files/2016presidentsreport.pdf. Accessed 31 March 2008.

Hall, C.M., 2008. *Tourism planning, policies, process and relationships*. 2nd ed. Haarlow: Pearson.

National Oceanic and Atmospheric Administration (NOAA), 2008. *About NOAA*. Available at: http://www.noaa.gov/about-noaa.html [accessed 2 April 2008].

National Ocean Service (NOS), 2008. *National Ocean Service*. Available at: http://oceanservice.noaa.gov/topics/oceans/nms/welcome.html [accessed 2 April 2008].

National Park Service (NPS), 2006. National Park Service Concession Environmental Management Program: *Greenline Newsletter* 5(1). Available at: http://www.concessions.nps.gov. [accessed 23 April 2008].

National Trust for Historic Preservation, 2008. Available at: http://www.preservationnation.org/issues/heritage-tourism/) [accessed 15 May 2008].

Office of Travel and Tourism Industries (OTTI), 2008. Available at: http://tinet.ita.doc.gov/about/index.html [accessed 12 May 20080].

Personal Communication, September 19, 2008. United Nations Foundation, meeting summary.

Southeast Tourism Policy Council, 2008. Available at: http://www.southeasttourism.org/south_T_policy_council.html [accessed 8 May 2008].

Sustainable Slopes Environmental Charter, 2005. Available at: http://www.nsaa.org/nsaa/environment/sustainable_slopes/Charter.pdf [accessed 2 May 2008].

Sustainable Tourism International (STI), 2008. Available at: http://www.sustainabletravelinternational.org/documents/au_mission.html [accessed 10 May 2008].

The Tourism Policy Council (TPC), 2008. Available at: http://tinet.ita.doc.gov/about/tourism_policy.html [accessed 10 May 2008].

Travel Industry Association (TIA), 2008. *Climate change and the travel community*. Available at: http://www.tia.org/resources/PDFs/Gov_affairs/Environmental_Primer_3_11_08.pdf [accessed 29 April 2008].

United States Environmental Protection Agency (USEPA), 2000. *waste reduction tips for hotels and casinos in Indian country*. Solid Waste and Emergency Response (5306W), EPA530-F-00–07, April 2000. Available at: http://www.epa.gov/tribalmsw [accessed 1 May 2008].

United States Environmental Protection Agency (USEPA), 2005a. *Everyday choices: opportunities for environmental stewardship*. EPA Innovation Action Council, November 2005. Available at: http://www.epa.gov/NCEI/pdf/rpt2admin.pdf [accessed 1 May 2008].

United States Environmental Protection Agency (USEPA), 2005b. *States join Energy Star challenge to cut costs by 10 percent or more.* EPA Innovation Action Council, December 2005. Available at: http://yosemite.epa.gov/opa/admpress.nsf/a4a961970f783d3a85257359003d480d/d54f75a8b788a56c8525 6fc4006f5065!OpenDocument [accessed 1 May 2008].

United States Environmental Protection Agency (USEPA), 2005c. *Evaluation report: ongoing management improvements and further evaluation vital to EPA stewardship and voluntary programs.* Office of Inspector General, Report Number 2005-P-00007, February 17, 2005. Available at: www.epa.gov/oig/reports/2005/20050217–2005-P-00007-Gcopy.pdf [accessed 12 May 2008].

United States Environmental Protection Agency (USEPA), 2008a. *The National Environmental Policy Act and Environmental Impact Statements.* Available at: http://www.epa.gov/compliance/basics/nepa.html#eis [accessed 15 April 2008].

United States Environmental Protection Agency (USEPA), 2008b. *About the Environmental Protection Agency.* Available at: http://www.epa.gov/epahome/aboutepa.htm [accessed 15 April 2008].

United States Environmental Protection Agency (USEPA), 2008c. *The Environmental Protection Agency timeline.* Available at: http://www.epa.gov/history/timeline/index.htm [accessed 15 April 2008].

United States Environmental Protection Agency (USEPA), 2008d. *History of the Energy Star program* http://www.energystar.gov/indx.cfm?c=about.ab_history accessed 15 April 2008.

United States Environmental Protection Agency (USEPA), 2008e. *Green Power Partnership.* http://www/epc.gov/greenpower accessed 15 April, 2008.

United States Environmental Protection Agency (USEPA), 2008f. *Green Power Purchasers* http://www.epa.gov/greenpwoer/toplists/partner100.htm accessed 15 April 2008.

United States Forest Service (USFS), 2008. *Forest service tourism program.* Available at: http://www.fs.fed.us/recreation/programs/tourism/ [accessed 11 May 2008].

United States Green Building Council (USGBC), 2008a. *About USGBC.* Available at: http://www.usgbc.org/DisplayPage.aspx?CMSPageID=124 [accessed 4 May 2008].

United States Green Building Council (USGBC), 2008b. *LEED certification.* Available at: http://www.usgbc.org/DisplayPage.aspx?CMSPageID=1721 [accessed 4 May 2008].

Western States Tourism Policy Council, 2008. *About the WSTPC.* Available at: http://www.dced.state.ak.us/wstpc/About/Objectives.htm [accessed 25 March 2008].

5 Argentina and Its Approach to Environmental Quality in Tourism
From Hotels to Destinations

Albina L. Lara

INTRODUCTION

Recognition of environmental issues in the tourism sector is the basis of a number of declarations, policies, and actions on the part of the Argentinean environmental public sector. This recognition appears in an evident way in a number of recent key policy instruments, notably in this context the Strategy for Tourism Development and the National Law of Tourism (2005). An essential principle of this law is to promote a process of continuous improvement, based on the commitment of all the actors, the development and management of tourism products, services, and related activities. At the same time, it aims to promote the generation of value and innovation through knowledge transfer, as key tools to assure the quality and competitiveness of the sector (National Secretary of Tourism, 2007). Even so, there is a clear lack of progress in some areas which has not been helped by the fact that existing tourism regulations have not been updated, many of which were promulgated some two decades ago. Conversely, progress is evident through initiatives designed to promote and coordinate the activities of public agencies at the national level, for example, between the National Secretary of Tourism (SECTUR) and the National Secretariat of Environment and Sustainable Development (SAyDS). Other alliances have also been established between the public and private sector, such as the joint work between IRAM[1] and SECTUR. These initiatives, it is argued, have accompanied the dynamic growth in tourism that characterises Argentina today.

In this chapter, we aim to provide first an analysis of the normative/institutional framework that encompasses tourism and the environment. Subsequently, the analysis turns to those developments which relate to environmental quality management, in particular those standards developed by the state as well as voluntary initiatives, such as those developed by IRAM. The development of a model for an integrated quality management system to be applied in tourist destinations is then discussed.

NATIONAL POLITICAL FRAMEWORK

The process of incorporation of environmental policies into government policies has progressed significantly in recent years. Nevertheless, there are many gaps that need to be addressed before current policy for planning and environmental management turn into effective tools for sustainable development. Even so, the key point is that the environmental variable is now present in various economic sectors as well as within public agencies at different levels of the administration. The voluntary sector, particularly environmental nongovernment organizations, has also grown and increased in influence, especially in relation to the quest for sustainable development. An important factor in this process of institutional and environmental maturity is the promulgation of the Environmental General Law (2002), as well as the outcomes of initiatives and joint declarations between the government and the provinces on environmental issues. Nevertheless, in order for environmental issues to be more prominent in the decision-making process, it is required that such issues be given a higher priority in the economy, in investment and funding and within the institutions of the country.

Argentina, as with other developed countries, faces numerous challenges regarding tourist development and the objectives of sustainability, especially arising from the directives of ill-conceived developments—both past and present. Addressing these challenges is essential because of the intimate relation between the protection of the visual amenity and the natural resources on which so much of tourism is based. Therefore, environmental protection is not incidental; it is essential and this must be reflected at all levels of government administration and recognized by the private sector.

In November 2004, the National Secretariat of Environment and Sustainable Development signed the "Frame Agreement" with the National Secretary of Tourism in order to strengthen the relationship between "Environment and Tourism," through the co-coordinated implementation of programmes, projects, and activities. To this effect, various key elements were accentuated, among which are:

- Sustainable management of tourist destinations, based on environmental quality.
- Promotion of the environmental certification of services and activities to encourage the sustainability of tourist operations.

Subsequently, in November 2005, a Unit of Sustainable Tourism was established by the SAyDS in order to strengthen the capabilities of the agency, to take proactive managerial actions regarding environmental protection and the promotion of more sustainable approaches to tourism, within the framework of inter-institutional cooperation with SECTUR.

This unit has now been transformed into a Programme of Sustainable Tourism under the responsibility of the Under-secretary for Promotion and Sustainable Development.

INSTITUTIONAL FRAMEWORK

The National Law of Tourism 2005 aims to regulate tourist activity and, of most significance in this context, that tourism should be developed in harmony with natural and cultural resources in order to guarantee their presence for future generations. Thus the aim is for a balance between the environment, society, and economy. The main objectives are thus to establish that the development, promotion, and regulation of tourist activity is guided by appropriate mechanisms for its sustainable development and the optimization of quality. In this, it recognized the need for:

- establishing mechanisms for participation and agreement between public and private sectors involved in tourism;
- the need to promote sustainable tourist development in different regions, provinces, counties, and the autonomous region of the city of Buenos Aires;
- the promotion of sustainability as a priority initiative within the "Incentives for Tourist Promotion."

In support of these objectives, it was proposed that an Inter-ministerial Committee of Tourist Facilitation be established, with the specific function of co-coordinating and assuring the compliance of the administrative functions of government institutions which have related competencies and/ or are related to tourism, to promote sustainable development and the competitiveness of the tourism sector. In sum, the National Law of Tourism deals, to a considerable extent, with the problems of environmental management and that due consideration is given not only to ecological factors but also the social and economic dimensions of tourism. This law is supported through the provincial institutional framework and thus discussion , albeit briefly, now moves forward to focus on those provincial regulations relating to tourism which explicitly refer to environmental quality.

Province of Rio Negro. Decree N° 657/03—Tourist Accommodation

This province establishes that to qualify as tourist accommodation such enterprises must demonstrate compliance with all necessary regulations; including construction and building, facilities and machinery operation, water provision, waste disposal, conservation of green spaces, and general management functions such as environmental health and safety. The latter areas are also addressed through Resolution N° 228 (2005), which deals with the Classification System for Tourist Accommodation.

Province of Salta, Law N° 7045—On Tourist Activities

This provision incorporates the environment dimension in the responsibilities and duties of the Provincial Secretary of Tourism; specifically it aims to:

- promote agreement and coordinate: local governments, policies, information, and territorial planning in order to optimise the plans of tourist development of the province;
- promote agreement and coordinate national and other provincial organisations, policies for the preservation of architectural and cultural patrimony, and the protection of the environment in the development of tourist operation.

Further, it established the principle that tourism projects must give due consideration in their design and development to policies for preserving and protecting historical, natural, and cultural resources of the province. In the process, noting that especial care should be given to the landscape, architectural, and archaeological aspects of the environment.

Province of Jujuy, law N° 5013—Promotion of Tourist Development

This Law essentially supports the promotion and development of resources for tourism whilst emphasising the need to conserve/preserve the environment, landscape, and architectural heritage. Complementary to this, the Provincial Law of Tourism N° 5198 establishes that the primary responsibility for all aspects of tourism lies with the Secretary of Tourism of the Province and that the emphasis should be on progress towards the sustainable development of tourism.

THE FEDERAL PLAN AND THE ARGENTINE SYSTEM OF TOURIST QUALITY

In 2005, the Argentine government, through the Secretary of Tourism, made public a Federal Strategic Plan of Sustainable Tourism (PFETS) 2006–2016. Its general objective is "To become a process to guide and articulate actions that, in synergetic form, reaffirms intentions, optimizes resources and directs these efforts towards a concentrated model of tourist development for the Argentine Republic" (SECTUR, 2005). It proposes decentralized management, at provincial and municipal level, with strong national principles, with the emphasis on the " . . . economic development with social inclusion and the conservation of the tourist National Patrimony." (SECTUR, 2005) as the guiding principle of Argentine's Tourist Policy. This strategic plan incorporates "Vision 2016," the objective of which is to position Argentina as the top tourist destination in South American; recognized for the quality and diversity of services offered, based on a tourist sector that respects the territorial equity,[2] the quality of natural environments and diverse communities.

The plan is being implemented through a number of "operational plans," designed for specific aspects of tourist activity. In particular, during 2007, a plan relating to quality management was prepared and included a set of policies, programmes, and specific actions for various aspects relating to the quality of tourism offerings. One of the programmes, designed to help integration, is the Argentine System of Tourist Quality, which consists of a set of operational tools designed to promote the principles of quality and continuous improvement on the part of every actor involved in the tourism value chain. Table 5.1 shows the basic scheme and tools of the quality system that are being implemented in the country. The main instruments are analysed synthetically.

Table 5.1   Basic Tools for the National System of Tourist Quality

Level of quality culture	Beneficiaries		
	Destinies	*Sectors*	*Products*
Initial	SIGO Good Practices	Management Bases for beaches, thermal areas, hotels, etc.	
Advanced		Sectoral Standards (IRAM–SECTUR Standards) Evolutionary Plan to Quality Certification Working Competences certification[3]	
Excellence	WTO.SBEST	WTO (World Tourism Organization. OMT in Spanish). TEDQUAL National Quality Prize[4]	*Excellence Clubs*, voluntary initiative of business that forms a cluster for implementing excellence in the subsector, for example, hotels.

Source: Based on SECTUR, SACT (2007). WTO (2008).

At the same time, the Secretary of Tourism established the System of Management for Small and Medium Size Companies (SIGO). This system aims to promote and support the modernisation of SME, by means of the adoption of 'best management' systems and international standards of quality and service. The overall objective is to satisfy the increased demands of domestic and international tourists whilst simultaneously seeking to increase profitability and competitiveness. To accomplish these goals, SIGO provides specific training opportunities for the development of management skills across a spectrum of management practices. Two other initiatives that have been implemented (at pilot project level at this stage), both of which have a strong emphasis on sustainability, are the Excellence System SBest and the Spanish SCTE (see following).

PUBLIC–PRIVATE ALLIANCES

The National Secretary of Tourism has placed substantial emphasis on the maintenance of several strategic alliances. The most important of these in terms of environmental quality are the following:

- Alliance with the Argentine Normalisation and Certification Institute (IRAM). IRAM was created in 1935 and is a nongovernmental organisation, recognised by successive governments as the National Organisation for Normalisation. This organisation elaborated the guide IRAM 30400 to promote the implementation of ISO 9001 in the tourism sector. Moreover, it established a plan for the certification of ISO 9001 and worked with the National Secretary of Tourism in formulating the "IRAM–SECTUR" (see following).
- Alliance with the Argentine Chamber of Tourism (CAT) (together with the National Foundation Award for Quality, CAT developed the "Guide for Excellence Management in Travel and Tourism Companies") and the Argentine Association of Travel Agencies (AAAVyT) Premiro Nacional de Colidad, 2008. In liaison with CAT, the secretary formed in October 2007 the Joint Commission for Tourist Quality, which seeks to develop strategies and joint actions to encourage and to strengthen the competitiveness and sustainability of all the actors of the tourist sector (SECTUR, 2007a).
- The agreement between Argentina and Spain to implement the Spanish Good Practices Model for Quality in tourism enterprises in Argentina.
- The relationship between the National Law of Tourism and the Federal Strategic Plan for Sustainable Tourism (PFETS) 2016, including the alliances between the public and private sector and promoting marketing based on the "country brand" (see Figure 5.1).

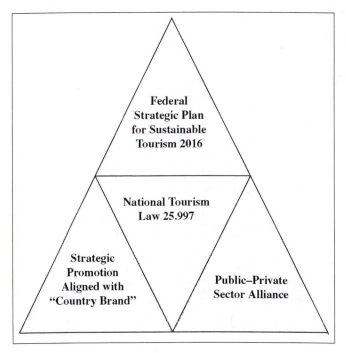

Figure 5.1   Outlook of the current Argentine tourism sector (Normalisation, ramework). Source: SECTUR (2007b) National Direction of Quality Management, Catalinas Park, September.

ENVIRONMENTAL MANAGEMENT

Further to the foregoing initiatives is the Federal Strategic Plan for Sustainable Tourism, which aims to improve quality management in the tourism sector and specifically addresses the conservation of national tourism resources and seeks to ensure that the development of habitats is both territorially balanced and sustainable. This objective has been furthered through the establishment of a number of standards developed by IRAM since 2006, at times in conjunction with SECTUR. Whilst these initiatives are seen as steps towards consolidating the government's approach to environmental performance, they are but promissory and thus require continuous and appropriate efforts in order for them to be implemented effectively. Lately, we have witnessed some progress in this through the participation of key actors in the development of tourism becoming involved in a strategic planning initiative wherein quality management is a key element.

Lately, we have witnessed some progress in this through the participation of key actors in the development of tourism becoming involved in a strategic planning initiative wherein quality management is a key element. For example, the Argentine Chamber of Tourism elaborated a *Manual: Guide for the Excellence Management of Tourism and Travel Companies* in 2005 (Cámara Argentina de Turismo [2005], www.fundacionfidccop. org/cat). This guide includes questions on leadership and management system. Each of these issues contains different indicators to measure the level of quality achieved. Included in the area of Management System in Resources, there are indicators related to natural resources conservation and measures applied to mitigate negative impacts on the environment. At the same time, the Chamber of Food and Hotels (Federación Empresaria Hotelera Gastronómica FEHGRA in Spanish) developed in 2005 a manual to guide the rational use of energy for hotels and food establishments (FEHGRA, 2005).

At present, the national administration is seen to have become a proactive and innovative actor in the development and promotion of management practices based on a culture of quality, which serves to demonstrate government commitment to the improvement of the economic, social, and environmental development conditions of tourist activity. For this reason, the National Direction of Tourist Quality Management proposed the creation of a National Plan for Tourist Quality, involving the formulation of a model to monitor and evaluate the delivery and development of quality management. This model considers the main characteristics of Argentina, its products, the managerial structure, and the institutional framework (see following).

In December 2007, a framework (known as the Programme for Normalisation [REF]), led by the National Secretary of Tourism, established eleven standards [IRAM–SECTUR norms] with a further fourteen expected in 2008. Grouped together, these standards encompass general and more specific guidelines, according to the different modes of service provision (see Table 5.2). In total, they cover approximately half of the requisites of ISO 9001:2000 (Quality Management) but additionally include aspects of environmental management and a set of best practices. They are designed to promote best practice in the development of tourism and delivery of tourist services by the enterprises involved. All are based on the principle that quality generates customer satisfaction and favours competitiveness. It is expected that the adoption of these standards will contribute to enhancing professionalism in the management of tourism enterprises and become recognised as key tools in the implementation of services to increase the level of customer satisfaction.

Enterprises are being encouraged to adopt these standards and gain the accompanying accreditation, but so far such adoption has been slow. SECTUR estimates that by the end of 2008 there will be approximately one hundred certified enterprises that have implemented some of these standards and plan to publish a regular record of the enterprises achieving certification. We now turn to a number of other initiatives which merit consideration.

Environmental Management of Beaches

Recognition of the impact of tourism on the environmental quality of beaches, and due to community pressure in some dense coastal municipalities

Table 5.2 Standards for Quality Management, Safety, and the Environment for the Tourism Sector (IRAM–SECTUR)

General tourist area of application	Main environmental topics	Standard Number	Specific tourism sub sector
Accommodation	Energy, water, solid waste management, personnel training, guests awareness and information to the providers' education. It includes an informative Appendix on environmental practices.	42200	Hotels
		42210	Huts
		42220	Bed & Breakfast
Natural Areas	Energy, water, residues, contamination of the soil, emissions to the air, control of noises, propitiates the use of alternative sources of energy and diffusion in the local communities of the importance of the values of the natural protected area.	42300	Tourist services in natural protected areas
Adventure tourism and ecotourism	Flora and fauna, emission to the air, spilled to the water, local communities and original inhabitants, discharge to the soil, use of raw materials and natural resources, wastes. It includes an appendix with rules of the international Program Leave No Trace (LNT, in English, http://www.int.org or NDR in Spanish)	42500	Tourist services hiking and trekking
		42510	Tourist services Mountain
		42520	Tourist services Horseback riding
		42530	Tourist services Bicycle
		42540	Tourist services Rafting
		42550	Tourist services Canoeing
Gastronomy	Energy, water, treatment of effluents, solid waste, buying policies, personnel participation. It includes an informative appendix on environmental practices for restaurants, solid waste, buying policies, personnel participation. It includes an informative appendix on environmental practices for restaurants.	42800	Restaurants

NOTE: "Leave No Trace" is a national and international program designed to assist outdoor enthusiasts with their decisions about how to reduce their impacts when they hike, camp, picnic, snowshoe, run, bike, hunt, paddle, ride horses, fish, ski, or climb. The program strives to educate all those who enjoy the outdoors about the nature of their recreational impacts as well as techniques to prevent and minimize such impacts. Leave No Trace is best understood as an educational and ethical program, not as a set of rules and regulations (www.int.org, consulted September 2008).

of the province of Buenos Aires, led to establishing a broad, cross-sectoral Interdisciplinary Commission with a remit to prepare guidelines for the environmental management of beaches. This initiative constitutes an interesting improvement for several reasons. First, because it integrates various governmental organisations: the National and Provincial Secretaries of Tourism, the highest environmental authority of government—the SAyDS. IRAM and three municipalities of Buenos Aires and also representatives of the National Council of Scientific and Technological Research, the College of Architecture, Design and Urbanism (University of Buenos Aires), and the Centre for Tourism Investigation (University of Mar del Plata). Secondly, it produced guidelines that apply principles of environmental quality management and included attention to the need for training, monitoring, and the principle of continuous improvement. These guidelines were presented in a framework encompassing both quality management and environmental management known as the Quality Management and Environmental Management in Beaches and Spas (2005). The main areas covered are:

- *Environment, resources, and scenery*, especially regarding swimming-water quality, resources management, quality of the soil, fauna and flora, visual contamination, and scenery.
- *Infrastructure and basic services*, especially related to building structures, the immediate environment, accessibility, signalling, and basic services.
- *Safety*, includes swimming areas, nautical activities, personnel and infrastructure.
- *Information and environmental education*, in order to educate users and tourists in the basic principles of environmental management and its role in the environmental quality of beaches and spas.
- *Management system documentation*, includes a self-assessment guide covering all aspects of the framework in order to evaluate the degree of compliance reached in the application of the requisites stated in the guidelines.

A direct outcome of these guidelines is the standard IRAM 42100 (2005) "Quality management and environmental safety in beaches and swimming settings"—which includes reservoirs, lakes, etc. (irrespective of whether or not there is recreational swimming) and requires that enterprises gain the appropriate certification. To be certified not only requires compliance but also the introduction of a process of continuous environmental improvement and to be proactive in the sustainable use of natural and cultural resources in the activities developed in these settings. The first beaches to gain certification were San Jose and Colon, in the province of Entre Ríos, in 2007. Both beaches are under municipal authorities, which reflects their commitment to IRAM 42100; other areas have since followed their lead.

Certification "WTO-SBest": Environmental Management in St. Martin of the Andes

This certification scheme, designed by the World Tourism Organisation in 2005, aims to improve the competitiveness and sustainability of tourist destinations by means of better management and promotion. The first accreditations of the certification "WTO-SBest"—Excellence Tourism Governance—were granted to just five destinations, St. Martin of the Andes being one of the first (2006). The others were Blackstone River Valley (United States), Durban KwaZulu-Natal (South Africa), Valencia (Spain), Cancun and the State of Tabasco (Mexico).

Excellence System for Sector Management: WTO.TedQual

The Certification Program WTO.TedQual was created by the Foundation WTO.Themis for promoting educational and professional capacity building in the tourism sector. WTO.TedQual is a tool that allows to assure a quality system for educational and training of tourism professionals.

Spanish System of Tourist Quality—Good Practices (SCTE)

The city of San Miguel de Tucumán (located in the northwest) was chosen as the tourist destination to pilot the implementation of the Spanish System of Tourist Quality (SCTE, acronym in Spanish) "Good Practices" (http://www.sgt.tourspain.es).[5] This is the first time that this system has been applied outside of Spain. The methodology is tackled from the perspective of the tourist destination and is directed to small and medium-sized enterprises. The process takes four months with three stages, involving field work, with the overall objectives of information provision and advice, workshops and training sessions, and evaluating enterprises. Almost sixty enterprises participated fully, which involved training provided by an international team of specialists from SCTE, SECTUR, and Tucumán's Tourism Organisation. In May 2007, Tucumán gained the award of "Destination Tucumán for the Successful Implementation of the Model of Tourist Quality Approach" (MACT)-SCTE: Good Practice in tourism enterprises, including an identification seal of commitment to quality (http://www.turismo.gov.ar/esp/prensa/gacetillas/2006/g12072006bol.htm).

Environmental Management of Thermal Waters

Argentina has fifteen provinces which exploit thermal resources by means of the development of thirty-six thermal facilities with more than ten thousand hotel beds, accompanied by a variety of related activities such as spa centres, golf courses, and ecological tourism activities (SECTUR, 2007a, www.turismo.gov.ar). At present SECTUR coordinates the development of guidelines, by means of the national standard IRAM 42600 regarding the "Quality, Safety and Environmental Management of Thermal

Establishments," following a successful pilot project in the province of Entre Rios, which has witnessed a large expansion in this field in recent years. This development is conducted within the framework of the signed agreement between SECTUR and IRAM. Its objective is to work on quality and the development of thermal products. Moreover, a manual of good practices is being derived for the thermal centres, in order to ensure quality and to establish criteria in the provision of services.

Environmental Management and the Hotel Sector

The hotel sector has shown a weak engagement in sustainability. Nevertheless, there are some interesting initiatives in the sector, and, promoted by the government and/or sectoral chambers, that show that the greening of the sector is in progress, although slow and concentrated in few hotels, predominantly part of an international chain. One example is that of NH hotels, an international chain, which in 2006 elaborated its Environmental Plan 2006–2012. Since 2003, the hotel has registered energy use and applied energy efficiency measures (http://www.iarse.org/new_site/site). Further, the Argentine Institute of Corporate Social Responsibility (IARSE), a reference centre in relation to CSR in Argentina, has two businesses related to the tourism sector among its members: Holiday Inn, Cordoba, in the centre of the country, and Turismo Integral Patagonico, a travel agency in the Patagonian province of Rio Negro in the South of the country (www.tipargentina.com). Also, three hotels are members of the Argentine Global Compact Network: one in the province of Entre Ríos, Empresa Hotelera Yañez Martìn, S.A., and two in the province of Mendoza, Hotel International and Carollo and Princess. Apart from the hotels, the Hotel and Food Association of Mendoza province is part of the Global Compact. (Argentine Global Compact Network, 2007)

In 2005, SECTUR prepared a report presenting a synthesis of successes in the implementation of quality systems (SECTUR, 2005), which identified three travel agencies, six hotels (singling out the Intercontinental Hotel as a particularly successful example), two recreation businesses, and one restaurant. The report also highlights the specific implementation of "Good Practices in Hotels," citing six huts (lodges) and a number of resorts, noting them as "Participants of the Good Practices."

Environmental Management of Biosphere Reserves and RAMSAR sites

Tourism can have negative impacts on Biosphere Reserves and RAMSAR sites. Moreover, some of them are not well prepared to prevent these kinds of impacts because they do not have the appropriate infrastructure or a basic environmental knowledge for planning in a more sustainable fashion. At the same time, it is also noted that some local authorities do not have proactive attitude towards conservation of these areas whilst local communities may not understand its environmental importance.

A UNDP project (ARG/PNUD 05/015, www.pnud.org.ar) implemented by the SayDS aims to promote the sustainable development of protected natural areas, especially Biosphere Reserves and Ramsar Sites (see Figure 5.2). The project was implemented into two pilot cases in the Northwest of Argentina: Biosphere Reserve, Laguna Blanca (province of Catamarca) and RAMSAR site Laguna Brava (province of La Rioja), both in the northwest of the country. After that, pilot experiences have been replicated in two more areas, located in different ecosystems: the Parana Delta Reserve, Jaukanigas, and Chaco Wetland, in the northeast of Argentina (www.ambiente.gov.ar).

Environmental Monitoring Initiative

The Federal Council of Investment (CFI, Consejo Federal de Inversiones in Spanish) financed a project (http://www.cfired.org.ar/Default.aspx?nId=525) that developed sustainable tourism indicators, based on the WTO methodology. This project was specifically applied in two counties of Catamarca Province, in the northwest of Argentina. The tool includes indicators for measuring:

- Conservation of cultural and archaeological patrimony.
- Conservation of natural patrimony, fragile areas, endangered species, and critical ecosystem.
- Community participation.
- Scarce natural resources management.
- Tourism seasonality.
- Environmental impacts of tourism activity.

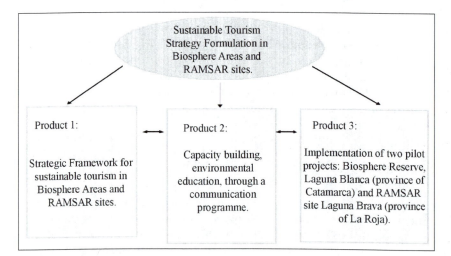

Figure 5.2 Scheme of the sustainable tourism project in Biosphere Reserves and RAMSAR sites.

TOURIST DESTINATION ENVIRONMENTAL MANAGEMENT

Tourism managers have recognised that individual businesses' efforts to improve their competitiveness are sometimes debilitated by the environment deterioration occurring at the destinations. This is because the tourism sector's success mainly depends on the quality of its environment. In this context, implementing an integrated destination management approach provides an effective structure to encourage the competitiveness of the sector. In 2005, the Argentine Chapter of Foundation Carolina[6] funded a research project to develop a public–private partnership management model for destination development: known as the "Model for the management of an integrated public–private system applicable to tourism destinations in Argentina." From the outset, the project was founded on the philosophy—what we might term the "Tourism Philosophy"—that a tourist destination is a place comprising images and expectations; where the relationship between the individual, the symbolic, and the collective take place. It is where the meanings are interwoven. Collectively these aspects define the destination. In a sense the 'personality' of that place, which then leads to the 'brand.' The outcome of the project was the formulation of the Tourist Destination Integrated System for Quality Management (Lara et al., 2006b) (see Figure 5.3).[7]

The model is based on the following requisites:

- facilitates articulation with tourism policies;
- encompasses the concept of Integral Quality (Product, Process, Environmental, and Safety Quality);
- the principles of sustainability, recognition of economic development, the preservation/conservation of the historical, cultural, and environmental heritage;
- replicable in any destination;
- facilitates a global vision of quality, which integrates products, process, environment, and risks;
- builds on existing experience of countries with proven development in tourism.

The model developed basically comprises the key elements of tourism destinations—the 'central processes'—which primarily encompass the development of the resources for tourism, and the delivery processes, which on the one hand comprise those processes involved in product design and development, marketing, and access. The named 'destination orientated processes' include management and product delivery (see Figure 5.3). These involve establishing the necessary requisites to meet the needs and expectations of visitors and developing the resources to meet those needs, including the appropriate funding, investment, facilities, management, and personnel. On the other hand, there are the 'delivery processes'—those operations

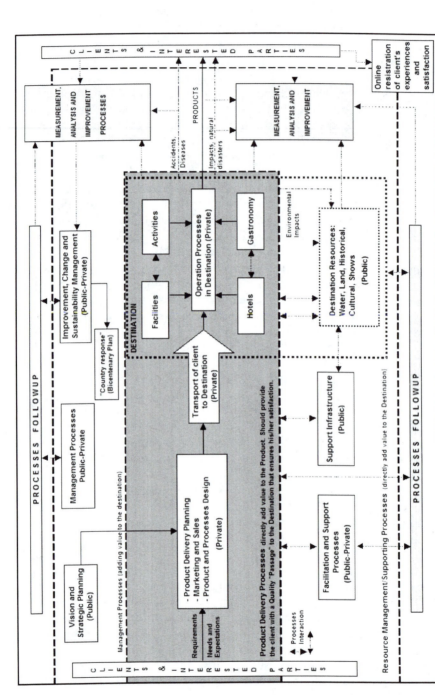

Figure 5.3 Integrated (Public–Private) quality management system model. Source: Lara et al. (2006a) Fundación Carolina.

processes in the destination itself (see Figure 5.3). Further to this due attention must be given to the need for the provision and/or development of other resources such as appropriately qualified personnel, facilities and equipment (including maintenance), and foreign currency exchange. The interaction between those processes in the delivery of tourism, and associated facilities and services, and those involved in resource management gives rise to the need for 'internal and external relations management,' personnel management and development, facilitation processes as well as information management, financial and resource management, and facility maintenance and the essential supporting infrastructure (Lara et al., 2006b).

For successful implementation it is essential that these processes—resource management and delivery—are integrated and further that performance in any area is monitored through an ongoing system of assessment, analysis, evaluation, the outcomes of which are then reviewed and used to inform further development and progress to achieve better performance and enhanced quality. A key factor in this is the need for well-founded partnerships between the public and private sectors. Finally, to manage each one of the three types of processes enunciated in an effective, coherent, and sustainable way, it is necessary to develop strategic management and planning process (encompassing 'vision,' communications, monitoring, and improvement), which is typically the domain of the public sector. Environmental management is an essential part of these processes in order to ensure the objectives of sustainability are genuinely evident in all aspects of tourist destination management.

To facilitate adoption and implementation of the model, a manual has been produced the purpose of which is to provide an operational instrument for applying the Model System to any specific tourism destination, at all the stages of evolution and development. The general character of the manual seeks to include, at least initially, all actors involved in the system's processes. But, in turn, it establishes specific guidelines for variances according to the destination's own activities. It is a step-by-step implementation guide that provides the tools for the effective start-up of a new enterprise. Nevertheless, it is a complex system and its application requires political will on the part of the authorities involved and the commitment of the main actors in the destination. This is not easy to achieve if there is not enough maturity[8] in the community and a clear understanding that a process of this nature needs time, coordinated effort, and involves change.

CONCLUSION

This chapter has sought to provide a broad and comprehensive view of the progress of the inception of environmental management aspects in the Argentine tourism sector. The analysis of the diverse initiatives designed to promote environmental management in tourism leads to the conclusion that many of the initiatives discussed do not approach tourism as a complex sector which, in turn, is part of, and predominantly within, an even more complex environmental and territorial system. In spite of an apparently high engagement in 'sustainability' principles and practices within the tourism sector in Argentina, it is uncertain if any subsector, such as hotels, much less the tourism sector as a whole, can declare to have achieved a significant level of 'sustainability.' This is mainly because each tourist subsector has developed without considering the relationship with other subsectors nor the effects they may have on the environment. Nevertheless, there are a number of promising initiatives, notably the cross-sectoral partnerships, which, for example, have led to the guidelines on beach management and the standards developed by IRAM/SECTUR. However, the Integrated Quality Management System for Tourist Destinations (IQMS), which constitutes an innovative improvement, has yet to be implemented.

Whilst these are indicative of progress, the implementation of principles of environmental quality has to be tackled slowly and gradually, bearing in mind the complexity of the problem and the heterogeneity of the actors involved. However, such progress, as has been seen, will be limited until such time as the existing obstacles, such as the entrepreneurial culture that does not perceive environmental management as a necessity and/or an obligation, are addressed and appropriate actions implemented. For example, the implementation of the quality guidelines in the IQMS to be effective will depend essentially on the environmental management capability of the municipalities involved. They are the ones that must take the first steps to mobilise this process.

Overall, the incipient development of environmental quality in the tourism sector requires not only time but also a strengthening of cross-sectoral partnerships and joint working to achieve a strategic vision, shared by the main actors, of the environmental needs of the tourism sector and of the advantages that the aforementioned vision could bring forth.

ACKNOWLEDGMENTS

The author would like to acknowledge the contributions of Alicia Gemelli, Eduardo Goldenhorn, and Norberto Esarte in the writing of this chapter and Sergio Otaño, who translated the chapter.

NOTES

1. IRAM represents Argentina in the International Organisation for Standardisation (ISO), in the Pan-American Commission of Technical Norms (COPANT), and in the Association MERCOSUR of Normalisation (AMN).
2. Territorial equity: principle of the sustainable development and the regional planning that search to decrease existing disparities between

regions, provinces, and communities of a country. For this reason, tourism policy should create comparable conditions of economic and social development, so that diverse geographic areas can have, at a certain level, equal opportunities.

3. This program intends to improve employment capacities (initiative implemented with the Minister of Labour, Employment and Social Security and main tourism unions).
4. National Quality Prize was institutionalized in 1992 by National Law 24.127 for different economic activities. It is applicable for the public and private sectors.
5. Spanish Institute for Quality Tourism (ICTE) operates the Spanish Quality Tourism Mark and was established in 2000 and is a nonprofit association whose founding members are the national business associations of the main subsectors of the tourism industry that have developed quality standards. Prior to the establishment of ICTE, the State Secretariat for Trade and Tourism had designed the Spanish Quality Tourism System (SCTE). The SCTE certifies the service, facilities, and management of Spanish tourist companies. It is a voluntary-type certification that indicates managers' level of commitment to applying improvements in the quality of their products and services. The SCTE consists of a series of specific standards for each sector and the system is flexible, open, self-regulated, and voluntary. With the creation of ICTE, the sectors consolidated their efforts into a single intersectoral management body with one overall quality label. The Spanish Quality Tourism Mark is based on service Quality Standards, and compliance with these is obligatory for obtaining certification. According to ICTE, the mark is at an intermediate stage between ISO 9000 and the European Business Excellence Model (EFQM).
6. Fundación Carolina of Argentina (FCA) promotes the cultural and scientific cooperation between Argentina and Iberoamerican countries. The FCA funded the selected research project:
7. For a complete report on this project go to: http://www.fundacioncarolina. org.ar/2006/trabajosapoyofca.asp.
8. A community is considered mature when its social network is strong and diverse, its institutional framework is well developed, and when community involvement is high. Also it should embrace sustainable development principles.

REFERENCES

Argentina Global Compact Network, 2007. *Annual report of activities 2004—2007.* Buenos Aires, Argentina: PNUD.

Argentine Chamber of Tourism, National Prize of Quality, 2005. *Guide to excellence management of tourism and travel companies.* Buenos Aires, Argentina: Edición 2005.

FEHGRA, 2005. *Rational use of energy manual for hotels and food establishments of the Argentina Republic.* Buenos Aires, Argentina: Federacion Empresaria Hotelera Gastronomica De La Republica Argentina, 1° edición 2005.

Lara, A.L., Goldenhorn, E & Esarte, N.E., 2006a. *Integrated public-private quality management model for tourism destinations in the Argentine Republic.* Argentina: Internet Publication. Foundation Carolina. Available at: www.fundacioncarolina.org.ar (accessed 10 March, 2008).

Lara, A.L., Goldenhorn, E. & Esarte, N.E., 2006b. *Basic application manual integrated public-private quality management model for tourism destinations in the Argentine Republic*. Internet Publication. Foundation Carolina. www.fundacioncarolina.org.ar (accessed 10 March, 2008).

Premio Nacional de Calidad, 2008. National Quality Award of the Argentine Republic. Bases for the National Quality Award, Argentina. Internet report. Available at: http://www.premiocalidad.com.ar/.

San Martin de los Andes Municipality, SBest St. Martin of the Andes Certification, 2007. http://www.sanmartindelosandes.gov.ar/turismo/items_de_interes/omt_sbets.html [accessed 22 April 2008].

SECTUR, 2005. *Federal strategic plan for tourism development*. Argentina, SECTUR. Argentina. Available at: http://2016.turismo.gov.ar/wp_turismo/wp-content/uploads/2007/12/dngct07.pdf (accessed 22 February, 2008).

SECTUR, 2007a. *Argentine system of tourism quality*. Internet report. Available at: http://2016.turismo.gov.ar/wp_turismo/wp-content/uploads/2007/10/sact-completo-final.doc (accessed 22 February, 2008).

SECTUR, 2007b. *Joint Commission on Tourism Quality* (SecTur-CAT): Internet report. Available at: http://www.turismo.gov.ar/esp/prensa/gacetillas/2007/g20071005cat.htm (accessed 22 February, 2008).

WTO, 2008. *SBest certification*. Available at: http://www.unwto.org/education-new/english/sbest.php [accessed 15 March 2008].

6 Strata Titled Tourist Development in Australia

Calling in the Sorcerer's Apprentice?

Jan Warnken and Chris Guilding

INTRODUCTION

After noting the significant growth of strata titled tourism accommodation (STTA) in Australia over the last twenty-five years, this chapter provides a consideration of using STTA for financing the construction of short-term accommodation infrastructure and its effects on the sustainability of a destination. More specifically, ways are outlined in which STTA developments have the potential to both contribute to and compromise meeting sustainable development criteria for tourism destinations.

INVESTMENT IN AUSTRALIAN TOURISM PROJECTS PRIOR TO THE 1990S

Introducing Western European concepts and ideas to Australia has always been a challenge. The supply of international competitive tourism accommodation infrastructure is no exception. Many of Australia's key natural attractions are located in sparsely populated regions that are a long distance from major conurbations and transport hubs. Unlike Canada or countries in Scandinavia with comparable remote attractions, Australia has no source population in close proximity (i.e., driving distance) that is large, affluent, and familiar with the English language and/or driving on the left side of the road. The vast majority of Australia's international visitors have to take a flight trip of at least eight hours' duration. For many, this consumes a substantial portion of their overall travel budget. These basic geographic factors underscore some of the key challenges associated with developing tourist accommodation facilities and associated infrastructure in Australia. The Snowy Mountain Hydro Scheme in the 1960s was Australia's last major international development grant or loan extended by an international institution such as the World Bank. Since then, most capital for major tourist accommodation projects has been raised from within the country or from large international investors. Private investment has, and still is, forthcoming for major hotel developments located in the central business districts of Australia's larger cities that experience high volumes of business travel visitation.

In developing leisure destinations and regional areas, the history of investment in tourism projects has been less conventional and at times controversial, especially in Queensland during the 1980s and early 1990s. Double-digit growth figures in international arrivals (Figure 6.1) and a strong belief in the 'trickle-down effect' of 'critical mass' development, i.e., large project development triggering multiplier effects for the middle and lower end markets (Craik, 1991), paved the way for a small number of influential entrepreneurs in the development industry and government to ride the tide of, at times, euphoric optimism over investments in tourism and real estate ventures. In the second half of the 1980s, i.e., at the height of the Japanese bubble economy, this optimism was further fuelled by a strong interest from large Japanese investors in the four- to five-star resort market (Daly et al., 1996) and private overseas investors with an interest in holiday and second-home real estate (Hajdu, 1993). The bursting of this bubble economy and the following recession in Australia led to a string of collapses of high profile projects (Warnken & Buckley, 1997), entrepreneurs, and even some banks, leaving many professional investors with substantial losses (Horwath & Horwath, 1993, cited in Daly et al., 1996). At the height of the recession, Australian hotels' negative return of 3.3 per cent was the lowest of seventy countries studied by Stewart (1992, cited in Daly et al., 1996).

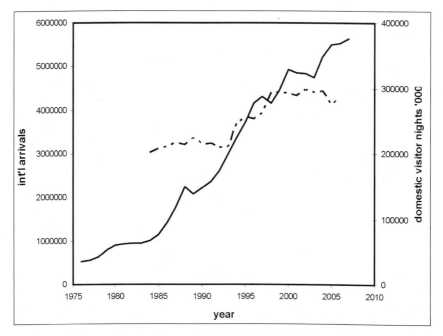

Figure 6.1 International visitor arrivals (solid line) and domestic visitor nights (broken line) in Australia from 1976 to 2007 (data compiled from ABS data set 340101, BTR domestic visitor monitor and the *Australian Yearbook* [ABS]).

Despite this poor period, demand for the Australian tourism product has remained generally strong (Hohl & Tisdell, 1995). With the increasing commoditisation of long-haul air travel over the past twenty-five years, the growth in international arrivals (Figure 6.1) and spending of foreign tourists has continued. Some of the international investors have maintained their interest and contributed to the financing of regional airports and other infrastructure (Stimson et al., 1998). Major international airports were upgraded (Craik, 1991: 6) and the number of flights increased while the costs for international airfares remained largely unchanged (i.e., a decrease in real terms). This trend extended to the domestic air travel market when the first low-cost airline (Virgin Blue) took to the skies in August 2000. This signified sustained demand for Australian tourism which in turn encouraged further investment in tourism infrastructure, most notably in accommodation facilities.

THE STRATA AND COMMUNITY TITLE TOURISM ACCOMMODATION DEVELOPMENT CONCEPT

Following the boom and then bust turbulence of the 1980s, banks and developers of short-term accommodation premises gradually moved away from large integrated resort projects financed through direct foreign investment where the original investor retained full ownership of the accommodation precinct. Even at the height of the 1980s boom, most of the then popular integrated tourist resort models were planned with large precincts containing housing lots that could be sold to smaller individual investors (a principally American concept [ULI, 1997]).

This concept of selling residential property was extended to the short-term, i.e., tourist, accommodation sector. Even in the late 1970s, a long time before the Japanese bubble economy burst, developers started to sell units in mixed-use apartment complexes on the Gold Coast which provided future owners with the option of either placing their unit in a short-term (holiday) letting pool, entering into a long-term letting contract, or residing in the unit. The notion of investing into real estate rather than a tourism business was established by introducing strata title legislation (Everton-Moore et al., 2006). Establishing a strata scheme involves vertical and/or horizontal subdivision of a multi-unit building with each unit being covered by a deeded title inferring indefeasible property rights and lot entitlements to the common property. These deeded property titles available to individual owners, together with providing options for switching to non-tourism use, opened avenues for major lending institutions to reduce their exposure to risk, especially when having to on-sell a unit as a mortgagee in possession after an investor had defaulted on a loan repayment. In essence, therefore, STTA opened the doors for housing-style mortgage financing to small investors who, when considered holistically, constituted a significant source of new private investment capital. It also facilitated the pre-sale of units, i.e., "off the plan sales," which, if sufficient, opened opportunities for local developers to obtain more favourable loans from major lending institutions.

It is notable that STTA appears to be particularly appropriate for the Australian market. It is often commented that Australian investors enjoy a love affair with brick-and-mortar investments. There has been a protracted and unbroken history of substantial capital gains earned over long-term property investments. The tax rules are favourable, as interest paid on an investment property mortgage is tax deductible, capital gains tax has been reduced on investment property capital growth, and the inheritance tax has been abolished in Queensland. These same tax rules do not extend to time-share because in Australia time-share does not qualify as a housing-type loan (Hovey, 2002). By slightly increasing the size of individual units and changing a few design parameters (e.g., including a small kitchen and laundry facility), units in tourist accommodation complexes could be sold as apartments on a separate property title. Banks treat this type of investment object the same as residential property, signifying relatively favourable loan terms.

GROWTH IN STRATA TITLED TOURISM ACCOMMODATION

In Australia, the STTA concept has penetrated almost all accommoda-tion market segments: from campsites and backpacker units (Warnken & Guilding, 2006) to accredited ecoresorts, mass tourism holiday units, and iconic five-star resorts; and from small two-unit complexes to seventy-seven-storey high rises with more than four hundred units. Accordingly, STTA can be found across almost all facets of tourism accommodation, from tourism cities to remote islands and national parks.

The growth in multi-ownership tourist accommodation facilities is noto-riously difficult to demonstrate (e.g., Warnken and Guilding, forthcoming; Warnken et al., 2008; Warnken and Guilding, 2006). With its quarterly tourist accommodation surveys (ABS Publication Series No. 8635.0), the Australian Bureau of Statistics is one of the very few organisations to regu-larly collect data about STTA complexes. Even these data are incomplete and vary in scope over time. In January 1998, the ABS began to list a subset of STTA units, i.e., 'serviced apartments,' in complexes with fifteen or more units in the letting pool. Prior to this date, serviced apartment complexes had been included in a broadly defined category described as "holiday apartments and holiday homes" with more than four units per let-ting entity. The replacement of four units per letting entity by fifteen units per letting entity as the recording threshold has also been applied to hotels and motels. This has resulted in a significant reduction in the number of establishments represented in the survey, although only minor changes in the record of room or unit nights sold (Quarterly tourism accommodation statistics, Australia—Warnken et al., 2008).

Further to this information, every three years the ABS provides data for holiday flats and homes managed by real estate agents. These, together with 'serviced apartments' data, allow comparisons with pre-1998 data. Figure 6.2 depicts the reported counts for establishments, bed spaces, room nights, and revenue for the four states receiving an estimated number of foreign visitor nights in excess of five hundred thousand (Table 11, ABS, 2008). For all variables and all states, serviced apartments showed the highest growth rates for the period 2000–2006. As predicted by Warnken and Guilding (2006), the number of bed spaces and guest nights in serviced apartments surpassed those recorded for hotels for the first time in 2006 (Figure 6.2, Queensland data).

It is further noteworthy that serviced apartments managed by a professional hotel operator in conjunction with their hotel business are being recorded as hotels under the ABS classification system. The same applies to units in hotels that have been converted to apartments, and subsequently sold to individual investors under a deeded (strata) title. On the other hand, time-share units are likely to be included as serviced apartments. In Australia, time-share is largely sold on a contractual basis, thereby avoiding the need to issue up to fifty-two separate titles (for each week) for a single unit.

SUSTAINABILITY INDICATORS FOR TOURIST ACCOMMODATION DEVELOPMENT

Following promulgation of the concept of (ecologically) sustainable development in the late 1980s and early 1990s, the tourism industry started to join other industry sectors on their, at times lengthy, journeys in a quest for defining sustainability criteria and indicators. Tourism's many stakeholders and its complex interactions with other sectors provided some additional challenges in the search for a consensus concerning such criteria and indicators for tourism. Over the past fifteen years, however, international organisations, industry, and academics have developed a number of key documents and publications that spell out sustainability criteria and parameters for tourism systems (Choi & Sirakaya, 2006; Hobson & Essex, 2001; IHEI, 1996; Manning, 1999; Miller, 2001; UN, 1996; UNEP & WTO, 2005; WTO, 1995).

Weaver (2006; see Chapter 2) suggests a number of parameters as an extension to the triple bottom line components, i.e., economic, social, environmental dimensions, but admitted that not all parameters were always applicable or easily ascertainable. The same three dimensions or 'pillars' were used by UNEP & WTO (2005) to formulate twelve aims for their "Agenda for Sustainable Tourism" (Table 6.1). Choi and Sirakaya (2006) used five dimensions (economic, social, cultural, ecological, and political) and a wide range of indicators to prioritise three top indicators for each dimension in the context of sustainable community tourism. Table 6.1 provides an overview of a number of these and other parameters relevant to accommodation providers.

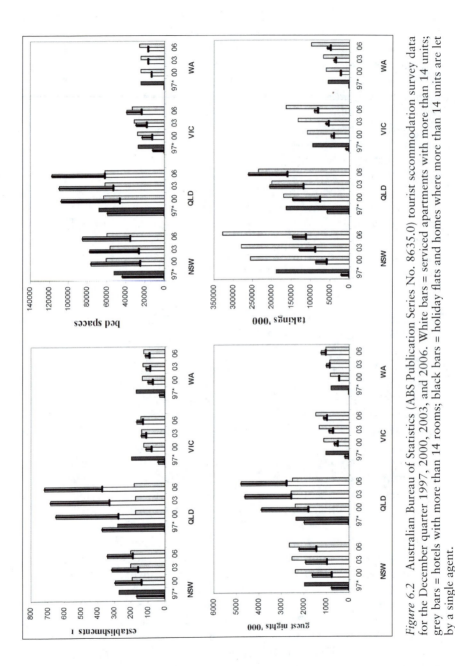

Figure 6.2   Australian Bureau of Statistics (ABS Publication Series No. 8635.0) tourist accommodation survey data for the December quarter 1997, 2000, 2003, and 2006. White bars = serviced apartments with more than 14 units; grey bars = hotels with more than 14 rooms; black bars = holiday flats and homes where more than 14 units are let by a single agent.

Table 6.1 Criteria and Selected Sustainable Tourism Development Indicator Parameters (with an STTA Complex Orientation)

Dimensions or 'pillars'	Broad aims	Main concepts	Potential indicators for short-term accommodation businesses (modified after Butler, 1980; Warnken et al., 2004; Weaver, 2006; Choi & Sirakaya, 2006)
Economic	Economic Viability	Viability and competitiveness of destination and its (local) enterprises.	• Growth in visitor numbers, tourism earnings, and employment; • Percentage and growth in repeat visitors; • Average length of stay; • Seasonality of tourism/tourist visitation; • Percentage of profit/revenue re-investment in the upkeep, conservation, and redevelopment of tourism assets (accommodation premises, contributions to natural and cultural attractions).
	Local Prosperity	Maximise contribution of tourism to the economic prosperity of the host destination, including the proportion of visitor spending that is retained locally.	• Contribution to employment growth in tourism and in general; • Percentage of total visitor spending captured by accommodation businesses in local ownership (and percentage of external ownership of business ownership in general); • Entrepreneurial and business opportunities for local community members; • Average period of ownership in local accommodation businesses.
	Employment Quality	Provision of local jobs with fair pay, conditions of service, and availability without discrimination by gender, race, disability, etc.	• Opportunities for career paths; • Comparative ratio of wages in the accommodation sector to local average; • Proportion of staff in regard to gender, cultural background, length of employment with current business.
Social	Social Equity	Widespread and fair distribution of economic and social benefits from tourism throughout the recipient community, including income and services available to the poor.	• Percent of managerial or supervisory employment from local residents; • Resident/non-resident ownership of homes or percentage of second homes in equivalent locations; • Unrestricted or discounted access for permanent residents to accommodation infrastructure and tourism attractions.
	Visitor Fulfilment	A safe, satisfying, and fulfilling experience for visitors.	• Visitor satisfaction with accommodation services; • General crime rate and proportion of reported incidents involving tourists.
	Local Control	Empowering and engagement of local communities in planning and decision making.	• Involvement of residents (resident input) in the planning and decision-making process for new development and redevelopment of accommodation premises.

(continued)

Table 6.1   (continued)

Dimensions or 'pillars'	Broad aims	Main concepts	Potential indicators for short-term accommodation businesses (modified after Butler, 1980; Warnken et al., 2004; Weaver, 2006; Choi & Sirakaya, 2006)
	Community Well-being	Maintenance and strengthening of quality of life, including social structures and access to resources, amenities, and life-support systems without social degradation or exploitation.	• Basic community health parameters (child mortality, suicide and divorce rates, average life expectancies, literacy and numeracy skills, education levels); • Significant increases in visitor densities at key community (recreational) sites; • General crime rate, alcoholism, and reported incidences of vandalism in relation to the overall population size.
	Cultural Richness	Respect and enhance historic heritage, authentic culture, traditions, and distinctiveness of host communities.	• Percentage of tourism accommodation complexes comparable with local vernacular buildings/architecture; • Percentage of local and vernacular building materials and processes used; • Percentage of sites/area of heritage properties protected from development.
Environmental	Physical Integrity	Maintenance and enhancement of the quality of landscapes (urban and rural) while avoiding physical and visual degradation of the environment.	• Percentage of accommodation buildings erected without approval, with violations of planning provisions, or subject to special planning relaxations; • Percentage of accommodation buildings and/or their precinct area located in environmentally high-risk (e.g., floodplains) or sensitive (habitats of threatened communities or species) sites; • Rate of incorporating recommendations from EIA and planning studies into development approval conditions.
	Biological Diversity	Support of conservation of natural areas, habitats and wildlife, minimise damage to them.	• Rate of encroachment into rural and nature conservation areas; • Rate of land swap (development sites/properties with high conservation values).
	Resource Efficiency	Minimise use of scarce and non-renewable resources in the development and operation of tourism facilities and services.	• Per capita (visitor night) energy and water consumption; and waste and wastewater production; • Proportion of renewable energy used; • Area of habitat or urban space modified per bed space or holiday unit.
	Environmental Purity	Minimise air, water, and land pollution and waste generation.	• Per capita (visitor night) waste and wastewater production; • Per capita air pollution (e.g. CO_2-e; NOx; SO_2; particulate matter [PM10]; etc.).

STTA AND SUSTAINABILITY

Before trying to gauge the extent that STTA fulfils some of the specific indicators identified in Table 6.1, it is worth emphasising that the majority of STTA complexes are not part of a large hotel corporation or franchise. This signifies that they are subject to less public scrutiny and experience and, therefore, less pressure to adopt sustainability programs through an environmental policy and environmental management system. Many operators (resident unit managers) are small husband-and-wife teams who bought the business for lifestyle reasons, and not entirely for commercial gains (Cassidy & Guilding, 2007).

THE ECONOMIC DIMENSION

At first glance, the STTA concept appears to carry quite a promising potential for assisting sustainable development. STTA's strong growth was documented in the previous section. These positive figures are further supported by a longer average length of stay relative to hotels (ABS statistics). At the same time, STTA complexes are heavily dependent on outsourcing a range of maintenance and service tasks such as room and linen cleaning, ground and landscaping works, and pool maintenance. This outsourcing provides small business opportunities (as opposed to employment opportunities) for members of the local community. There are also more opportunities for local entrepreneurs through STTA developments. The purchase of management rights by husband-and-wife teams circumvents what can be a lengthy negotiation period with a hotel operator who frequently insists on a contractual arrangement that locks in a certain number of units into the letting pool (which, in turn, would increase the potential risks to major lending institutions).

In theory, local residents and operators can also benefit from STTA complexes. The purchase of an individual holiday accommodation unit opens up an additional opportunity for local residents and operators to diversify and re-invest in their local tourism industry at an affordable entry level. Further, apartments in STTA complexes provide mechanisms to ameliorate seasonality by attracting different types of visitors during different times of the year: the same STTA unit can accommodate long-term stays of retirees who want to escape adverse climate conditions at their principal place of residence, as well as short-term stays of small families and other visitors during major holiday periods.

The achievement of other economic sustainability criteria are more difficult to gauge. As indicated earlier, the operation of an STTA complex relies heavily on outsourcing its maintenance and services, mostly to small specialised service companies. As a result, career paths associated with STTA operations are more akin to small to medium enterprise business paths, i.e., staff move from being employed to becoming self-employed owner-operators and, later, managers of their own extended businesses. This also impedes a comparison of wages between employees associated with STTA complexes and those in other tourism subsectors or the whole of a destination. Many small owner-operator and family businesses may not accurately record the actual hours worked to eschew social welfare payments. Instead they invest money into their business assets to increase its future value. Many STTA service businesses are not entirely tourism specific—they also provide services to non-tourism strata complexes and private residences (owner-occupied or long-term rentals). Probably the most compromising factor in calculating tourism-related contributions associated with STTA complexes is their deliberate mix of residential, tourism, and often retail or commercial uses. Costs for upkeep and maintenance services for the building itself, or in strata terms the common property, are either allocated based on individual lot entitlements and incorporated into body corporate levies or charged to separate subsidiary bodies corporate based on their particular assets or their responsibility for particular parts of the common property. Tracing such information for a number of STTA complexes would consume considerable resources in terms of time and money.

There are, however, a number of economically orientated problems. The majority of STTA units are marketed, and purchased, on the expectation of strong capital gains. The development of STTA complexes, therefore, tends to be driven more by building demand borne from real estate speculation, rather than an analysis of tourism-demand fundamentals. This can result in the building and sale of STTA properties during times of overoptimistic forecasts of tourism demand. Subsequent releases of new tourism accommodation products without a commensurate growth in visitor nights reduces occupancy levels, which then places a downward pressure on room rates charged. Purchasers of STTA units from the original developer are frequently initially insulated from this concern over returns, as many developers provide a guaranteed return for the first three years of ownership. This guaranteed return provides unit owners with little over the long term, however. By guaranteeing a rental income for this limited period, the developer stands to gain all of the potentially inflated price resulting from the guarantee. The new owner will only benefit from the guaranteed income for a small portion of the unit's life, however. Despite this rationale, the guaranteed return can fuel ill-informed, shortsighted purchases of STTA units, especially 'serviced apartments,' which in turn can fuel developers' building of more similar complexes, especially at times of bourgeoning real estate markets. The problem of dwindling room rates will be exacerbated if 'serviced apartment' operators are not applying a unit pricing regime based on appropriate yield management principles (see Cassidy & Guilding, 2007). This spectre of declining room rates is particularly threatening to hotels located in areas experiencing high levels of speculative real estate development and investment. The decreased yields that can arise in these areas are likely to be more acutely felt by hotel operators (generally remunerated on a basis linked to hotel revenue and profit) than hotel owners, who stand to benefit from any increasing real estate values resulting from the real estate speculation. The reality of this problem of declining rooms is best illustrated by comparing growth in takings per guest night for serviced apartments (AUS$54.7, AUS$60.2, AUS$68.6 for 2000, 2003, and 2006, respectively) and hotels (AUS$87.1, AUS$91.8, AUS$106.0 for 2000, 2003, and 2006, respectively) and the corresponding overall growth in takings from these two accommodation types. Average takings per guest night increased by 25.2 per cent (serviced apartments) and 21.7 per cent (hotels) between 2000 and 2006, whereas overall takings for these two categories only grew by 18.8 per cent—due to an increase in guest nights of 56.0 per cent versus 12.9 per cent in serviced apartments and hotels, respectively (values calculated from ABS data presented in Figure 6.2).

Experience suggests that local developers, who have successfully completed one or several STTA buildings, try to persuade their local planning authority to grant further approvals for similar projects, preferably through changes to local planning instruments that will permit the building of such developments without the need for special approval. This in turn can inflate land values based on the simple principle of the value of the sum of the parts (units) being greater than the value of the whole. Such pressure on land values and, as indicated above, room rates detracts from any incentive to develop traditional hotels on a single title. STTA developers can react to high land values by building large complexes and selling the units at inflated prices. Hotel developers, however, have to offset inflated land prices by selling room nights at higher rates if at all possible or, alternatively, by accepting reduced returns on investment.

In summary, STTA can provide opportunities for strong growth in accommodation capacity, greater business prospects (rather than employment) to local community members, and, therefore, greater flow-on effects within a destination. However, these positive sustainability aspects carry the potential of rendering the development of traditional hotels on a single title economically unsustainable. It comes as no surprise, then, that practically all post-1998 'hotels' on Australia's Gold Coast have been developed with some or even all units under strata title. While STTA's sustainability can be seen to be good for a destination, the negative implications for hotels obviously carry negative implications for those destinations with a high accommodation dependency on hotels.

THE SOCIAL DIMENSION

A literature review reveals that there has been a paucity of examination of social implications arising from STTA growth. The relative contemporary nature of Western European settlement in Australia is too young to have created the type of deep-rooted, long-standing, and very locale-specific cultural identities that are particular to individual destinations evident in villages in mountainous and coastal regions all over Europe. If the 'laid-back' perspective generally claimed for Australians in regional coastal areas qualifies as a distinguishing facet of their cultural identity, then STTA growth with its creeping urbanisation carries the potential to erode such a culture (Mullins, 1991; Smith, 1992; see also discussion following). One of major issues with STTA complexes and their impact on cultural richness and identity relates to the fact that most new buildings aim to maximise residential densities. This commonly translates into buildings with three storeys or a high rise, which, in most cases, prohibits the use of traditional local construction styles and materials.

Australia, in general, is also perceived to be a very safe travel destination, although some exasperation amongst local residents was felt in the early 1990s during the height of the Japanese investment interest (Daly et al., 1996; Hajdu, 1993; Stimson et al., 1998). Overall, crime rates are considered relatively low. Crime could become a problem, however, should clusters of aging STTA complexes prevent the redevelopment of tourism infrastructure and a ghetto scenario result (Warnken et al., 2003).

It is hard to conceive of any general community health issues arising from an increased incidence of STTA. Even if some health issues were to be conjectured, it would likely be hard to determine the presence of any such effects due to the confounding effects of many other concomitant factors.

In terms of social equity and local control, STTA can provide opportunities for local residents who are not in a position to inherit or acquire large land holdings to take an equity stake in a complex by purchasing a unit or setting up in business to provide one of the many STTA sub-contracted services. Resident input into planning decisions is very much dependent on local planning schemes and planning legislation. In Australia, the latter vary from state to state (Bates, 2006). Although this can restrict the degree of influence of local government authorities when drafting their local planning schemes, the general planning tradition in Australia has been, and still is, focused on powers granted to local communities represented by their elected aldermen. Such a system carries the potential for greater community involvement in drafting planning schemes and subsequent decision making. On the other hand, the development of Australian tourism infrastructure has been noted for the strong influence of a few entrepreneurs, who often used their skills to either manipulate state governments to overturn local sentiment or, alternatively, lobby at the local authority level with promises for employment to influence approvals required from higher levels (Craik, 1991; Russell & Faulkner, 1998, 1999). Not surprisingly, the quality of environmental impact assessment for tourism developments has not always been at a high-quality level (Warnken & Buckley, 1998).

THE ENVIRONMENTAL DIMENSION

From a long-term perspective, this dimension of sustainability probably presents the most controversial aspects of STTA developments in Australia. During the early stages of STTA-mediated destination development, large floor spaces (relative to hotel rooms) and mixed residential and tourism use STTA buildings can be seen to constrain tourist visitation densities.[1] This feature, combined with a history, in some areas, of being constructed with either no development approvals (e.g., Costa del Sol, Spain) or subject to violations of planning provisions, can lead to an unplanned growth of urban structures that have the potential to reduce the competitiveness and attractiveness of the tourist attraction that created the demand for the properties in the first place.

At a later stage in the life cycle of a destination (Butler, 1980), STTA-inflated land values tend to encourage developers to push for relaxations of urban densities and a "reach for the sky" philosophy, i.e., to seek special approval for increasing the number of units per base lot area. The incremental cost of building each additional floor is low relative to the total cost of building the initial floor which requires land acquisition, building design, development of building application documentation, laying of foundations, etc. Once the fixed cost of constructing the initial floor has been incurred, the spreading of this cost over more and more floors constructed signifies that the total cost per floor (total cost of the building divided by the number of floors built) is reducing with each incremental floor constructed. This highlights a fundamental motivation for developers seeking to maximise the number of floors in high-rise building projects. If allowed to run unchecked, this "reach for the sky" philosophy will ultimately increase residential and tourist densities and dominate the skyline of a destination (Plate 6.1).

A "build, sell, and move on" philosophy appears to characterise the STTA development sector; however, Blandy et al. (2006) note the lasting influence of developers long after they have "moved on." A large proportion of STTA unit sales are made to individuals who cannot be described as sophisticated investors. Although legislation has been subjected to a series of amendments to increase consumer (i.e., buyer) protection (Everton-Moore et al., 2006), the fundamental legal principle of *caveat emptor* (buyer beware) still applies. By enabling the entry of unsophisticated investors due to the greatly diminished cost of the investment required, strata titling can be seen to be giving a license to developers to take more shortcuts that have an increased likelihood of passing undetected by unit purchasers. This signifies that when building STTA properties, developers will have a greater propensity to adhere to little more than minimum building standards and to seek low-value undeveloped property that may be of high environmental value and carry risks, for example, in floodplains, acid sulphate soil areas, or areas with unstable soils. Such a mind-set is less likely to result in

Plate 6.1   Skyline surfers paradise, Gold Coast, Australia, November 2005 (courtesy of the first author).

successful sales to professional hotel operators, who will have experience and training that heightens their awareness of the long-term financial costs that can result from the pursuit of substandard building practices.

Environmental performance is another increasingly important issue for the sustainability of accommodation premises. Because of their inclusion of kitchen, laundry, and living room areas, STTA complexes tend to require larger floor area per bed space (i.e., larger units) relative to hotel rooms. This can translate to larger areas of land sealed by impermeable surfaces, which increases surface runoff and risks of local flooding, as well as greater investment (per bed space) of materials and grey energy (energy required for construction). On the other hand, many STTA units are serviced by their own separate hot-water and air-conditioning or heating systems, which can be turned off when the unit is not occupied, thereby providing a saving in energy and water consumption (Warnken et al., 2005).

CONCLUSION

Like the brooms summoned by the sorcerer's apprentice, the last twenty-five years has seen the strata title concept enjoy substantial success as an ownership framework upon which a wide variety of tourism accommodation types are based. With the necessary financial, taxation, and town planning conditions now in place to support STTA, government and industry are faced with the challenge of harnessing the rising tide of these developments without compromising the long-term sustainability of Australian tourist destinations. New planning and approval policies are required to find the right balance to:

i. retain and promote those elements of STTA that are consistent with sustainable development,
ii. mitigate those elements of STTA that could compromise the tourism focus of destinations, and
iii. control unfettered growth of STTA that might come at the cost of traditional hotels that provide much in terms of tourism equity to destinations.

An initial step in this regard has been taken in Western Australia, where the state government has released a number of documents and guidelines (Tourism Western Australia, 2008; WA Tourism Planning Taskforce, 2006) to control the spread and design of STTA complexes within and outside identified key destinations.

NOTES

1. It has come to the attention of the authors that the Aspen ski resort suffers from a problem that much of the Aspen 'condominium' accommodation is owned by wealthy investors who choose not to rent out their holiday property.

REFERENCES

ABS (Australian Bureau of Statistics), 2008. *Overseas arrivals and departures.* Series 3401.0—June 2008, ABS, Canberra.
Bates, G., 2006. *Environmental law in Australia.* 6th ed. Sydney: Butterworths.
Blandy, S., Dixon, J. & Dupuis, A., 2006. Theorising power relationships in multi-owned residential developments: unpacking the bundle of rights. *Urban Studies,* (43)13, p.2365–83.
Butler, R.W., 1980. The concept of tourist area life cycle evolution: implications for management of resources. *Canadian Geographer,* 14, 5–12.
Cassidy, K. & Guilding, C., 2007. An exploratory investigation of tourist accommodation price setting in Australian strata titled properties. *International Journal of Hospitality Management,* 26, p.277–92.
Choi, H.C. & Sirakaya, E., 2006. Sustainability indicators for managing community tourism. *Tourism Management,* 27, p.1274–89.
Craik, J., 1991. *Government promotion of tourism: the role of the Queensland Tourist and Travel Corporation.* Research paper No. 20. Brisbane: The Centre for Australian Public Sector Management, Griffith University.
Daly, M.T., Stimson, R.J. & Jenkins, O., 1996. Tourism and foreign investment in Australia: trends, prospects and policy implications. *Australian Geographical Studies,* 34(2), p.169–84.

Everton-Moore, K., Ardill, A., Guilding, C. & Warnken, J., 2006. The law of strata title in Australia: a jurisdictional stocktake. *Australian Property Law Journal*, 13(1), p.1–35.

Hajdu, J., 1993. The Gold Coast, Australia: spatial model of its development and impact of the cycle of foreign investment in property during the late 1980's. *Erdkunde*, 47, p.40–51.

Hobson, K. & Essex, S., 2001. Sustainable tourism: a view from accommodation businesses. *The Service Industries Journal*, 21(4), p.133–46.

Hohl, A.E. & Tisdell, C.A., 1995. Peripheral tourism: development and management. *Annals of Tourism Research*, 22(3), p.517–34.

Hovey, M., 2002. Is timeshare ownership an investment product? *Journal of Financial Services Marketing*, 7(2), p.141–60.

IHEI (International Hotel Environment Initiative), 1996. *Environmental management for hotels: the industry guide to best practice*. Boston: Butterworth-Heinemann.

Manning, T., 1999. Indicators of sustainable tourism. *Tourism Management*, 20, p.179–81.

Miller, G., 2001. The development of indicators for sustainable tourism: results of a Delphi survey of tourism researchers. *Tourism Management*, 22, p.351–62.

Mullins, P., 1991. Tourism urbanization. *International Journal of Urban and Regional Research*, 15, p.326–42.

Russell, R. & Faulkner, B., 1998. Reliving the destination life cycle in Coolangatta: a historical perspective on the rise, decline and rejuvenation of an Australian seaside resort. In E. Laws, B. Faulkner, & G. Moscardo eds., *Embracing and managing change in tourism: international case studies*. London: Routledge, p.95–115.

Russell, R. & Faulkner, B., 1999. Movers and shakers: chaos makers in tourism development. *Tourism Management*, 20, p.411–23.

Smith, R.A., 1992. Coastal urbanization: tourism development in the Asia Pacific. *Built Environment*, 18, p.27–40.

Stimson, R.J., Jenkins, O.H. & Roberts, B.H., 1998. The impact of Daikyo as a foreign investor on the Cairns–Far North Queensland regional economy. *Environment and Planning A*, 30, p.161–79.

ULI (Urban Land Institute), 1997. *The resort development handbook*. Washington, DC: Urban Land Institute.

UN (United Nations), 1996. *Indicators for sustainable development: frameworks and methodologies*. New York: UN.

Warnken, J., Bradley, M. & Guilding, C., 2004. Exploring methods and practicalities of conducting sector-energy consumption accounting in the tourist accommodation industry. *Ecological Economics*, 48, p.125–41.

Warnken, J., Bradley M. & Guilding, C., 2005. Eco-resorts vs mainstream accommodation providers: an investigation of the viability of benchmarking environmental performance. *Tourism Management*, 26, p.367–79.

Warnken. J. & Buckley, R.C., 1997. Major 1987–93 tourism proposals in Australia, 1987–1993. *Annals of Tourism Research*, 24(4), p.974–78.

Warnken, J. & Buckley, R.C., 1998. Scientific quality of tourism EIA. *Journal of Applied Ecology*, 35, p.1–8.

Warnken, J. & Guilding, C. 2006. Serviced apartment complexes in Australia: a critical analysis of their potential and challenges for sustainable tourism. In, C.B. Brebbia & F.D. Pineda eds., *Sustainable tourism II, Bologna 2006*. Ashurst, U.K.: WIT Press, p.47–58.

Warnken, J. & Guilding, C., forthcoming. Multi-ownership of tourism accommodation complexes: a critique of types, relative merits and challenges arising. *Tourism Management.*

Warnken, J., Guilding, C. & Cassidy, K., 2008. A review of the nature and growth of multi-titled tourism accommodation premises. *International Journal of Hospitality Management,* 27(4), p.574–83.

Warnken, J., Russell, R. & Faulkner, B., 2003. Condominium developments in maturing destinations: potentials and problems for long-term sustainability. *Tourism Management,* 24, p.155–68.

WTO, 1995. *What tourism managers need to know: a practical guide to the development and use of indicators of sustainable tourism.* Madrid: WTO.

7 Tourism Enterprises and Sustainable Development in Australia

Ralf Buckley

INTRODUCTION

In Australia as worldwide, tourism enterprises may produce both negative and positive consequences for sustainable development (Buckley, 2009). The broad categories are reviewed in Chapter 3. The main focus of this chapter is therefore to illustrate these various links through recent research and case studies in an Australian context. The dates when data were collected, and the degree to which coverage can be considered as comprehensive or otherwise, differ from one issue to another.

GOVERNMENT POLICY CONTEXT

Environmental Impact Assessment for Major Tourism Developments

Australia is a federated nation with three tiers of government, and provisions for environmental impact assessment at local, state, and federal level depending on the scale of the development application. The majority of tourism developments, particularly in urban areas, are subject only to local government planning controls. Larger developments, particularly stand-alone resorts in undeveloped sites, or those which require major public works such as port or harbour facilities, are generally subject to formal environmental impact assessment (EIA) at state government level. Federal EIA legislation is triggered only if a new tourism development, or sometimes associated infrastructure, falls under one of the heads of power allocated to the federal government under the Australian Constitution. In a tourism context, the most common of these is the international affairs power, which includes obligations under international treaties such as those associated with World Heritage.

Triggers and thresholds for various levels of EIA for tourism developments in Australia were reviewed recently (Buckley, 2007), drawing on earlier work by Warnken and Buckley (1995, 1996). The principal patterns may be summarised as follows. There are considerable differences in the way which individual local government authorities (LGAs) treat tourism development applications. There are differences between LGAs in different states, because of different state legislation; but there are also differences between neighbouring LGAs within any one state, because of local politics. For major tourism developments which trigger EIA at state government level, the technical quality of the EIA documents is relatively poor (Warnken & Buckley, 1998, 2000), commonly with inadequate baseline information to detect any future impacts.

For those tourism development applications which trigger a federal government involvement, the technical quality of EIA is generally much higher, even if the EIA process itself is managed by the state government. This includes, for example: tourism within the Great Barrier Reef Marine Park, which is managed by a federal agency; developments within or adjacent to land managed by Parks Australia, the federal protected area management agency; and developments which might affect World Heritage sites. Since most of Australia's 14 World Heritage areas are in fact managed by state government agencies, the federal government does not automatically become aware of tourism development proposals which may affect them. Commonly, it is left to voluntary conservation organisations to alert the federal environment agency. Indeed, such nongovernment organisations often have to enlist the voluntary assistance of university ecologists to prepare a dossier of likely impacts, in order to convince the federal agency to exercise its powers.

Tourism in Parks

Much of the Australia tourism industry relies heavily on the outdoor natural attractions for which the country is internationally known. Relatively few of these tourism operations take place on private land and most of these are adventure activities aimed principally at the self-drive domestic market. By far the majority rely on public national parks, and especially on World Heritage areas, as the primary attraction. Commercial tourism operations simply package transport, accommodation, and guides to bring commercial clients to these parks, where they use the same publicly funded infrastructure and take part in the same activities as private individual visitors. The precise conditions under which commercial tour operators (CTOs) are granted access to public protected areas, including fees and charges payable, legal liability and special privileges, are somewhat contentious (Buckley, 2004a; Buckley et al., 2003).

Most of Australia's national parks are managed by state government parks agencies, and these agencies have established both formal and informal coordinating arrangements for management of CTOs. Formal consultation occurs both at ministerial level and between the heads of agencies responsible for park management. Informal consultation occurs through the Tourism in Australia's Protected Areas Forum (TAPAF). Originally, TAPAF consisted simply of the most senior visitor management staff in each of the state national parks agencies, and acted principally as a mechanism for information exchange, with any implementation occurring state by state through the heads of agencies. Subsequently, representatives of the state government tourism agencies lobbied hard to take part in TAPAF meetings, which may now serve more as a negotiating forum between parks and tourism interests. For example, TAPAF has helped to harmonise insurance requirements, and the use of certification programmes, between states.

General principles for commercial tourism operations within public protected areas were discussed at a national conference hosted by the Australian Academy of Science in 2001 (Buckley 2002, 2004b; Buckley et al., 2003). Broadly speaking, in Australia as in other developed nations, protected area management agencies need political support to continue their primary conservation functions, and this support derives from people with interests in private or commercial outdoor recreation as well as those with interests in conservation. Parks agencies are thus generally pleased to retain a congenial working relationship with commercial ecotourism operators whose environmental performance they respect, but not at the expense of large-scale tourism development, or loss of their ultimate management control.

TOURISM ENTERPRISES

Urban Accommodation

The design, materials, and construction of urban tourist accommodation are determined principally by building regulations set by state governments, and standards established by professional organisations in architecture, engineering, and urban development. Historically, as in most countries, the supply of water and energy has been subsidised from general taxpayer revenue, so economic incentives for water and energy conservation have been relatively weak. In some states at least, there are currently various publicly funded incentives for both business and residential premises to install water- and/or energy-saving measures.

An analysis of water- and energy-saving technologies in all standards of tourism accommodation in the Gold Coast, one of Australia's principal tourist towns, found that inexpensive measures such as fluorescent light globes and energy-saving showerheads had been adopted widely, in the sense that many hotels, motels, and caravan parks had at least a few such fittings; but not deeply, in the sense that very few of these accommodation providers had installed even the simplest water- or energy-saving measures comprehensively (Buckley & Araujo, 1997; Warnken et al., 2004). Much publicised examples such as the so-called green hotel at the Sydney Olympics also proved, on investigation, to have rather limited measures in place.

Recycling programmes are commonplace for some resources, such as back-office paper; but very limited for others, because of a variety of constraints. The provision and potential re-use of guest toiletries, for example, is restricted by health regulations as well as client expectations. Composting facilities for organic garbage proved to be relatively commonplace in low-key tourist accommodation with ample space available, such as caravan parks; but very uncommon in upmarket accommodation with space restrictions, such as five-star city-centre high-rise hotels.

In more recent years, water restrictions associated with an extended drought have focused more attention on water conservation, in tourist accommodation as well as residential housing, in many regions of Australia. Similarly, the expectation of increased energy prices associated with climate change mitigation measures has focused more attention on options for energy conservation. These price signals are not yet strong enough to lead to significant retrofitting of existing tourism accommodation, but may have some influence on new construction.

Leading Tour Operators

Several of Australia's larger nature-tourism operations provide globally representative examples of companies which have successfully applied eco-tourism principles at mainstream tourism scale. Three different but equally successful models have been used to increase the volume of clients and scale of operations.

The first approach relies simply on selling a single product to a large number of clients, and increasing the scale of infrastructure and operations without sacrificing environmental performance. This model is exemplified by Quicksilver Cruises, which operates high-speed wave-piercing catamarans from Cairns and Port Douglas in tropical North Queensland, to a large purpose-built pontoon on the outer Great Barrier Reef. Operational details, including equipment and technologies, were outlined by Buckley (2006: 186–88) and environmental management issues and practices by Buckley (2003: 115). All sewage and rubbish are held on board the catamaran or pontoon and taken ashore. Videos outlining environmental issues and management practices in the Great Barrier Reef Marine Park are shown on board the catamaran on the way to the pontoon, and leaflets distributed. The same messages are reiterated by dive and snorkel guides. The pre-dive briefing includes instruction to avoid touching any coral or marine organisms.

The second successful model is to offer a similar product in many different geographic locations. An example is provided by Aurora Expeditions, which specialises in polar and subpolar expeditionary natural history cruises in both Northern and Southern Hemispheres. Aurora has recently reached a scale where it has purchased its own polar expedition vessel, the 100-passenger *Marina Svetaeva*. A similar business model, but with much smaller boats, is employed by Southern Sea Ventures, which offers sea-kayak tours in a wide variety of destinations and latitudes. Of these, the warm-water tours provide camping accommodation on secluded coasts or islands, whilst the cold-water tours run in conjunction with Aurora Expeditions, with shipboard accommodation and overnight cruising, and sea-kayak excursions by day at particular destinations.

Operational, social, and environmental management practices for two of the warm-water sea-kayak tours run by Southern Sea Ventures, in Fiji and subtropical Australia, are described by Buckley (2006: 128–34). Environmental management issues and practices for an Arctic expeditionary cruise and sea-kayak tour run jointly by Australia-based operator Aurora Expeditions and Southern Sea Ventures are described by Buckley (2003: 191–93) and may be summarised as follows. Non-biodegradable wastes are bagged and later taken ashore. Food scraps are dumped overboard. Sewage is treated on board and the treated effluent discharged. Passengers are taken ashore once or twice each day in inflatable rubber boats powered by outboard engines. Potential impacts from the inflatables include noise disturbance and two-stroke fuel and oil residues. Both of these are unavoidable, as with outboard-powered recreational boats worldwide. The Aurora staff drove with care and discretion around seabird colonies and marine mammals. Onshore, the guides were careful to keep passengers far enough away from wildlife that the latter seemed undisturbed, albeit alert. Svalbard residents hunt the larger native mammals, and the impacts of tourism are presumably low relative to those of hunting. Sea kayaking has negligible impact on water quality or noise, except through human voices. There was no indication that the sea kayakers disrupted breeding by cliff-nesting birds, potentially the most critical concern.

The third model, adopted by Sydney-based World Expeditions, offers a broad portfolio of different activities at different destinations worldwide. World Expeditions provides the retail shop-front, packaging, and quality control. In some cases it also owns the equipment and hires the guides so as to run the entire tour itself. More commonly, however, these on-ground components are subcontracted to local tour operators which are prepared to meet World Expeditions' standards. At a corporate level, World Expeditions has its own environmental code of practice, the *Responsible Travel Guide Book*, which covers the social as well as the natural environment. The company also supports developing-country community health programmes such as the Fred Hollows Foundation. Several tours operated by World Expeditions are described by Buckley (2006: 78–81, 128–31, 291–93).

Australian Ecolodges

Australia now has a number of tourist lodges which are within or adjacent to well-known national parks or World Heritage areas and can also lay claim to a high standard of environmental management. Some examples are listed in Table 7.1; more detailed descriptions of several of these are available in Buckley (2003). Some of these, such as Crocodylus Village in the Daintree area, cater principally to backpackers and budget travellers, but most of them are relatively upmarket. In addition to those lodges listed in Table 7.1, there are many more which advertise nature-based attractions but do not seem to have made any particular claims with regard to environmental management. Several of the upmarket properties in the Voyages portfolio, for example, might fall into this category. Some of these Voyages lodges, however, such as the Latitude 131 lodge in Uluru National Park, run social or community programmes (Buckley, 2004c).

Controversial Proposals

A number of major tourism development proposals in Australia have given rise to major political controversies on environmental grounds, even though other proposals which are not dissimilar in design have successfully been approved and in some cases even considered as ecotourism. The distinctions seem to lie partly in location and land use history, and partly in the political approach of the proponents.

These issues are illustrated particularly well by a proposal some years ago to construct a tourist cableway in the hinterland of the Gold Coast, a well-known tourist town on Australia's central eastern seaboard. Essentially, the proponents aimed to copy an existing cableway in the hinterland of Cairns, a smaller but also well-known tourist town further north. The Cairns cableway company, known as Skyrail, is not a publicly listed

Table 7.1   Some Well-Known Australian Ecolodges

Lodge	Park	State
Binnaburra	Lamington	Qld
O'Reillys	Lamington	Qld
Silkyoaks	Wet Tropics	Qld
Crocodylus Village	Wet Tropics	Qld
Oasis	Carnarvon Gorge	Qld
Crystal Creek	Border Ranges	NSW
Jemby-Rinjah	Blue Mountains	NSW
Freycinet	Freycinet	Tas
Cradle Mountain	Cradle Mountain	Tas
Lemonthyme	Cradle Mountain	Tas
Latitude 131	Uluru	NT
Seven Spirit Bay	Gurig	NT

corporation, but is understood to be highly profitable. Effectively, it is a ski-resort gondola which runs over the top of tropical rain-forest canopy and provides an easy and comfortable view of both the forest and the coastal scenery. There are a number of alighting points along the route, with boardwalks, lookouts, and interpretive displays; and souvenirs, food, and toilets. The Skyrail trip to the Kuranda Tablelands and back is ranked high amongst the "must do" experiences for visitors to Cairns.

The Skyrail cableway was approved and constructed as part of a political package when the tropical rain forests of North Queensland were converted from logging to World Heritage national park. This process involved national political and legal controversy, large-scale payments to the timber industry and its employees, and active and successful promotion of tourism as an alternative source of regional employment. In fact, the total regional revenue derived from tourism rose very rapidly to many times that previously derived from the timber industry, and Skyrail contributed significantly to this. It was, however, not without its social and economic costs. In particular, small-scale tourism operators in the village of Kuranda itself, which is accessible from Cairns by road and rail, complained that Skyrail captured their clients. Instead of going into Kuranda itself to buy food, drink, and locally made products, most of the cableway passengers simply ate in the café at the upper terminus of the cableway itself, and then went back to Cairns.

There were several key economic, social, environmental, and political differences between Skyrail and the Gold Coast proposal, which was named Naturelink. The principal proponent for the Naturelink proposal was a former mayor of the Gold Coast City Council, and the proposed route ran as far as possible along council-owned land. The key section, however, would have crossed part of a World Heritage national park, as for its northern counterpart. In contrast to the Cairns case, however, the protected area in the Gold Coast case was established many decades ago, is relatively small, and is threatened more by visitor pressure, residential encroachment, and urban invasive species than by logging, which halted more than half a century ago. The Springbook Plateau, the proposed inland terminus, already had a thriving tourism industry catering for both day trippers and overnight visitors.

The political strategy adopted by the Naturelink proponents contained a number of rather remarkable components. There is a local newspaper, strongly favourable to property development interests, and the first public announcement of the proposal was a front-page article which gave the impression that construction had already been approved and was about to commence. In fact, however, no applications had been lodged and the parks service had not been consulted. The proponents then sent a mailout to several thousand residents living in suburbs far enough from the proposed starting point that they would not suffer any immediate impacts from noise and traffic, but close enough that they might be interested in employment opportunities. The mailout was purportedly an opportunity to register for potential future employment; but in order to register, respondents had to tick a box accepting a pre-printed endorsement of the project. Not surprisingly, the response rate to this mailout was minuscule, but a high proportion of those who did respond were indeed interested in potential employment opportunities, since this was the only issue addressed. The project proponent, and the local newspaper, presented this as if it were an unbiased public opinion survey reflecting public attitudes to the proposal.

At the time this proposal was put forward, the state government minister for the tourism portfolio held a seat in a Gold Coast electorate, in a coastal rather than hinterland area. The proponent offered to donate quite significant sums to voluntary surf lifesaving clubs within this electorate if the project went ahead. The proponent also commissioned a well-known tourism academic to produce an economic model for the proposed development, but with very tightly restricted terms of reference. Most importantly, the consultancy brief apparently specified the number of customers and the ticket price, but the proponent then later publicised these figures as if they were an independent output from the model rather than inputs which he had specified himself. The model also made a number of other unrealistic assumptions which considerably underestimated the likely negative economic impacts on other existing tourism businesses.

As the controversy over this project developed, one particular local resident, who later won an environmental award for her determination, began to publicise the unusual features of this development proposal, and seek formal environmental impact assessment by the federal government, under its powers associated with World Heritage. This drew the attention of other university academics with expertise in environmental law and impact assessment, who began to make public comments in the mass media. A number of such academics were then contacted by a company based in the state capital city, offering them unspecified consultancies if they would first sign a confidentiality agreement. Those with prior commercial experience were suspicious of this approach, but others did indeed sign the agreement and then discovered that it was an attempt to prevent them making any public comment on the cableway proposal. One of those concerned, however, was also a Supreme Court barrister and thus well qualified to repudiate this manoeuvre.

Ultimately, the project proponents did produce an environmental impact statement under state legislation, despite arguing at one point that the cableway should be considered as public transport rather than a private tourism development and hence granted exemption. By the time the state government came to consider the EIS, the federal minister for the environment portfolio was well briefed on the World Heritage issues, and it was clear that the proposal would be prohibited under federal legislation, even if it were granted permission by the state government. As it turned out, the state government did not approve the proposal, and it did not go ahead.

Another highly controversial tourism development, but one which did in fact proceed, is at Hinchinbrook Harbour in the mid Queensland coast. The proposal was for a large-scale, resort-residential development on a narrow strip of low-lying coastal land between two World Heritage areas. The proponent was a somewhat outspoken property developer who had built a previous resort on a large rock island close to the central Queensland coastline. There was apparently a certain degree of residual commercial resentment associated with that previous development.

The key environmental issue for the Hinchinbrook Harbour proposal was the likelihood that it would increase recreational and commercial boat traffic in the narrow channel between Hinchinbrook Island and the mainland. This is a relatively shallow channel with extensive sea-grass beds, which provide grazing and habitat for the endangered dugong, a relative of the North American manatee. A significant proportion of the manatee population off the coast of Florida has suffered cuts from boat propellers, and dugong experts in Australia expressed considerable concern that the same effect was already occurring in Hinchinbrook Channel, and was likely to be greatly exacerbated by the proposed new marina development. Concerns were also expressed over the proposed destruction of an area of coastal mangroves, though these species were not endangered.

The critical legal issue was whether federal environmental impact legislation could be triggered by the potential impact on World Heritage areas and values, notably the dugong, even though the development itself was outside World Heritage areas. The upshot was that the development proposal was indeed evaluated under federal as well as state legislation, and did receive approval to proceed. Take-up of the residential land components was apparently rather low, so even a decade later the development is still significantly smaller than originally proposed. As yet, therefore, the predicted impacts on dugong populations do not seem to have been tested.

It is interesting to compare the Hinchinbrook Harbour development with two others, each of which has some similarities but some significant differences. A close parallel in terms of the physical design is provided by Couran Cove on South Stradbroke Island near the Gold Coast, which is also a coastal resort-residential development. Couran Cove, however, made use of a pre-existing harbour dug for a failed development proposal some decades ago. It is neither in nor adjacent to World Heritage areas. The development proposal included a number of environmental measures and technologies which allowed it to be marketed as an ecoresort; even though, in fact, most of these were simply dictated by its greenfields island location and were hence unavoidable. In addition, the Couran Cove proponent was a well-respected public figure, a former long-distance runner who had represented Australia internationally and who had made significant contributions to well-regarded voluntary conservation organisations. Because of all these distinctions, the development received approval with general support, and has apparently been successful.

Another interesting parallel is provided by the Kingfisher Bay Resort on Fraser Island, a large sand island off the south-central Queensland coast between the Gold Coast and Hinchinbrook Island. Thanks to an extended conservation campaign by one particular local resident several decades ago, the unique sand forests of Fraser Island and nearby mainland areas were protected from previous logging and sand mining through the declaration of a national park and subsequent listing as a World Heritage site. The Kingfisher Bay Resort was built on an enclave of private land within the Fraser Island protected area, and once again was marketed heavily as an ecoresort. It does indeed have a high standard of environmental management, due largely to the early efforts of a single individual; but it is still a large-scale resort-residential development with associated impacts, and many of the environmental management and technologies which it advertises were in fact mandated either by its island location or by legal conditions of development consent.

Most recently, another resort-residential development in a private enclave within a World Heritage national park has also been subject to both state and federal environmental impact assessment before approval. This particular example, the Mountain Bowers development at O'Reillys Rainforest Resort in Lamington National Park, is in the subtropical forest hinterland of the Gold Coast, rather than a coastal development as for those outlined earlier. O'Reillys is a well-respected and internationally known forest lodge, frequently referred to in compendia of ecotourism case studies. Originally established by the pioneering O'Reilly family as a dairy cattle property, it long predates the declaration of Lamington National Park or the Gondwana Rainforests World Heritage area. Although the O'Reillys management and the Queensland Parks and Wildlife Service disagree about some issues, such as feeding of birds by tourists, in general the relationship between the tourism enterprise and the park management agency is cordial.

The principal product at O'Reillys is mid-market tourist accommodation, with all meals provided in a large central dining room accompanied by members of the O'Reilly family, and a variety of nature and wildlife walks, drives, and presentations. An associated facility, also owned and operated by O'Reillys, caters for day visitors to this section of the national park. The proposal to construct a large residential development on another section of the private enclave, with individual residences to be sold to private investors under a strata-titled or condominium-style arrangement, was thus a significant departure from the previous model. Concerns were raised regarding potential impacts on World Heritage ecosystems, notably including particular endangered frog species. The proposal was thus assessed under federal as well as state legislation and was approved. As of early 2008, construction is nearing completion.

There are many other tourism developments around Australia, actual and proposed, which have generated their own particular environmental concerns. Wilsons Promontory National Park, in the southern Australian state of Victoria, is a popular destination for self-drive tourists who bring tents and caravans to a large campground near the entry gate, a site known as Tidal River. Parks Victoria itself proposed to construct a large hotel at Tidal River as an alternative to extending the camping facilities. This, however, met with enormous opposition from existing users, who feared that this would place it outside the financial reach of family visitors. Whilst the parks service believed that replacing a campground by a hotel would allow greater control of environmental impacts, principally those associated with noise, litter, and human waste, the park users were concerned about social impacts and felt that other approaches could be taken to control environmental impacts.

Another controversial tourism development within Victoria was at Seal Rocks on Phillip Island. The state government granted development consent to a private enterprise, which constructed a tourist resort. When the tourist enterprise later wished to expand the development, it apparently relied on an unusual clause in the development consent which required the government to allow the enterprise to operate profitably. The owners claimed that the only way they could run at a profit was to expand. The issue was ultimately resolved in court, at a cost to the taxpayer of some $56 million (Buckley, 2004c; O'Connor, 2003).

Industry Associations

Australia has several tourism industry associations at various scales and with various interests. The roles of three such associations are outlined following. The peak tourism industry association in Australia currently goes under the name of TTF Australia. It was previously known as the Tourism Task Force and later the Tourism and Travel Forum. Whilst the principal role of TTF Australia is to represent the tourism industry's interests to the federal government, in a similar way to associations in other industry sectors, it has also taken an active role in promoting tourism enterprises with good environmental performance, and in debates regarding large-scale tourism development within public protected areas. Best known of its contributions in this regard is a three-part report under the general heading of *A Natural Partnership*, covering marketing, visitor satisfaction, and infrastructure (Buckley, 2004c).

For some years there was a competing tourism industry association to TTF Australia, known initially as the Australian Tourism Industry Association and later as Tourism Council Australia. This collapsed, but its state subsidiaries re-formed as independent state councils. The director of the Queensland Tourism Industry Council has on a number of occasions represented tourism industry interests in issues relating to protected area management, in a very positive light. QTIC has added its voice, for example, to calls by conservation groups for the protection of forests against logging; and has made submissions to national parliamentary enquiries, arguing in favour of increased funding for protected-area management agencies.

The principal public roles of Ecotourism Australia are to operate a tourism product ecocertification programme and an annual ecotourism conference. The association also acknowledges quite openly on its Web site, however, that one of its goals is to increase access to public protected areas for the commercial tourism enterprises which are its members, and it appears that this was the principal reason why it was originally established. In assessing the net contribution of Ecotourism Australia to sustainable development, therefore, there are several considerations. On the negative side, it is possible that its lobbying campaigns have increased the volume and hence impacts of commercial tourism within the conservation estate. Since private recreational visitation to protected areas appears to be falling in a number of developed nations, however, it is arguable that commercial tours are simply substituting for independent visitation.

Since various commercial tourism enterprises are in fact permitted to operate in public protected areas, a mechanism to select only those enterprises with high standards of environmental management and education, which is what the ecocertification programme intends to provide, arguably represents a positive contribution to sustainable development. In addition, not all of the enterprises which are members of Ecotourism Australia necessarily operate in protected areas; and the association has helped to publicise the importance of good environmental management practices throughout the Australian tourism industry as a whole. In particular, some of its leading members have also won a series of national and international tourism awards, which has provided publicity for the association as well as the individual enterprises concerned.

CONCLUSIONS

When the term *ecotourism* first gained widespread international currency in the early 1990s, it was adopted rapidly within Australia because there was no previous terminology for it to displace. The North American term *outfitter* and the African term *safari* were not used in Australia, and the federal government at the time produced a *National Ecotourism Strategy* which was endorsed largely without opposition, even though it had rather little practical effect. At least partly because of this report, the Australian tourism industry and its government agencies were able to promote the perception internationally that environmental management within the Australian tourism sector was of a high standard. In reality, however, it appears to be neither better nor worse than any other developed nation.

As internationally, there are particular individual tourism enterprises which appear to have achieved high standards of environmental management performance, and have contributed to environmental education and in some cases to conservation of the natural environment. As worldwide, however, these are a small minority. The majority of the industry simply complies with applicable environmental and social legislation. There is also a sector of the industry which routinely seeks to flout, subvert, or modify environmental legislation in its own favour. Once again, this is probably no different from any other industry sector or any other country.

The tourism industry is of particular interest in sustainable development because, unlike most sectors, it does have the potential to make positive triple-bottom-line contributions to sustainable development: i.e., to make net positive contributions to conservation and communities whilst still remaining profitable for shareholders. Whilst a limited number of tourism enterprises do indeed pursue such an approach on their own behalf, the industry as a whole certainly does not; and there is no particular reason why we should expect it to do so. If the speed limit is 60 kph, we do not expect people to drive routinely at 50 kph. If we want them to drive at 50 kph, we change the speed limit. Likewise, if we want tourism property developers and tourism enterprises to improve their environmental management across the entire industry sector, the only realistic approach is to establish legislation, regulations, audit and enforcement mechanisms that require all such enterprises to do so equally; and to recognise that industry claims that this approach is unnecessary because the industry will regulate itself are not borne out by historical evidence.

REFERENCES

Buckley, R.C., 2002. Draft principles for tourism in protected areas. *Journal of Ecotourism*, 1, p.75–80.

Buckley, R.C., 2003. *Case studies in ecotourism.* Oxford: CAB International, 264pp.

Buckley, R.C., 2004a. Partnerships in ecotourism: Australian political frameworks. *International Journal of Tourism Research*, 6, p.75–83.

Buckley, R.C. ed., 2004b. Tourism in parks: Australian initiatives. Gold Coast: Griffith University, 194pp.

Buckley, R.C., 2004c. A natural partnership, vol 2. Innovative funding mechanisms for visitor infrastructure in protected areas. Sydney: TTF Australia.

Buckley, R.C., 2006. *Adventure tourism.* Oxford: CAB International, 528pp.

Buckley, R., 2007. Thresholds and standards for tourism environmental impact assessment. In M. Schmidt, J. Glasson, L. Emmelin, & H. Helbron eds., *Standards and thresholds for impact assessment.* Heidelberg: Springer,p.205–15.

Buckley, R.C. & Araujo, G., 1997. Environmental management performance in tourism accommodation. Annals of Tourism Research, 24, p.465–69.

Buckley, R.C., Pickering, C.M. & Weaver, D. eds., 2003. *Nature-based tourism, environment and land management.* Oxford: CABI, 213pp.

O'Connor, A., 2003.Workers' lament at Seal Rocks. *The Age*, 21 November, Fairfax, Melbourne.

Warnken, J. & Buckley, R.C., 1995. Triggering EIA in Queensland: a decade of tourism development. Environmental Policy and Law, 25, p.340–47.

Warnken, J. & Buckley, R.C., 1996. Coastal tourism development as a testbed for EIA triggers: outcomes under mandatory and discretionary EIA frameworks. Environmental Planning and Law Journal, 13, p.239–45.

Warnken, J. & Buckley, R.C., 1998. Scientific quality of tourism EIA. Journal of Applied Ecology, 35, p.1–8.

Warnken, J. & Buckley, R.C., 2000. Monitoring diffuse impacts: Australian tourism developments. Environmental Management, 25, p.453–61.

8 Environmental Performance of Tourism Enterprise in Ghana
A Case Study of Hotels in the Greater Accra Region (GAR)

Ishmael Mensah

INTRODUCTION

The importance of the accommodation sector in tourism cannot be over-emphasised. It usually becomes the psychological base of the tourist during his/her stay at the destination (Cooper et al., 1993) and the pivot around which other tourism activities revolve; and accounts for a substantial share of international tourists' expenditure, which has been estimated at 31 per cent (WTTC, 2000). The importance of accommodation to tourism is also underscored by the fact that the number and class of hotels at a destination indicate the level of tourism development. In the words of Pearce: "Hotels are the most visible and pure manifestation of tourism in the city" (1995:151). The accommodation sector is also one area where activities such as construction of buildings, landscaping, cooking, laundry, disposal of waste as well as use of water and energy tend to affect the environment adversely if not properly managed. The construction of hotels also leads to the development of other supporting facilities, e.g., parking lots, restaurants, kitchens, swimming pools, and laundries; all of which make great demands on environmental resources such as minerals, timber, water, and energy. Foster et al. (2000) have identified four inherent characteristics of hotels that exacerbate their potential environmental impacts; these are:

- Time perishable capacity: a hotel room, if not occupied by midday today, cannot be stored and resold at this moment tomorrow and therefore represents lost revenue.
- Heterogeneity: each guest or customer needs to be treated individually during service provision, so that the amount of resources used cannot be cut down through standardisation.
- Labour intensity: the large workforce in the sector renders automation almost impossible and this has implications for resource utilization.
- Customer involvement: unlike other industries, the customer participates in the production process rather than the final good being sent to him/her, and this could also lead to wastage of resources by customers.

Marin and Jafari (2002) are of the view that hotels mark and distinguish destinations and tourists who reside in those hotels temporarily, have non-ordinary consumption, and generate unnecessary waste during their short stays. In most coastal tourist destinations in developing countries, it is common to see a huge concentration of hotels along the beachfront which are often out of scale and clash with the surrounding environments, a phenomenon described as 'architectural pollution' (Mathieson & Wall, 1982), and this results in a commensurate huge generation of waste with its attendant environmental problems. Furthermore, the impacts of hotels on the environment include depletion and degradation of host communities' source of water (Holder, 1988; Tyler, 1989; Shah, 2000); displacement of local communities (Eber, 1992; Hunter & Green, 1995); depletion of energy resources (Jackson, 1984; Eber, 1992; Kirk, 1998); and generation of pollutants and waste (Mathieson & Wall, 1982; Chan & Lam, 2001). To date there has been little research on the impacts of tourism enterprises, in particular hotels, on the environment in Ghana and even less in terms of their environmental performance (Mensah, 2006). It is therefore the aim of this chapter to examine the environmental performance of hotels in the GAR against the background of the policy and institutional framework provided by the government through its ministries, departments and agencies (MDAs). However, first and providing the broader context, a brief introduction to Ghana and an overview of the hotel sector.

Ghana, which is situated in West Africa (Figure 8.1), is one of the most popular tourist destinations in the subregion, due to its tropical climate, pristine beaches, warm hospitality, World Heritage status slave forts and castles, connections with the transatlantic slave trade, and relative political stability within the West African subregion.

Tourist arrivals increased from 145,780 in 1990 to 530,827 in 2003 and are projected to reach the one million mark by the year 2010. United Kingdom, USA, and Germany represent the three top generating markets in the Northern Hemisphere whilst Nigeria, Cote d'Ivoire, and Togo represent the top generating markets in Africa. In response to the growth being experienced by the tourism sector, there is a proliferation of hotels. Hotel accommodation has increased from 8,518 rooms in 1995 to 19,010 rooms in 2005. This increase is largely accounted for through the growth in budget hotels whilst the five-star category has remained about the same over this period.

The increases in hotel accommodation stock has also been attributed to the Structural Adjustment Programme (SAP) embarked upon by the government in 1986 (Konadu-Agyemang, 2001) and the generous investment incentives provided by the Ghana Investment Promotion Council (GIPC Act 478) in 1994 for investors (Mensah, 2006). This steady increase in the country's hotel accommodation stock has put pressure on the environment and natural resources, especially in the Greater Accra Region (GAR), which accounts for an average of 40 per cent of the total number of rooms

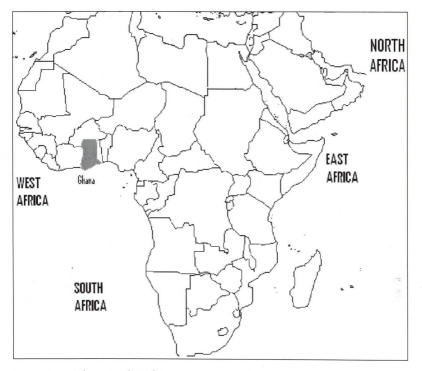

Figure 8.1 Ghana in the African context.

in the country (Table 8.1). There have been increasing concerns over the environmental problems posed by the proliferation of hotels in every part of the GAR, especially in Accra and Tema. The 1996 Tourism Development Plan for the region concedes that sewerage and solid waste disposal is a problem in some hotels. The plan further recognised that there could be pollution of rivers, lakes, and coastal water from sewerage outfall lines and of groundwater through the seepage of waste materials due to improper development of sewerage and solid-waste disposal systems in hotels and other facilities. As evident, for example, from a number of instances where hotels in Accra have discharged waste into their surrounding environments (Mensah, 2006; Akyeampong, 2007).

Another issue that raises serious concern is the unsanitary nature of the environment in which tourist facilities, including hotels, especially in Accra, operate and its implications for the environmental health and safety of tourists (Asiedu, 1999). Accra, like most capital cities in developing countries, suffers from environmental problems: inappropriate sewage, liquid, and solid waste disposal, contamination of food and water sources, inadequate potable water supply, unsanitary conditions and insect infestation (Songsore, 1992; Benneh et al., 1993). Thirteen significant diseases in Accra, including diarrhoea, malaria, and respiratory infections, are attributed to poor housing

Table 8.1   Number of Hotel Units and Rooms, 1995–2005

Years	Budget	Guest House	1 Star	2 Star	3 Star	4 Star	5 Star	*Other	Total	No. in GAR (%)
1995	4,825	305	1,455	1,286	196	347	104	—	8,518	3,231 (37.9)
1996	6,236	438	1,498	1,491	260	364	104	—	10,391	3,928 (37.8)
1997	6,217	460	1,861	1,391	488	465	0	39	10,921	4,752 (43.5)
1998	5,916	525	1,850	1,544	517	518	0	9	10,879	5,125 (47.1)
1999	5,776	655	1,694	1,655	594	414	104	4	10,896	4,317 (39.6)
2000	7,200	796	2,065	1,955	808	234	104	479	13,641	5,874 (43.1)
2001	8,127	840	2,282	1,988	885	414	104	813	15,453	6,211 (40.2)
2002	8,701	975	2,487	2,315	953	554	104	188	16,277	6,873 (42.2)
2003	8,730	1,002	2,675	2,768	970	658	104	49	16,956	7,157 (42.2)
2004	9,479	1,104	2,866	2,848	998	558	104	52	18,009	7,846 (43.6)
2005	10,076	1,270	2,821	2,752	1,190	658	104	139	19,010	7,777 (40.9)

* Other forms of accommodation include accommodation facilities that have not been graded, hostels, home lodges, tourist homes, and other supplementary accommodation. Source: Ghana Tourist Board (GTB), 2006.

and ventilation, unsanitary environment, contaminated drinking water, poor drainage, and lack of waste-disposal facilities (World Bank, 2002). Since hotels in Accra are not insulated from these environmental problems, they owe a corporate social responsibility to help address the problem rather than exacerbating it. This includes the need to address their environmental performance and introduce environmental management, which is defined by Hewitt and Gary (1998) as the management of an organisation's impact on the environment. The purpose of environmental management, according to the Environmental Protection Agency (EPA) of Ghana, is to identify human activities that may impact on the quality of the environment, to implement appropriate mitigation measures to address these effects, to ensure that predicted effects are kept within the levels projected so that they do not become a problem, and to enhance environmental protection (EPA, 2002).

THE POLICY AND INSTITUTIONAL FRAMEWORK

To help ensure that hotels and other establishments do not degrade or pollute the environment, the government, through MDAs, provides the policy and legal framework for environmental management. The Ministry of Tourism and Diasporan Relations (MOTDR), Ghana Tourist Board (GTB), Environmental Protection Agency (EPA), and District, Municipal and Metropolitan Assemblies (DMMAs) are all involved in shaping environmental policies and exacting compliance with environment policies by hotels in the region.

The Ministry of Tourism and Diasporan Relations (MOTDR) is the tourism policymaking arm of the government. In fulfilment of its role, the ministry, in collaboration with the World Tourism Organization (WTO), developed the Integrated Tourism Development Plan (ITDP) in 1996 to provide the general direction for tourism development in the country. The ITDP, which is a fifteen-year tourism development plan, is based on the development of tourism on a sustainable basis in order to balance the generation and distribution of the economic benefits of tourism with the protection of the environmental, historical, and cultural heritage of the country (Inskeep, 2000). The policy goal of the plan is "To develop tourism as a leading socioeconomic sector of the country and a good quality, internationally competitive tourist destination, within the framework of maintaining its permanent sustainability" (Inskeep, 2000: 85). The plan makes a number of considerations based on the principles of sustainability which have implications for environmental management in hotels. The considerations are:

- the natural, historic, cultural, and other resources for tourism are conserved and where necessary enhanced for continuous use in the future, while still bringing benefits to the present society. Tourism development is planned, developed, and managed so that it does not generate serious environmental or socio-cultural problems;

- the overall environment quality of the tourism areas is maintained and improved where needed;
- a high level of tourist satisfaction is maintained so that the country retains its marketability and popularity;
- the socioeconomic benefits of tourism are spread widely throughout the country and society (Inskeep, 2000).

Tourism enterprises, by abiding by these considerations, could contribute their quota towards the achievement of sustainable development by meeting the needs of both present and future hosts and tourists (Burton, 1995) and not degrading or altering the environment (Butler, 1993; Middleton & Hawkins, 1998).

The Environmental Protection Agency (EPA) was established in 1994 to replace the erstwhile Environmental Protection Council by an act of parliament (Act 490), and by Legislative Instrument (LI) 1652 of 1999 and 1703 of 2001. The act states that the role of the EPA is "To ensure compliance with any laid down Environmental Impact Assessment (EIA) procedures in planning and execution of development projects." The procedures for EIA are described in the 'Ghana Environmental Impact Assessment Procedures of 1995.' Under the EPA Act 490, the functions of the EPA include

- advise the minister on the formulation of environmental policies;
- issue environmental permits and pollution abetment notices for controlling waste discharges, emissions, and pollutants;
- prescribe standards and guidelines relating to the pollution of air, water, land, and other forms of environmental pollution; and
- ensure compliance with any laid down EIA procedures in the planning and execution of development projects (EPA, 1994).

This act requires new hotel developers to register with the EPA, conduct an environmental impact assessment of their proposals, and submit an environmental assessment report to the EPA for review. If the EPA is satisfied, an environmental permit is granted for the hotel development to commence. Hotels are further required to submit Environmental Management Plans (EMP) after eighteen months of operations. The creation of the EPA also resulted in the formulation of the National Environmental Action Plan (NEAP) in 1991, which is Ghana's most elaborate environmental policy document. NEAP "defines a set of policy actions, related investments and institutional strengthening activities to make Ghana's strategy more environmentally sustainable" (EPA, 1994). The NEAP contains six main working documents on mining, industry, and hazardous chemicals, marine and coastal ecosystems, human settlements, forestry and wildlife, land management, and water management (EPA, 1994). The NEAP aims at ensuring a sound management of resources and the environment so as to avoid exploitation of these resources in a manner that might cause irreparable damage to the environment (EPA, 1997).

The Ghana Tourist Board (GTB), which is the implementing agency of the MOTDR, was created in 1977 to serve as the National Tourism Organization (NTO) and therefore tasked with monitoring and regulating tourism establishments, including the licensing and classification of hotels. The Accommodation and Catering Enterprises Regulations of 1979 (Legislative Instrument 1205) empowers the GTB in the discharge of its duties. As part of the requirements for the issuance of license by the GTB, hotels are supposed to submit environmental permits from the EPA. Also, they have to be physically inspected each year by quality assurance officers of the GTB in order for them to be reclassified. Among the areas inspected is the level of sanitation or environmental health of the hotels. Before a hotel is licensed by the GTB, it must also submit certificates of suitability from the district, municipal, or metropolitan assembly where it is located, as well as the Ministry of Health, Department of Town Planning, Fire Service, and Police Service. All these are to ensure that the hotels meet high environmental and safety standards; however, this is only mandatory when the hotel is initially licensed and no further license is required for the reclassification in subsequent years (Vine, 1994).

District, Municipal and Metropolitan Assemblies (DMMAs) are also major enforcers of sound environmental management practices in hotels. The DMMAs in the GAR are Accra Metropolitan, Tema Metropolitan, Ga District, Damgbe East District, and Damgbe West District (Figure 8.2). The DMMAs are the decentralized units in the country which also issue licenses

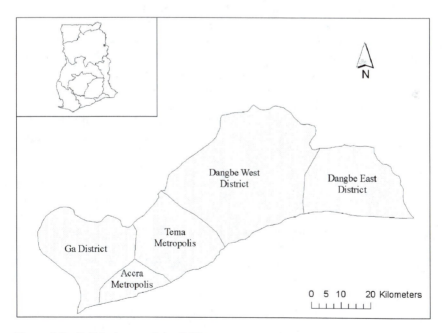

Figure 8.2   Political map of the GAR.

to all businesses, including hotels, before they can commence operations. Although the approval of site plans by the DMMAs is to ensure that the hotel is not located on public lands or waterways and does not conflict with the area's development plan, there have been instances whereby hotels have been located on waterways, thereby causing flooding to outlying areas.

A case in point was the Secaps Hotel in Accra, which was washed away by a rainstorm (Harruna Attah & Alhassan, 2001). The town or city engineer inspects the site to ensure that it is not on public land or on a waterway. The health officer also has the mandate to inspect all hotel premises in order to ascertain the lighting, ventilation, toilet facilities, and general sanitation on the compound. There must be re-inspection every year by the DMMA before licenses are renewed. The DMMAs also have environmental health officers who are supposed to inspect the hotels regularly.

ENVIRONMENTAL PERFORMANCE OF HOTELS

To determine the environmental performance of hotels in the country against the background of the cited regulations, data for this study were collected from both primary and secondary sources. Primary data were obtained by means of survey of hotel managers designed to elicit information on their environmental management practices. The areas covered and of concern in environmental management in hotels are energy conservation (Stipanuk, 1996; Williams, 1992; Chan & Lam, 2001); recycling of waste (Faulk, 2000); water conservation (Zhao & Merna, 1992); support for local communities (Middleton & Hawkins, 1998) and environmentally responsible marketing (Miles & Munilla, 1993). The GAR was chosen for the study because, apart from having the largest number of hotels in the country, Accra, which is also the capital town of Ghana, and Tema, the industrial hub of the country, account for over 80 per cent of businesses that employ ten or more persons in the country. Accra has the only international airport, which contributes immensely to the tourist traffic. There are also a number of travel and tour agencies, car hire agencies, transport companies, restaurants, nightclubs, and hotels. Hotels in the region could generally be described as small to medium enterprises. The Ghana Ministry of Trade and Industry defines a small enterprise as an organisation employing six to twenty-nine people with fixed assets valued at $100,000, whilst a medium enterprise employs between thirty and ninety-nine people with fixed assets amounting to $1 million.

A stratified random sample of hotels in the GAR comprising ten budget, ten one-star, ten guest houses, ten two-star, and twelve three- to five-star hotels were surveyed (n = 52). This was because there was the need to have a representation of the various categories of hotels, drawn from the GTB list of 486 licensed hotels in the GAR, in the sample for the purposes of comparison and objective analysis. The four-page questionnaire was categorized into four modules. Module A was on environmental management practices and questions on managers' perception of environmental management; module B was on environmentally responsible marketing; module C dealt with the characteristics of the hotel facility; and module D was on the socioeconomic characteristics of respondents. The questionnaires were either self-administered or administered by field assistants who were assigned to the different categories of hotels. Though some of the hotel managers declined taking part in the survey, other hotels were randomly selected from the same category to replace them due to the relatively small sample size. Most of the hotels surveyed employ less than thirty workers (73%). The majority (69%) are within the budget/one-star category with less than thirty rooms (71%) and mostly owned by private individuals or sole proprietors (63%), as indicated in Table 8.2. Apart from their basic functions of providing accommodation and food, they also provide other services, e.g., laundry, secretarial services, conferencing, and banqueting. The provision of these services nonetheless leads to the consumption of energy and water as well as the generation of waste.

Table 8.2   Characteristics of Hotels Sampled

Variable	Frequency	Percentage
Number of rooms		
< 30	37	71.2
30–59	10	19.2
90–119	2	3.8
120–149	1	1.9
150+	2	3.8
Number of workers		
< 30	38	73.1
30–59	4	7.7
60–89	1	1.9
90–119	4	7.7
120+	5	9.6
Ownership		
Local sole proprietor	33	63.5
Local partnership	6	11.5
Local/foreign partnership	8	15.4
Local limited liability company	5	9.6
*Other services offered		
Conferencing	22	50
Banqueting	19	43.2
Laundry	40	90.9
Secretarial services	33	75
Health/fitness/sports	13	29.5

*Other services offered apart from accommodation adds up to more than 100 due to multiple responses.

The hotel managers were asked to indicate the environmental management practices undertaken in their hotels and thus the results therefore relate to what the hotel managers indicated. The specific environmental management practices of the hotels encompassed within the survey are categorised as follows: environmental policy; waste reduction and recycling; conservation of water and energy; education and awareness creation; social responsibility; and environmentally responsible marketing as it pertains in the literature. The hotels undertake some of these environmental management practices (see Table 8.3). Generally, more hotels were engaged in activities geared towards conservation of energy and water, probably due to the fact that such practices have implications for the level of profitability of the hotels. This conforms to the literature that the priority action areas for

Table 8.3   Environmental Management Practices in Hotels in the GAR

Environmental management practice	Frequency	Percentage
Environmental policy		
Environmental policy	29	58
Manager in charge of environmental management	22	42.3
Submitted EMP to EPA	15	30
Waste and recycling		
Recycled waste	9	17.3
Used ecofriendly cleaning products	36	72
Reused linen and towels	37	74
Purchased in bulk to reduce packaging	27	54
Composted food leftovers	4	8
Conservation of water and energy		
Used energy-efficient light bulb	49	94.2
Used low-flow shower heads and sink aerators	35	63
Switched off air conditioners	17	32.7
Installed dual flush toilets	15	28.8
Installed solar hot-water system	4	8
Provided energy-efficient appliances	34	68
Education and awareness creation		
Encouraged guests to be ecofriendly	32	64
Trained staff to be ecofriendly	36	72
Advised guests on local customs and traditions	28	53.8
Educated guests on environmentally friendly practices	29	55.8
Social responsibility		
Supported environmental NGOs in cash or kind	20	40
Supported local community in which hotel is located	35	70
Sponsored research on an environmental issue	7	13.5
Environmentally responsible marketing		
Encouraged guests to try new experiences	32	61.5
Produced brochure on recycled paper	4	7.7
Provided accurate information to guests	37	71.2

environmental management programmes in hotels are water, waste, and energy management (Stipanuk, 1996; Faulk, 2000).

The most popular environmental management practices identified were use of energy-efficient light bulbs (94%); reuse of linen and towels (74%); use of ecofriendly cleaning products (72%); training of staff (72%); provision of accurate information to guests (71%); and support for local communities where the hotel is located (70%). A greater majority of the hotels, however, do not practice the following: production of brochure on recycled paper (8%); composting of food waste (8%); installation of solar hot-water system (8%); sponsoring of research (14%); and recycling of waste (17%). Though more than half of the hotel managers (58%) claimed they had an environmental policy, taken to be a written statement on the enterprises' attitude towards the environment, only one hotel had an environmental policy statement clearly displayed. This is particularly noteworthy because the first and most important step towards environmental action in an organisation is the formal adoption of a written policy statement (Forte, 1994; Kirk, 1998). Recycling, though considered one of the cost-cutting practices, is not popular among hotels in the region as it pertains in the developed world because of a lack of technical know-how and recycling plants. The EPA have acknowledged that there is a lack of waste recycling/treatment or proper management practices in the country (EPA, 2002).

Another problem is non-compliance with environmental regulations and legislations. Though hotels are required to submit an Environmental Management Programme (EMP) to the EPA every eighteen months of operation, only about a third (30%) had fulfilled this statutory requirement. In a related study by Hens and Boon (1999), it was discovered that in 1995, 114 environmental assessment applications were received by the EPA, out of which twenty-nine required environmental impact statements (EIS). However, applications for projects in the public utility sector were most numerous, followed by mining, manufacturing, infrastructure, and forestry. There was only one application from the tourism sector. The low compliance in the tourism sector could be due to the fact that hotels with less than twenty rooms are exempted. Also, there is a lack of an effective monitoring mechanism by the EPA, which enables hotel managers to flout this regulation. Moreover, penalties for non-compliance are as low as GH¢10 (about $10).

Most of the hotels did not have appropriate waste management and recycling programmes in place. As a result, most of the waste they generate is not treated but dumped into the environment to further compound the worsening waste management problem in Accra (Songsore, 1992; Benneh et al., 1993) and the other districts. The three main types of waste generated by the hotels—food, water, and sewage—are usually dumped inappropriately. On a positive note, bottles are returned to distributors for onward transmission to manufacturers for reuse. As indicated in Table 8.4, food

Table 8.4   Waste Disposal Practices in Hotels in the GAR

Form of waste	Disposal method	Frequency	Percentage
Food waste	Recycling/animal feed	8	15.4
	Garbage bin/disposal site	34	65.4
	Open space (free range)	6	11.5
	No response	3	5.8
Wastewater	Drainage/soak away system	37	71.1
	Sewage treatment plant	8	15.3
	River/stream	1	1.9
	Irrigation of plants	1	1.9
	No response	5	9.6
Sewerage	Cesspit	35	67.3
	Sewerage treatment plant	7	13.5
	Drainage/soak away system	3	5.7
	No response	7	13.5

waste is mostly dumped into garbage bins or waste disposal sites (65%), though such waste could be recycled into animal feed and other usable materials or composted. In fact, only 8 per cent of the hotels composted their food leftovers. Waste water also goes down the drain of the majority of the hotels (71.1%), though it could be reused for irrigating ornamental plants and flowers or to flush toilets. Sewerage treatment is also a major problem in the hotels as only 7 per cent of the hotels had sewerage treatment plants. The greater majority of the hotels (67%) discharge their sewerage into cesspits, which are periodically emptied by tankers and dumped at designated sewerage treatment sites.

There were some differences in the extent of implementation of environmental management practices among the various categories of hotels comprising budget/one-star, guest house/two-star and three- to five-star (see Table 8.5).

A greater percentage of hotels in the three- to five-star category, compared with those in the budget/one-star category and guest house/two-star category, implemented most of the environmental management practices. About 83 per cent of the 3- to 5-star hotels, compared with 2-star/guest house (68%) and budget/1-star enterprises (32%), have an environmental policy. The differences in the environmental performance of the various categories of hotels were found to be significant at alpha level 0.05 (Table 8.6). To determine the relationship between hotel category and level of involvement in sound environmental management practices, a list of eighteen ecofriendly practices was used as a benchmark. Hotels that practised one to six (1–6) had a low level of implementation, seven to twelve (7–12) a medium level, and hotels that practised thirteen to eighteen (13–18) were

Table 8.5   Percentage of Hotels in Each Category Implementing Environmental Management Practices

Environmental Management Practice	Budget/ 1-star	Guest House/ 2-star	3–5 star
Environmental policy	31.6	68.4	83.3
Manager in charge of environmental management	25.0	25.0	100.0
Recycled waste	5.0	15.0	41.7
Used energy-efficient light bulb	85.0	100.0	100.0
Used low-flow shower heads or sink aerators	70.0	70.0	58.3
Switched off air conditioners	50.0	20.0	25.0
Installed dual flush toilets	25.0	35.0	25.0
Encouraged guests to be ecofriendly	77.8	45.0	75.0
Installed solar hot-water system	5.6	5.0	16.7
Trained staff to be ecofriendly	83.3	55.0	83.3
Provided energy-efficient appliances	72.2	55.0	83.3
Used ecofriendly cleaning products	77.8	75.0	58.3
Supported environmental NGOs in cash or kind	38.9	35.0	50.0
Supported local community where hotel is located	72.2	55.0	91.7
Submitted EMP to the EPA	22.2	15.0	66.7
Reused linen and towels	77.8	65.0	83.3
Purchased in bulk to reduce packaging	44.4	55.0	66.7
Composted food leftovers	5.6	5.0	16.7
Advised guests on local customs and traditions	30.0	55.0	91.7
Educated guests on environmentally friendly practices	60.0	45.0	66.7
Sponsored research on an environmental issue	20.0	0.0	25.0
Encouraged guests to try new experiences	55.0	55.0	83.3
Produced brochure on recycled paper	10.0	0.0	16.7
Provided accurate information to guests	85.0	65.0	58.3

N = 52

considered to have a high level of implementation of these environmental management practices. The significance level of 0.027 provides statistical evidence of a relationship between hotel category and level of implementation of environmental management practices.

The level of implementation of environmental management practices by 35 per cent and 30 per cent of budget/one-star hotels and guest house/

Table 8.6   Hotel Category and Level of Implementation of Environmental Management Practices

	Budget/ 1-star	Guest House/ 2-star	3–5 star	Total
Low implementation	7 (35.0)	6 (30.0)	3 (25.0)	16 (30.8)
Medium implementation	12 (60.0)	13 (65.0)	4 (33.3)	29 (55.8)
High implementation	1 (5.0)	1 (5.0)	5 (41.7)	7 (13.5)
Total	20 (100.0)	20 (100.0)	12 (100.0)	52 (100.0)

X^2 = 10.922 Df. = 4 Sign. = 0.027*
*Significant at 0.05.

two-star hotels, respectively, can be described as low, whilst 25 per cent of the three- to five-star hotels category also had low levels of involvement in environmental management. Also, whilst the performance of only 5 per cent of the budget/one-star hotels and guest house/two-star can be described as high, 42 per cent of the three- to five-star hotels can be described as such. Therefore, the higher the class of a hotel, the greater the involvement in environmental management practices. This coincides with the conclusions of Kirk (1998), Mowforth and Munt (1998), and Alvarez Gil and Cespedes (2001) that larger hotels have been at the forefront of environmental management. This is probably due to the fact that the larger hotels have more financial and material resources, technology, and well-qualified human resources. They also have better management structures in place. The majority of the three- to five-star hotels are also multinationals operating as franchises, management contracts, or have international affiliates and therefore have to yield to the environmental policies and guidelines of their headquarters in Europe or America. A typical example is NOVOTEL Accra, which abides by the environmental policies of Accor, its parent company. Among Accor's environmental initiatives is the creation of an environment department to integrate the efforts of other departments in the various hotels, formulation of the Accor environmental charter, and the establishment of a sustainable development department to execute company policies. In addition, each major business unit has an environmental coordinator. Specific actions undertaken by the hotel include water and energy conservation, prevention of greenhouse gas emissions, tree planting, waste management including numerous recycling activities, sustainable purchasing, building construction, customer awareness, employee awareness, and achievement of local certifications for performance related to environmental goals. To ensure effectiveness, specific actions are determined with regards to applicable issues in each country in which Accor hotels operate.

CONCLUSIONS

Environmental management is becoming an essential aspect of the operations of tourism businesses, leading to a number of initiatives and programmes by trade associations, international organizations, and individual tourism businesses. In Ghana, much of the environmental initiatives have been in the form of legal requirements, plans, and policies from government MDAs. Hotels in Ghana can undertake environmental management practices like recycling, use of solar energy as well as compliance with legislations and guidelines. However, the majority of hotels have adopted environmental management practices in the fields of energy and water conservation because these are cost-cutting measures which have implications for profitability. Also, the larger hotels (three- to five-star) were found to be at the forefront of the adoption and implementation of sound environmental management practices. This study has also revealed that recycling of waste is one of the least popular environmental management practices in the country. The principle of 'reduce, reuse, recycle' which guides environmental management in hotels in most parts of the world is not adhered to by the majority of hotels in Ghana. This is because recycling is perceived as a high-tech activity. Hotels should be encouraged to sort their waste into, for instance, paper, food, plastic, and metals instead of putting them together and dumping them. A recycling plant could then be established where these wastes could be sent to for recycling at the close of every day.

One of the practical ways of ensuring that hotels and other tourism enterprises engage in environmental management practices is by certifying them or awarding ecolabels. There are over one hundred ecolabels for tourism, hospitality, and ecotourism (Font, 2002); however, there is not a single ecolabelling scheme developed by Ghana's tourism sector. Whilst the claims by hotels to be environmentally friendly could be untrue, or amount to 'ecoexploitation' (Wight, 1994), ecolabelling and certification provides the opportunity for a third party to verify such claims against some set criteria before the ecolabel is issued. Ecolabelling and certification therefore represent more credible ways of assessing the environmental performance of tourism businesses and should be encouraged in Ghana, especially against the background that the agencies established by the government to monitor environmental performance and enforce standards have been sometimes ineffective due to resource constraints.

In spite of the existence of numerous laws, policies, and plans, as well as MDAs to exact compliance with such legal instruments, a number of hotels are able to flout certain legal requirements like submission of Environmental Impact Assessment to the EPA. Furthermore, though Ghana has a number of legislations and guidelines for the environmental performance of hotels and other tourism businesses, the study suggests that a number of these businesses are not complying. The non-compliance suggests a lack of an effective monitoring mechanism. The number of hotels in the GAR keeps increasing by the day, but this is not accompanied by a corresponding increase in logistics and human resources for the Ghana Tourist Board, the DMMAs, and Environmental Protection Agency. There is the need to strengthen these institutions tasked with monitoring the environmental performance of the hotels in order for them to live up to their responsibilities. They should also adopt technology and some of the latest methods for monitoring these hotels and other tourism businesses.

There is also the need for education of managers of smaller hotels, which constitute the bulk of the region's accommodation stock, who may lack the capacity to manage effectively the environments in which they operate. As the study indicates, the three- to five-star hotels are at the forefront of environmental management but they are in the minority in terms of supply. The cumulative effects of wastes and pollutants generated by the other hotels could be very substantial. The monitoring agencies should therefore team up and organise training programmes for managers of these hotels on the country's environmental legislation, waste management practices, water and energy conservation practices, pollution control, and some of the industry's standard best environmental practices.

REFERENCES

Akyeampong, O.A., 2007. *Tourism in Ghana: the accommodation sub-sector.* Accra: Janel Publications Ltd.

Alvarez Gil, M.J. & Cespedes Lorente, J.J., 2001. An analysis of environmental management organizational context and performance of Spanish hotels. *Omega*, 29(6), p.457–71.

Harruna Attah, A.R. & Alhassan, A.R., 2001. Accra drowns again. *Accra Mail.* Wenesday, October 17.

Asiedu, A.B., 1999. The environmental health safety factor in international tourism promotion in Ghana—evidence from university exchange students. *Bulletin of Ghana Geographical Association*, 21.

Benneh, G. et al., 1993. *Environmental problems and the urban household in the Greater Accra Metropolitan Area (GAMA)—Ghana.* Stockholm: Stockholm Environmental Institute.

Burton, R., 1995. *Travel geography* 2nd ed. London: Pitman Publishing.

Butler, R.W., 1993. *Pre- and Post-Impact Assessment of Tourism Development, Tourism Research: Critiques and Challenges.* New York: Routledge, p.135–55.

Chan, W.W. & Lam, J., 2001. Environmental accounting of municipal solid waste originating from rooms and restaurants in the Hong Kong hotel industry. *Journal of Hospitality and Tourism Research*, 25(4), p.371–85.

Cooper, C., Fletcher, J. & Wanhill, S., 1993. *Tourism principles and practices.* Essex, UK: Longman Group Ltd.

Eber, S., 1992. *Beyond the green horizon, principles for sustainable tourism.* A discussion paper commissioned from tourism concern by WWF, UK, p.10–31.

EPA, 1994. *Ghana Environmental Action Plan, vol. 2,* ed. E. Liang, technical background papers by the six working groups, Environmental Protection Council, Accra.

EPA, 1997. Overview of some environmental management practices in Ghana. *EPA Newsletter*, 1(7).

EPA, 2002. *State of Environment Report 2001.* Environmental Protection Agency, Accra, Ghana.

Faulk, S.E., 2000. *A survey of environmental management by hotels and related tourism businesses.* A presentation at Oikos PhD. Summer Academy, University of St. Gallen, Switzerland, p.3–6, 11–17.

Font, X., 2002. Environmental certification in tourism and hospitality: progress, process and prospects. *Tourism Management,* 23, p.197–205.

Forte, J., 1994. Environmental-friendly management in hotels. In B. Taylor et al. eds., *Environmental management handbook.* London: Pitman Publishing, p.97–113.

Foster, S.T., Samson, S.E. & Dunn, S.C., 2000. The impact of customer contact on environmental initiatives for service firms. *International Journal of Operations and Production Management,* 20(2), p.187–203.

Ghana Tourist Board, 2006. *Tourism statistical factsheet.* Accra.

Harruna Attah, A.R. & Alhassan, A.R., 2001. Accra drowns again. *Accra Mail.* Wednesday, October 17.

Hens, L. & Boon, E.K., 1999. *Institutional, legal and economic instruments in Ghana's environmental policy.* Available at: http://iodeweb1.vliz.be/odin/bit-stream/1834/375/1/epghana [accessed 18 August 2008].

Hewitt, G. & Gary, R., 1998. *ISO 14001 EMS implementation handbook.* Oxford, UK: Butterworth-Heinemann Ltd.

Holder, J.S., 1988. Pattern and impact of tourism on the environment of the Caribbean. *Tourism Management,* 9(2), p.119–27.

Hunter, C. & Green, H., 1995. *Tourism and the environment, a sustainable relationship?* New York: Routledge.

Inskeep, E., 2000. Planning for sustainable tourism in Ghana. In P.U.C. Dieke ed., *The political economy of tourism development in Africa.* New York: Cognizant Communication Corporation.

Jackson, I., 1984. Enhancing positive impact of tourism on the built and natural environment. In OAS, vol. 5, *Reference guidelines for enhancing the positive socio-cultural and environmental impacts of tourism.* Washington, DC: Organisation of American States, International Trade and Tourism Division, Department of Economic Affairs.

Kirk, D., 1998. Attitudes to environmental management held by a group of hotel managers in Edinburgh. *International Journal of Hospitality Management,* 17, p.33–47.

Konadu-Agyemang, K., 2001. Structural adjustment programme and the international tourism trade in Ghana, 1983–99: some socio-spatial implications. *Tourism Geographies,* 3(2), p.187–206.

Marin, C. & Jafari, J., 2002. Sustainable hotels for sustainable destinations. *Annals of Tourism Research,* 29(1), p.266–68.

Mathieson, A. & Wall, G., 1982. *Tourism: economic, physical and social impacts.* Harlow, UK: Longman.

Mowforth, M. & Munt, I., 1998. *Tourism and sustainability, new tourism in the Third World.* New York: Routledge.

Mensah, I., 2006. Environmental management practices among hotels in the Greater Accra Region. *International Journal of Hospitality Management,* 25, p.414–31.

Middleton, V.T.C. & Hawkins, R., 1998. *Sustainable tourism: a marketing perspective.* Oxford: Butterworth-Heinemann.

Miles, M. & Munilla, L., 1993. The eco-marketing orientation: an emerging business philosophy. *Journal of Marketing Theory and Practice,* 1(2).

Pearce, D.G., 1995. *Tourism today, geographical analysis.* 2nd ed. Essex, UK: Longman.

Shah, K., 2000. *Tourism, the poor and other stakeholders: Asian experience.* Overseas Development Institute, fair-trade in tourism paper. London: ODI.

Songsore, J., 1992. *Review of household environmental problems in the Accra Metropolitan Area*. Ghana: Stockholm Environmental Institute working paper.

Stipanuk, D.M., 1996. The U.S. lodging industry and the environment—an historical view. *Cornell Hotel and Restaurant Administration Quarterly*, 37(5), p.39–45.

Tyler, C., 1989. A phenomenal explosion. *Geographical Magazine*, 61(8), p.18–21.

Vine, P.A.L., 1994. *Hotel and restaurant standards in Ghana; review, recommendations and training*. Accra: Ministry of Tourism/UNDP/WTO.

Wight, P., 1994. Environmentally responsible marketing of tourism. In E. Cater & G. Lowman eds., *Ecotourism: a sustainable option?* New York: John Wiley & Sons.

Williams, P.W., 1992. Tourism and the environment: no place to hide. *World Leisure and Recreation*, 34(2), p.13–17.

World Bank, 2002. *Upgrading of low income settlements, country assessment report, Ghana*. Washington, DC: World Bank.

Zhao, Jin-Lin & Merna, K.M., 1992. Impact analysis and the international environment. In R. Teare & M. Olsen eds., *International hospitality management: corporate strategy in practice*. New York: John Wiley & Sons.

9 Owner-Manager Perspectives on Environmental Management in Micro and Small Tourism Enterprises in the Bay of Plenty, New Zealand

Sophie Rainford and Craig Wight

INTRODUCTION

The issue of sustainable tourism continues to dominate industry and public forums such as conferences, textbooks, and corporate policy statements, yet there are still relatively few examples of established sustainable tourism initiatives the world over. Our aim here is thus to develop an understanding of why the tourism industry continues to display little evidence of sustainable tourism practices, especially among micro and small tourism enterprises (MSTEs). The actions taken by owner-managers to minimise negative impacts on the natural environment are important for the long-term survival of MSTEs. Consequently, the owner-managers of these enterprises have an implicit responsibility to sustain the earth's life systems. As such, an assessment of the levels of awareness, interest, and implementation of environmental management among MSTEs is a useful research endeavour. Thus, we explore the extent to which environmental management is implemented by MSTEs and the levels of awareness of sustainable practice amongst the owner-managers of these enterprises in the Bay of Plenty, New Zealand.

The greater Bay of Plenty region encompasses a land area of 12,447 square kilometres in the centre of New Zealand's North Island (McDonald & Patterson, 2003). The eastern boundary of the region follows the Bay of Plenty coastline while the west, south, and southeast boundaries are formed, respectively, by the Waikato, Hawke's Bay, and Gisborne regions. The region is characterised by volcanic activity and has numerous thermal pools and geysers. There is a strong interest in the long-term survival and enjoyment of these natural assets, and as such, there is a greater need for widespread implementation of environmental management among regional tourism operators.

The natural environment is a significant part of the Bay of Plenty region and is characterised by a diverse physical geography including 9,509 square kilometres of coastal marine area (Environment Bay of Plenty, 2006). Volcanic landscapes, including plateaus, cones, and lakes dominate the area around Rotorua, in the east, steep native forested terrain defines the Te

Urewera National Park and the Ruakumara Ranges, coastal lowlands and floodplains extend from Waihi Beach in the west to Opotiki in the east and exotic pine plantations cover large parts of the volcanic plateau between Rotorua and Taupo (University of Auckland, 2006). Volcanic and other natural resources are continually being utilised by tourism in this region. Thus, it is important for the MSTEs operating in the Bay of Plenty to implement activities that provide minimal negative impact on the natural environment. Environmental management is a significant part of local government policy in the Bay of Plenty region and businesses are encouraged to engage in related practices. However, there remains some ambiguity in understanding sustainable tourism in this region in terms of implementing practical environmental management initiatives effectively. Thus, within the current regional and national strategic frameworks, this chapter highlights the need for a redress of sustainable tourism to better suit the needs and concerns of owner-managers of MSTEs. First, the discussion brings into focus 'sustainability,' sustainable tourism and sustainable tourism development, in the process raising a number of issues before we move on to presenting an analysis of schemes concerned with the environmental improvement of business and, in particular, environmental management initiatives in New Zealand.

SUSTAINABILITY AND TOURISM

Whilst the concept of sustainability is increasingly used in tourism studies, the word *sustainability* is used in very different ways to mean vastly different things (Parliamentary Commissioner for the Environment, PCE, 2004) and is identified by Hall (1998) as a contestable concept with its use and application often being disputed. McKercher (1993) states that perhaps the inherent vagueness of 'sustainability' is its greatest weakness. The term is free floating and is used by both industry and the conservation movement to legitimise and justify activities and policies, although, in many instances, these are mutually exclusive (McKercher, 1993). Rather than acting as a catalyst for change, 'sustainability' may serve to entrench and legitimise extant policies and actions, thus exacerbating rather than resolving conservation and development conflicts (McKercher, 1993). It is suggested that the meaning of 'sustainability' is evolving and shaped by social and organisational institutional forces, with a focus on the evolution of environmental practices rather than sustainable businesses (Sharma, 2002). 'Sustainability' is not just about the environment, but the environmental dimensions of 'sustainability' are essential for long-term survival (Parliamentary Commissioner for the Environment, 2004).

Griffin (2002) suggests that tourism has been accused of being many things such as a despoiler of pristine natural environments, a destroyer of valued lifestyles and age-old cultures, and an exploiter of poor nations. Tourism, it is claimed, ultimately degrades the attractive natural and cultural features of places and thus can neither sustain the basic resources on which it relies nor rely on itself as an industry in the long term (Griffin, 2002). Signs are emerging, however, that the tourism industry has learnt some valuable lessons from the downside of its 'successes' and has taken steps to secure its own future. For example, codes of environmental ethics and accreditation schemes have burgeoned in the twentieth century and environmental management initiatives have been developed in key industry sectors keeping 'sustainability' firmly on the tourism agenda (Griffin, 2002). Many businesses, especially those that are linked to the tourism sector, rely on a 'clean and green' image for competitive advantage. Furthermore, if environmental realities do not meet the perceptions of overseas consumers and tourists, then economic interests may not be sustainable, leading to losses in the share of many high-value markets (Parliamentary Commissioner for the Environment, PCE, 2004). Essentially it is through lack of environmental management in the tourism sector that these risks associated with 'sustainability' became prevalent.

Ham and Weiler (2002) state that sustainable tourism is tourism that is developed and maintained in a manner, and at such a scale, that it remains economically viable over an indefinite period and does not undermine the physical and human environment that sustains and nurtures it (Ham & Weiler, 2002). The construct of 'sustainable tourism' provides an ideal and goal to work toward, and one moreover that is widely embraced in principle, however ambiguous and elusive the term may be (Weaver, 2004). With the complexity of tourism systems, and the practical problems in identifying, weighting, measuring, and monitoring sustainability indicators, there are associated challenges that impede sustainable tourism and thus implementation of environmental management within MSTEs (Weaver, 2004). Amongst the greatest concerns for owner-managers of these enterprises are the financial aspects of running a business. Sustainable tourism needs to be economically sustainable, because if tourism is not profitable then it is a moot question to ask whether it is environmentally sustainable (tourism that is unprofitable will simply cease to exist). However, Hunter (2002) states that the use of the term *sustainable tourism* brings with it the preconceptions and values of the user.

Sustainable tourism development embodies a range of variables and it is important to identify at what level do owner-managers of MSTEs understand each variable and how they can be implemented into their business through environmental management. The underlying assumption is that owner-managers are not aware of the complexity of sustainable tourism development and tend to see it as mostly economic sustainability or environmental sustainability. Wanhill (1998) argues, while the concept of 'sustainability' draws in the natural environment as an issue for the economic development of tourism, the concept of sustainable tourism development implies that issues to do with economic growth and environmental quality should not be mutually exclusive from each other.

ENVIRONMENTAL MANAGEMENT SCHEMES

Little has been written on the meaning and operation of sustainable organisations (Sharma, 2002). Griffin and DeLacey (2002) state that making MSTEs more environmentally sustainable requires action on a number of fronts, some of which include:

- regulation by government which can establish minimum standards of performance with regard to the generation of certain environmental impacts;
- strategic environmental planning of tourism, supported by laws related to land use and environmental impact assessment, which can anticipate a range of potential problems and establish protective measures to prevent them arising.

For effective sustainable development to occur throughout the tourism sector, regulation and legislation are required. Discourses concerned with the ethics of 'sustainability' or sustainable development have recently been muted and replaced by an apparently general tacit acceptance that the concept of sustainable development represents a kinder and more moral or ethical approach to development (Butler, 1998). Indeed, the concept of sustainable development is a holistic one and traditional separation of development and conservation (and preservation) has inevitably led to division and disagreement between proponents of these two approaches. Schemes aiming for the environmental improvement of business have emerged from earlier science-based models of sustained yield resource management, progressive conservation, and integrated resource management. These models link to the notion of sustainable development by incorporating and encouraging business activities which focus on sustaining natural resources in the physical location of the business. In relation to these environmental improvement schemes, Weaver (2004) reports that sustainable tourism development was popularised through the World Conservation Strategy, the Brundtland Report, and the Rio Earth Summit of 1992 and its Agenda 21 manifesto.

Environmental improvement schemes such as Green Globe and Blue Flag, as well as the implementation of 'green' practices such as recycling and energy use reduction, have stemmed from Agenda 21, a comprehensive programme of action adopted by 182 governments at the United Nations Conference on Environment and Development (UNCED), the Earth Summit, on 14 June 1992. Agenda 21 is a comprehensive plan of action to be taken globally, nationally, and locally by organisations of the United Nations system, governments, and major groups in every area of human impacts on the environment (Leslie & Hughes, 1997).

Green Globe (GG) is identified by Griffin and DeLacey (2002) as one of the more comprehensive environmental improvement and accreditation

schemes, which has been developed in the last decade. It is a global certification and environment programme that aims at improving quantifi-
able environmental performance in the travel and tourism sector (Kozak
& Nield, 2004) and therefore assists in environmental management. GG
is a multifaceted programme which uses a process-based system with an
ISO 9000 style approach involving environmental policy, a 'tick the box'
checklist, and sustainability performance outcomes (Griffin & DeLacey,
2002). ISO 9000 is an example of a quality system which enables and
organisation to know where it is weak or strong. In practice this is similar to benchmarking, a continuous learning process designed to compare
products, services, and practices with reference to external competitors and
then implement procedures to upgrade performance to match or surpass
these (Pigram, 1998).

ENVIRONMENTAL MANAGEMENT SCHEMES IN NEW ZEALAND

In terms of environmental management schemes in New Zealand, the
development of *Sustainable Tourism Charters, Qualmark, Sustainable
Business Network,* and *The Natural Step* are recognised as recent landmark schemes for New Zealand's tourism businesses. The Sustainable
Tourism Charter is a scheme unique to New Zealand which is based on a
community-developed vision for sustainable tourism incorporating environmental management in tourism enterprises. The scheme outlines what
businesses, community groups, local government, and Kiwi groups see as
the key characteristics of a tourism sector that can exist in the long term.
The tourism sector move towards Sustainable Tourism Charters has come
about because they are cheaper, self-policing, and have peer support systems (Zahra, 2006).

Qualmark[1]

Qualmark, and its scheme badged 'The Nature of Good Business,' is an
industry initiative encouraging tourism operators and organisations to
improve their environmental, social, and business performance. Guidelines
and supporting information have been developed to help businesses write
an environmental plan under Qualmark. The environmental plan has been
integrated into the Qualmark Endorsement Systems, and is based on the
Green Globe programme. Environmental plan is an environmental accreditation programme which has been developed by Qualmark New Zealand
Limited. Participation in the environmental accreditation programme is
encouraged to help businesses improve their environmental sustainability
in more depth (Knox, 2006). Over time, the goal is that all tourism businesses in New Zealand will require an environmental plan to achieve a
Qualmark endorsement.

Sustainable Business Network

The Sustainable Business Network (SBN) is a forum for businesses unique to New Zealand that are interested in sustainable development practice to collaborate and systematically implement environmental management. The SBN aims to promote sustainable practice in New Zealand and supports businesses on the path to becoming sustainable and effectively implementing environmental management. They link businesses and provide a forum for the exchange of ideas and experiences equipping members for success (Sustainable Business Network, 2006). 'Sustainable business' is defined by the network as the integration of economic growth, social equity, and environmental management, both for now and for the future, and the network has taken on the challenge of making sustainable practice 'mainstream,' to see business flourish through sustainable practice, and to design its services, resources, and activities to suit the needs of both small and medium-sized businesses (Sustainable Business Network, 2006).

The Natural Step

The Natural Step (TNS) scheme is a not-for-profit environmental education organisation founded by Dr. Karl-Henrik Robert. Robert, a Swedish paediatric oncologist, was motivated by an anomaly he observed in his work with children suffering from cancer (Osland et al., 2002). To prevent cancers resulting from pollution, Robert began a process of dialogue and consensus about building social and environmental 'sustainability' with scientists. After numerous iterations, fifty scientists agreed on four basic, non-negotiable system conditions for 'sustainability' (ibid). Essentially these system conditions reflect elements of identifying how a society or an organisation can negatively impact both natural processes and biodiversity and satisfying human needs. The scheme has applicability when aiming for environmental improvement in business, similar to Green Globe, though it is not tourism focused.

The environmental improvement of business aims to enhance and maintain:

- The life-supporting processes (ecological systems) that provide people with good quality air, water, soil, and marine life and a viable climate. This is essential for sustaining a world that humans and other species can survive and flourish in.
- Other environmental factors that contribute to people's quality of life. What people value about the environment is always changing, but most people in New Zealand today enjoy living in a good quality environment (Osland et al., 2002).

Hunter (2002: 18) identifies that any kind of improvement in the environmental functioning of tourism operations can be seen as beneficial, but environmental betterment comes in many forms and does not necessarily mean long-term 'sustainability.' Pigram (1998) argues that since the 1980s, the tourism industry has shown commendable preparedness to apply the principles of environmental management to its activities. The concept of an 'ecological footprint' has been developed to illustrate the demands that people place on the environment and measures how much land a person, or a population, needs to meet their current lifestyles (Parliamentary Commissioner for the Environment, 2004). The 'ecological footprint' considers food, housing, energy, mobility requirements, and demands for consumer goods and services. The Parliamentary Commissioner for the Environment (2004) identifies the ecological footprint for New Zealand as calculated at over eight hectares per person, compared with a world average of 2.3 hectares per person. New Zealand's ecological footprint is very large, being 25 per cent greater than the footprints of Germany, the United Kingdom, the Netherlands, or Japan (Parliamentary Commissioner for the Environment, 2004).

MSTES IN THE BAY OF PLENTY

Schaper and Carlsen (2004) state that there is a significant moral or value-based element to the arguments as to why firms should be involved in environmental matters and environmental management provides a practical element to value-based argument. Essentially the prevention or rectification of environmental problems should be carried out by individuals and by businesses because this is an ethically acceptable choice of action (Schaper & Carlsen, 2004). Tourism throughout regions in New Zealand is fundamentally dependant upon the attractive power of the destination's natural environment, that is, its primary resources of climate, scenery, wildlife, cultural and historic heritage. MSTEs have a role in supporting tourism visits to New Zealand to enjoy this natural environment in sustainable ways.

Indeed, MSTEs in all countries are a rapidly expanding and dynamic sector of regional tourism (Ateljevic & Doorne, 2003). According to Ahmad (2005), they dominate the tourism sector and yet there is only a small body of literature which deals specifically with MSTEs and their behaviour toward environmental management (Schaper & Carlsen, 2004). They are considered to be dominated by family businesses and owner-managers whose motivations have been found to encompass a spectrum that runs from commercial goals to lifestyle intentions (Wanhill, 2004). Hwang and Lockwood (2006) identify areas of common concern to MSTEs which include administrative regulations, access to finance, and a lack of skilled labour; ignoring such issues may lead to poor or inaccurate analyses of research. They are notable in terms of their significance and buoyancy (Thomas, 2000) for the New Zealand tourism sector, and thus are important to research and understand to ensure that inefficiencies are overcome and strengths capitalised upon in relation to environmental management.

The following section introduces the Bay of Plenty as a relevant unit of analysis for a study of environmental management amongst MSTEs.

The Bay of Plenty climate is largely influenced by the eastward movement of weather systems and the bold topography of New Zealand. In particular, the high country of the central North Island provides shelter from the prevailing winds that cross the country from the southwest. As a result, the Bay enjoys sunny weather with frequent dry spells and light offshore winds. Tauranga, for example, receives two hundred hours more sunshine per year than Auckland (University of Auckland, 2006). At times, however, the Bay of Plenty is exposed to northerly and northeasterly airstreams that are very humid and produce heavy rainfalls (ibid). McDonald and Patterson (2003) identify the climatic conditions of the Bay of Plenty to play a key factor in attracting people to the region for both migration and tourism.

The region depends heavily on the economic benefits of tourism; with a growing population it is important to ensure that natural resources are protected and that MSTEs (being the majority of tourism enterprises) engage in effective environmental management, aiming to significantly reduce business activities with negative environmental impacts. Maoris tend to have a strong spiritual bond to the land, especially ancestral land that may be owned by whanau, hapu, and iwi (Boyes, 2005). Within the Bay of Plenty region there are ten iwi groups, the largest being Te Arawa in Rotorua, followed by Tuhoe, centred in the eastern Bay of Plenty. Other iwi include Ngati Pukenga, Ngaiterangi, Ngati Ranginui, Ngati Awa, Ngati Manawa-Ngati Whare, Ngai Tai, Whakatohea, and Whanau-a-Apanui (Te Puni Kokiri, 2001). With such significant representation of indigenous people in this region, and a high level of indigenous involvement in the tourism sector, indigenous people play an important role in assisting effective implementation of environmental management in MSTEs.

Tourism is one of the region's major economic activities. In 2004, there were 3.78 million visitor nights, of which domestic visitors accounted for 78.1 per cent and international visitors for 21.9 per cent. Total expenditure was $411.2 million (Career Services, 2007). By 2011, the number of guest nights is expected to reach 4.25 million, with much of the increase coming from international visitors, and expenditure to rise to $553.4 million by 2011 (Career Services, 2007). This growth in tourism will benefit the large retail and distribution industry and particularly recreation services, which has witnessed steadily increasing employment opportunities as tourism activity has increased.

There are two organisations involved in the development of tourism in the region, Tourism Rotorua and Tourism Bay of Plenty. Both organisations in recent years have become proactive and supportive of sustainable tourism development and were instrumental in the implementation of a Sustainable Tourism Charter, which encourages environmental management. The charter scheme is funded by the New Zealand central government and is a joint initiative of the Ministry of Tourism and Ministry for the Environment aiming to assist tourism businesses in reaping the benefits of incorporating smart sustainable business practices into their operations (Tourism Bay of Plenty, 2005).

One of the objectives of the Sustainable Tourism Charter is to raise the profile in the region of the need for sustainable tourism through showing the public that being wise to environmental needs goes 'hand in hand' with future business success (Tourism Bay of Plenty, 2005). Similarly, the 'Rotorua Sustainable Tourism Charter' is an approach to adopt sustainability and requires member businesses to commit to a statement of intent to protect the physical (environmental/ecological) and social/cultural environment, in turn achieving long-term viability and economic prosperity of the Rotorua tourism industry (Rotorua Sustainable Tourism Charter, 2006). Essentially the Sustainable Tourism Charter has taken an incremental approach in that some improvement towards sustainability is better than no improvement at all.

A move towards sustainable tourism planning in the context of the region is evident in the policy and planning documents of various public sector institutions: Bay of Plenty Regional Council, Environment Bay of Plenty, Tauranga City Council, Western Bay of Plenty District Council, Eastern Bay of Plenty District Council, Whakatane District Council, and Rotorua District Council. An example of sustainable planning and development is the concept of 'SmartGrowth' as a programme aimed at developing and implementing a plan for managing growth in the Western Bay of Plenty (SmartGrowth, 2001). The programme has social, economic, and environmental goals which seek to be achieved in a sustainable way leading up to 2050 and is being led by Environment Bay of Plenty, Tauranga City Council, Western Bay of Plenty District Council, and Tangata Whenua, on behalf of the community.

Environment Bay of Plenty is the regional council for the area. Their work guides and supports the sustainable development of the Bay of Plenty, making sure the region grows and develops in a way that keeps its values safe for future generations (Environment Bay of Plenty, 2006). Environment Bay of Plenty (2006) see themselves as caretakers of the land, air, and water; they monitor the effects of human activities on our environment and promote the sustainable management of our natural and physical resources for present and future generations. As far as possible, principles embraced in their mission statement are employed—"working with our communities for a better environment" (Environment Bay of Plenty 2006).

The Regional Policy Statement, prepared by Environment Bay of Plenty Regional Council, establishes a directional framework for regional and district plans to promote the sustainable management of the region's natural and physical resources. The statement has been prepared in accordance with the requirements of the Resource Management Act 1991 and identifies and manages key resource issues in the Bay of Plenty Region by creating methods, policies, and initiatives to achieve environmental results (Boyes, 2005). Many people, agencies, and authorities are involved in using, developing, and protecting the region's resources (Environment Bay of Plenty, 1999). This policy statement identifies sections with relative importance to the implementation of environmental management in MSTEs in the region.

Resource management practice in the statement refers to relationships between agencies, users, and their values, legislation, policy statements, plans, resource consents, and other mechanisms, which enable the promotion of sustainable resource management (Environment Bay of Plenty, 1999). Resource users such as owner-managers of MSTEs should be able to find out what is required of them to practice sustainable management of resources or environmental management and be encouraged to adopt good practice, seeking quality, not just avoiding significant adverse effects. For example, sustainable land management practices can maintain and enhance soil productivity to enable long-term use of the resource. The use and development of land plays an important role in enabling people and communities in the Bay of Plenty region to provide for their social, economic, and cultural well-being (Environment Bay of Plenty, 2006).

The Bay of Plenty is therefore an effective case study region for this research based on

- its diverse and valuable natural environment that is an integral part of regional economic prosperity;
- its thriving tourism industry with the majority of operators dependant upon pristine natural assets and climate of the region as the main attraction for visitors;
- regional government demonstrating some level of endorsement for environmental management of business.

This chapter has so far outlined the paradigm for environmental management globally, regionally, and in the context of tourism MSTEs in the Bay of Plenty. The next section outlines the methodology undertaken to explore the research objectives and the key findings emerging from this.

RESEARCH METHODOLOGY

To address the objectives of this research, owner-managers of MSTEs in the Bay of Plenty were interviewed to explore viewpoints and underlying awareness and interest levels in environmental management. Interviews were carried out on seventeen owner-managers and co-owners from fourteen MSTEs located in the Bay of Plenty region. MSTEs were chosen as representative of the tourism industry in New Zealand (comprising up to 80% of the nation's tourism industry). Some of these at the time of writing were already participating in environmental management schemes such as Green Globe, the Sustainable Tourism Charter for Rotorua and the Bay of Plenty and Qualmark. MSTEs interviewed were located in the Whakatane, Mt. Maunganui, Tauranga, and Rotorua areas and included a cross section of tourism operations ranging from accommodation providers to activities and transportation.

Semi-structured interviews were carried out on participants with emphasis on the use of open-ended questions to facilitate frank and unprompted discussion. An outline of interview questions was provided prior to the interview taking place, providing an opportunity for respondents to orientate their thoughts along key topic lines. The key findings that emerged from this research are discussed in the following paragraphs.

FINDINGS

Profile of Respondents

Table 9.1 records the basic profile of owner-managers, including perceptions of role within the business, age, gender, family status, and ethnicity.

When outlining perceived roles within the business, a variety of responses were observed. Broadly, however, respondents perceived themselves as fulfilling a 'multi-tasking' role. Additionally, married couple respondents tended to share roles and responsibilities and can be described as 'copreneurs.' A common theme was a shared sense of the need to micro-manage all aspects of the business. Multi-tasking and multifarious skills therefore appear important. Of the MSTEs interviewed, business life cycles ranged from start-ups to incumbents with over forty years in operation. It is evident that the longer the life cycle observed, the larger the business, although there are variations in level of success and growth of the business.

ENVIRONMENTAL MANAGEMENT

Respondents commented on practices within their business that they considered encompassed 'environmental management.' Recycling represents the most cited environmental management procedure with little perceived environmental management practice undertaken beyond this (see Table 9.2).

It is evident that instances of practical environmental management initiatives among the MSTEs studied are low. Pigram (1998) discusses how the expertise, expense, and long-term commitment of resources involved in lifting environmental management performance inevitably mean that the adoption of environmental management is 'currently a minority activity, confined, in the main, to a few large enterprises.' Table 9.3 outlines a

Table 9.1 Owner-Manager Profile

Business	Perceived Role	Age	Gender	Family Status	Ethnicity
1.	Project Manager/ Entrepreneur	52	Male	Married 1 grown son	European/kiwi
2.	Operations/Feasibility	48	Female	Married 1 grown son	European/kiwi
3.	Sales and Marketing, Accounts and Office	41	Female	De facto Relationship No children	Dutch/kiwi immigrated 14 years ago
4.	Chief Executive	55	Male	Single	New Zealand
5.	Director	31	Male	Married, 2 children	New Zealander/Kiwi
6.	General Manager	23	Female	Single	New Zealand/European
7.	Adventure Tourism Operator	43	Female	Married, 4 children	Pakeha
8.	Owner	42	Female	Married to OM2 with 2 young children	English/New Zealand immigrated 19 years ago
9.	Owner	53	Male	Married to OM1 with 2 young children plus 3 from previous marriage	Maori
10.	Owner-Operator	64	Male	Married with children	New Zealander European
11.	Director	48	Male	Married to other OM with 2 grown children	Indian (on a business visa)
12.	Senior Guide	31	Male	Single	Pakeha
13.	Accommodation Provider	Mid 60s	Male	Married to OM2 2 grown children	New Zealander
14.	Accommodation Provider	Mid 60s	Female	Married to OM1 2 grown children	New Zealander
15.	Motelier	55	Male	Married to other OM, 2 grown children	New Zealander
16.	Partner	31	Female	Married to other OM	New Zealand European
17.	Operations Manager	33	Male	Married to other OM	New Zealander

When outlining perceived roles within the business, a variety of responses were observed. Broadly, however, respondents perceived themselves as fulfilling a 'multi-tasking' role. Additionally, married couple respondents tended to share roles and responsibilities and can be described as 'copreneurs.' A common theme was a shared sense of the need to micro-manage all aspects of the business. Multi-tasking and multifarious skills therefore appear important. Of the MSTEs interviewed, business life cycles ranged from start-ups to incumbents with over forty years in operation. It is evident that the longer the life cycle observed, the larger the business, although there are variations in level of success and growth of the business.

Table 9.2   Environmental Management in MSTEs

Environmental Management Activity	Total number implementing activity
Recycling	11
Composting	2
Reusing	3
Energy efficiency (switching off lights, solar water/natural heating, efficient lights)	7
Minimising vehicle usage/fuel efficiency	2
Minimising water usage	4
Using environmentally friendly cleaning products	5
Growing own vegetables	2
Passenger/guest education and involvement in environmental management activities	4

fuller account of environmental management practices undertaken by the 14 MSTEs that listed environmental management initiatives.

A total of six of the fourteen MSTEs had implemented more than three activities considered to count as environmental management. Of these six businesses, three have been in operation more than fifteen years and employ more than eleven staff. The MSTEs smaller in size and younger were not as likely to implement more than three environmental management activities due to a lack of access to finance and labour.

ENVIRONMENTAL IMPROVEMENT SCHEMES

Analysis of this sample suggests that those schemes demanding a great deal of effort and time from businesses experienced lower uptake. The following sections provide an overview of the perceptions of environmental schemes amongst the MSTEs interviewed.

Green Globe

Some respondents demonstrated low awareness of environmental improvement schemes to improve business processes unless participation in a specific scheme was evidenced (for example, Green Globe). Most respondents were aware of Green Globe but demonstrated varying levels of interest. Some regarded Green Globe as a business benefit and identifiable benchmark. Others, however, regarded Green Globe as expensive, time consuming, and impractical. Sasidharan and Font (2001) argue that despite the benefits of environmental

Table 9.3   Environmental Management Activities Implemented

Business	Type of Business	Environmental Management Activities Implemented	Years of operation	Total Employees
A	Tour company (2x OMs)	Recycling, energy efficiency, cleaning products, reusing, fuel efficiency	16	39
B	Tourism Aviation	Recycling, cleaning products	4	11
C	Geothermal Tourism Attraction	None	16	13
D	Kayak-Oriented Business	Recycling, reusing, energy efficiency, minimise water use, fuel efficiency, cleaning products	31	12
E	Tourism Accommo-dation Business	Recycling, energy efficiency, cleaning products	40	21
F	Adventure Tourism	Recycling	3	5
G	Guided Trekking	Energy efficiency	1	0
H	Luxury Transportation	Recycling, minimise water use	7	0
I	Hospitality	Recycling, energy efficiency	3	0
J	Kayaking	Recycling, minimise water use	5	0
K	Luxury bed and breakfast (2x OMs)	Energy efficiency, minimise water use, cleaning products, guest involvement	5	0
L	Hospitality (2x OMs)	Cleaning products, energy efficiency, recycling, guest involvement	3	3
M	Backpackers (2x OMs)	Recycling, composting, cleaning products, guest involvement, energy efficiency	5	0
N	Transport(2x OMs)	Recycling	7	5

improvement schemes such as Green Globe, no conclusive evidence exists to support claims that these schemes actually improve the environment or are effective in encouraging environmental management among MSTEs.

Sustainable Tourism Charter

Most respondents demonstrated awareness of the Sustainable Tourism Charter (STC) and regarded it as user friendly. However, respondents actually participating in this scheme regarded it negatively. Some demonstrated high awareness of the scheme but were concerned it did not promote a localised approach to environmental management. Essentially, levels of interest and awareness of the Sustainable Tourism Charter varied greatly amongst the sample.

Sustainable Business Network

The Sustainable Business Network (SBN) is a scheme which acts as a forum for New Zealand businesses, encouraging the exchange of ideas and experiences, aiming to promote and support businesses on the path to becoming sustainable (Sustainable Business Network, 2006). Respondents were not generally aware of this scheme and did not see participation as important. Indeed, Jurowski (2005) states how participation in this scheme is useful only for businesses with some prerequisite knowledge of environmental management and those committed to the implementation of sustainable practices.

The Natural Step

The Natural Step (TNS) provides a systemic perspective on environmental management that encompasses key dimensions of environmental sustainability along with inequality, labour conditions and rights, national sovereignty, and cultural and community impacts (Osland et al., 2002). Essentially, this scheme was relatively unfamiliar to respondents. Whilst awareness was generally low, six respondents were interested to learn about the Natural Step. The scheme was generally regarded as complex and more appropriate for a large company.

'The Nature of Good Business' (Qualmark)

Overall, respondents were negative and disinterested in respect of Qualmark and 'The Nature of Good Business.' It is interesting to note that five of the fourteen micro and small enterprises interviewed for this study were participating in the scheme at the time of writing. Some seven of the fourteen respondents were negative about the benefits of Qualmark whilst a further two did not comment. The remaining five respondents were positive about the scheme.

CONCLUSION

A key outcome of the foregoing analysis suggests that attitudes to environmental performance in MSTEs in the Bay of Plenty, New Zealand are subjective and depend on a number of factors including the commitment of time and resources, general awareness of schemes, and perceived benefits from participation. Findings imply limited knowledge of schemes and low motivation to participate in known schemes. Furthermore, analysis suggests that respondents perhaps do not link participation in such schemes with actively caring for the environment

Future research may include further enquiry as to why owner-managers of MSTEs do not appear to see the connection between their environmental performance and the overall environmental qualities of their region. In addition, respondents did not appear to appreciate their businesses' contribution to harmful environmental impacts, and thus did not see the need to address potentially harmful business activities. As such, future research may also seek to identify negative environmental impacts of 'day-to-day' business conducted by MSTEs in order to yield important information that may assist in increasing implementation of environmental management.

This study identifies that perceptions relating to the value of implementing environmental management are influenced by constraints such as a lack of financial and human resources to invest in scheme participation. Thus respondents, unable to appreciate truly the impacts of their business on the environment, generally limited environmental management activities to recycling. The low uptake of environmental management schemes amongst the Bay of Plenty's tourism MSTEs is potentially impacted by three background factors:

- the role of the owner-manager in the business as one that is 'needed' to be 'everywhere' in the business, and thus 'too busy' to think about effective implementation of environmental management;
- low levels of knowledge and experience in tourism; and
- limited human resource in their MSTEs.

However, in order for environmental management implementation to develop and grow, owner-managers must perceive the advantages of implementing initiatives. In addition, they must be convinced of the advantages of pursuing such approaches. As such, future research should aim to clarify the needs and concerns of owner-managers relative to achieving effective implementation of environmental management to yield important information in the pursuit of sustainable tourism business.

Findings from this study seek to pose avenues for effective future research and aim to further the understanding of why the suggested lack of sustainable tourism implementation remains evident in tourism. This case study has explored and provided insight into key themes relative to owner-manager perceptions towards environmental management in MSTEs located in the Bay of Plenty region of New Zealand. While important information in the pursuit of sustainable tourism business has been identified, significant further study is suggested using a larger sample size and greater geographic area for validation. Schaper and Carlsen (2004) state that while it is hard to gauge the overall negative environmental effect of tourism MSTEs around the world, it has been claimed that they may be responsible for up to 70 per cent of global environmental pollution. Thus, if the tourism sector is to become more consistent with ecological principles and sustain the environmental qualities on which it depends, activities must be examined thoroughly and the sector must be prepared to rethink what may well be a fundamentally flawed process.

NOTES

1. Since the completion of this research, Qualmark has launched the Qualmark Green award designed to be part of the total quality assessment—a fully integrated quality and environmental accreditation system.

REFERENCES

Ahmad, G., 2005. Small firm owner-managers' networks in tourism and hospitality. *International Journal of Business and Society*, 6(2), p.37–54.

Ateljevic, J. & Doorne, S., 2003. Diseconomies of scale: a study of development constraints in small tourism firms in central New Zealand. *Tourism and Hospitality Research*, 5(1), p.5–24.

Boyes, H., 2005. *Implementing sustainable tourism—a Northland case study*. Unpublished Thesis. Dunedin: University of Otago

Butler, R.W., 1998. Sustainable tourism—looking backwards in order to progress? In C.M. Hall & A.A. Lew eds., Sustainable tourism. Harlow, UK: Addison Wesley Longman, p.25–34.

Careers Service, 2007. Living and working in the Bay of Plenty. Available at: http://www.careers.govt.nz accessed 23 October, 2007.

Environment Bay of Plenty, 2006. *About us*. Available at: http://www.ebop.govt.nz/About-us/About-Us.asp [Accessed 1 December 2006].

Griffin, T., 2002. An optimistic perspective on tourism's sustainability. In R. Harris, T. Griffin, & P. Williams eds., *Sustainable tourism: a global perspective*. Sydney: Butterworth-Heinemann

Griffin, T. & DeLacey, T., 2002. Green Globe: sustainability accreditation for tourism. In R. Harris, T. Griffin, & P. Williams eds., *Sustainable tourism: a global perspective*. Sydney: Butterworth-Heinemann.

Hall, C.M., 1998. Historical antecedents of sustainable development and ecotourism: new labels on old bottles. In C.M. Hall & A.A. Lew eds., *Sustainable tourism* Harlow, UK: Addison Wesley Longman, p.13–24.

Ham, S.H. & Weiler, B., 2002. Interpretation as a centrepiece of sustainable wildlife tourism. In R. Harris, T. Griffin, & P. Williams eds., *Sustainable tourism: a global perspective*. Sydney: Butterworth-Heinemann.

Hunter, C., 2002. Aspects of the sustainable tourism debate from a natural resources perspective. In R. Harris, T. Griffin, & P. Williams eds., *Sustainable tourism: a global perspective*. Sydney: Butterworth-Heinemann.

Hwang, L.J. & Lockwood, A., 2006. Understanding the challenges of implementing best practices in hospitality and tourism SMEs. *Benchmarking: An International Journal*, 13(3), p.337–54.

Jurowski, C., 2005. B.E.S.T. think tank IV: mass sustainable tourism: challenges and opportunities. *Journal of Sustainable Tourism*, 13(3), p.296–309.

Kozak, M. & Nield, K., 2004. The role of quality and eco-labelling systems in destination benchmarking. *Journal of Sustainable Tourism*, 12(2), p.138–48.

Knox, J., 2006. *Green light for Qualmark*. Media release. Auckland: Qualmark New Zealand Ltd.

Leslie, D. and Hughes, G. 1997. Agenda 21, local authorites and tourism in the UK. *International Journal of Managing Leisure*. Volume 2(3) pp. 143–54.

McDonald, G. & Patterson, Dr. M., 2003. *Ecological footprints of New Zealand and its regions*. A technical paper for Ministry for the Environment Environmental Reporting. Available at: http://www.mfe.govt.nz/publications/ser/eco-footprint-sep03/eco-footprint-sep03.pdf [accessed 10 May 2007].

McKercher, B., 1993. The unrecognised threat to tourism: can tourism survive 'sustainability'? *Tourism Management*, 14(2), p.131–36.

Osland, J., Kanwalroop, K.D. & Yuthis, K., 2002. Globalisation and environmental sustainability: an analysis of the impact of globalisation using the Natural Step framework. In S. Sharma & M. Starik eds., *Research in corporate sustainability: the evolving theory and practice of organisations in the natural environment*. Cheltenham, UK: Edward Elgar.

Parliamentary Commissioner for the Environment (PCE), 2004. *See change: learning and education for sustainability*. Wellington: PCE.

Pigram, J.J., 1998. Best practice environmental management and the tourism industry. In C. Cooper & S. Wanhill eds., *Tourism development: environment and community issues*. Chichester, UK: John Wiley & Sons Ltd.

Rotorua Sustainable Tourism Charter, 2006. *Need for sustainability*. Available at: http://www.rotoruanz.co.nz/SustainableCharter/Sustainability.asp [accessed 20 November 2006].

Sasidharan, V. & Font, X., 2001. Pitfalls of ecolabelling. In X. Font & R. C. Buckley eds., *Tourism ecolabelling: certification and promotional sustainable management*. Oxon, UK: CABI Publishing.

Schaper, M. & Carlsen, J., 2004. Overcoming the green gap: improving the environmental performance of small tourism firms in Western Australia. In R. Thomas ed., *Small firms in tourism: international perspectives*. Kidlington, Oxford: Elsevier Ltd.

Sharma, S., 2002. Research in corporate sustainability: what really matters? In S. Sharma & M. Starik eds., *Research in corporate sustainability: the evolving theory and practice of organisations in the natural environment*. Cheltenham, UK: Edward Elgar.

Sustainable Business Network, 2006. *About the sustainable business network*. Available at: http://www.sustainable.org.nz/about.asp [accessed 6 September 2006].

Te Puni Kokiri, 2001. *Te Maori i Nga Rohe: Maori regional diversity*. Wellington: Ministry of Maori Development.

Thomas, K., 2000. The research process as a journey: from positivist traditions into the realms of qualitative inquiry. In J. Phillmore & L. Goodson eds., *Qualitative research in tourism: ontologies, and methodologies*. London: Routledge.

Tourism Industry Association New Zealand and the Ministry for the Environment, 2006. *The nature of good business*. Available at: http://www.tianz.org.nz/Current-Projects/Environmental-Plan.asp [accessed 6 September 2006].

University of Auckland, 2006. *Natural hazards in New Zealand: GEOG105 lab programme*. Available at: http://flexiblelearning.auckland.ac.nz/geog105/index.html [accessed 10 May 2007].

Wanhill, S., 1998. Tourism development and sustainability. In C. Cooper & S. Wanhill eds., *Tourism development: environment and community issues.* Chichester, UK: John Wiley and Sons Ltd.

Wanhill, S., 2004. Government assistance for tourism SMEs: from theory to practice. In R. Thomas ed., *Small firms in tourism: international perspectives.* Kidlington, Oxford: Elsevier Ltd.

Weaver, D., 2004. Tourism and the elusive paradigm of sustainable development. In A. Lew, C.M. Hall, & A.M. Williams eds., *A companion to tourism.* Oxford: Blackwell Publishing.

Zahra, A., 2006. *Destination management.* Unpublished research document. Hamilton: University of Waikato

10 Southern Africa, Policy Initiatives, and Environmental Performance

Anna Spenceley

INTRODUCTION

Over the past twenty years tourism development as a whole has been positive in Africa, and during the 1990s tourism grew on an average at an annual rate of 6.2 per cent in contrast to 4.3 per cent for the world. The World Travel and Tourism Council reports that travel and tourism in sub-Saharan Africa in 2007 is expected to generate US$ 90.1 billion of economic activity, and to account for 8.1 per cent of GDP and 10.4 million jobs (5.9% of total employment). Between 2008 and 2017 the industry is expected to grow by 4.5 per cent per annum (in real terms) between 2008 and 2017. However, in 2007 the total demand represented just 1.3 per cent of world market share (WTTC, 2007).

During 2002 Africa hosted 715 million arrivals, and approximately 60 per cent of international tourist arrivals visited Africa for the purposes of leisure, recreation, and holidays. In the 1990s Africa's share in the world tourism total rose almost one point from 3.3 per cent to 4.1 per cent in 2001. Africa earned on average US$414 per tourist in 2001—which is below the world average of US$670 and the lowest of all world continents. There are seventy-six countries in the world (i.e., 35% of the total) that receive more than one million international tourist arrivals. Only four of these countries are in Africa (8% of African Countries)—seven countries receive half a million to a million, while eighteen have between one hundred thousand and half a million and twenty-three less than one hundred thousand (Mukugo et al., 2004). The continent is heavily endowed with some of the exceptional attractions, including natural resources, biodiversity, and sites of historical importance. Nature-based tourism is the main component of the African tourism product and the continent boasts of a wide range of natural attractions (Mukugo et al., 2004).

Research commissioned by New Partnership for Africa's Development (NEPAD) and the Southern African Development Community (SADC) assessed tourism growth in southern Africa. The report indicates that in 2005 South Africa and Mauritius had advanced tourism sectors, contributing 2.9

per cent and 4.2 per cent to gross domestic product growth, respectively. Tourism markets in Botswana and Namibia are still maturing; Zambia, Mozambique, Tanzania, and Madagascar are emerging countries in terms of tourism growth; and Zimbabwe's market has regressed; and the tourism potential of Lesotho and Swaziland are promising. NEPAD has made tourism a priority sector with the potential to diversify economic opportunities and generate income and foreign exchange earnings for African countries. This is in line with the African Union and NEPAD tourism action plan, adopted at the union's third general assembly in Ethiopia in July 2004. However, the report noted that there was inadequate tourism education, training, and awareness for the general public, and a lack of protection for the environment (Gadebe, 2005).

OVERVIEW OF POLICY INITIATIVES

The NEPAD strategic framework document arises from a mandate given to the five initiating heads of state (Algeria, Egypt, Nigeria, Senegal, South Africa) by the Organisation of African Unity (OAU) to develop an integrated socioeconomic development framework for Africa. The 37th Summit of the OAU in July 2001 formally adopted the strategic framework document. NEPAD is designed to address the current challenges facing the African continent. Issues such as the escalating poverty levels, underdevelopment, and the continued marginalisation of Africa needed a new radical intervention, spearheaded by African leaders, to develop a new vision that would guarantee Africa's renewal. NEPAD has identified tourism as an important vehicle to address the current challenges facing the African continent. Tourism is located within the NEPAD under the market access initiative and its broad objectives are to:

- Identify "key" anchor projects at national and sub-regional levels which will generate significant spin-offs and assist in promoting inter-regional integration;
- Develop a regional marketing strategy;
- Develop research capacity; and
- Promote partnerships via sub-regional bodies (NEPAD, 2001: 45).

The actions proposed to address these objectives, which are particularly germane in this context, are to:

- Forge cooperative partnerships to capture the benefits of shared knowledge, as well as providing a base for other countries for entering into tourist-related activities;
- Provide the African people with the capacity to be actively involved in sustainable tourism projects at the community level;

- Market African tourism products, especially in adventure tourism, ecotourism, and cultural tourism; and
- Increase regional coordination of tourism initiatives in Africa for the expansion and increased diversity of products (NEPAD, 2001: 45–46).

Individual countries in southern Africa have taken different approaches to implementing the NEPAD tourism action plan, and towards promoting sustainable tourism growth. Interventions within a range of southern African countries are explored throughout this book. As an introduction, however, South Africa provides a good example of responsible tourism policy development, and their principles of responsible tourism have largely been adopted globally. This chapter focuses on progress on environmental sustainability in South Africa, and particularly on performance by specific nature-based tourism enterprises, progress in environmental certification, and the demand for responsible tourism in Africa.

RESPONSIBLE TOURISM POLICY IN SOUTH AFRICA

In 1996 the Department of Environmental Affairs and Tourism (DEAT) published its White Paper on the Development and Promotion of Tourism, which recognised that tourism had largely been a missed opportunity for South Africa, but which also considered that tourism could provide the nation with an 'engine of growth, capable of dynamising and rejuvenating other sectors of the economy.' A foresighted part of the paper promoted the development of "responsible and sustainable" tourism growth. The key elements of responsible tourism were to

- Ensure communities are involved in and benefit from tourism;
- Market tourism that is responsible, respecting local, natural, and cultural environments;
- Involve the local community in planning and decision making;
- Use local resources sustainably;
- Be sensitive to the host culture;
- Maintain and encourage natural, economic, social, and cultural diversity; and
- Assess environmental, social, and economic impacts as a prerequisite to developing tourism (DEAT, 1996: section 3.4).

Following the white paper, DEAT also produced national *Responsible Tourism Guidelines*, which included targets for the tourism sector and emphasised the need to address the triple bottom line of sustainable development (economic, environmental, and social sustainability) (DEAT, 2002). It was envisaged that tourism industry groups will take the guidelines and develop subsector guidelines that are applicable to their business, and that codes of best practice would be derived. Through such voluntary systems, it was hoped that enterprises would achieve market advantage over their competitors by being demonstrably 'responsible (Spenceley, 2003).

As a tool to assist the tourism sector, a Responsible Tourism Manual for South Africa was published by DEAT in 2002. This aimed to provide 'mainstream' as well as community-based tourism enterprises (CBTEs) with information about responsible tourism and the opportunities that it presented for improving their business performance. Specific to South Africa, and in line with international best practice, the manual provided a range of practical and cost-effective responsible actions available to tourism businesses, and referred to many useful sources of information that could guide their implementation of responsible business activities (Spenceley et al., 2002).

Also in 2002, South Africa hosted the first conference on Responsible Tourism in Destinations, just prior to the Johannesburg World Summit on Sustainable Development. The Cape Town Conference was attended by 280 delegates from twenty countries, and resulted in a declaration that called upon tourism enterprises to " . . . adopt a responsible approach, to commit to specific responsible practises, and to report progress in a transparent and auditable way, and where appropriate to use this for market advantage" (Cape Town, 2002: 3). In particular, the Cape Town Declaration states that responsible tourism:

- minimises negative economic, environmental, and social impacts;
- generates greater economic benefits for local people and enhances the well-being of host communities, improves working conditions and access to the industry;
- involves local people in decisions that affect their lives and life chances;
- makes positive contributions to the conservation of natural and cultural heritage, to the maintenance of the world's diversity;
- provides more enjoyable experiences for tourists through more meaningful connections with local people, and a greater understanding of local cultural, social, and environmental issues;
- provides access for physically challenged people; and
- is culturally sensitive, engenders respect between tourists and hosts, and builds local pride and confidence (Cape Town, 2002: 2).

The declaration makes a commitment to ' . . . work with others to take responsibility for achieving the economic, social and environmental components of responsible and sustainable tourism.' The term "responsible tourism" is also attracting increasing attention globally. So by 2002 South Africa had a strong policy basis for responsible tourism, and it was hoped that this would be followed by concrete and tangible evidence of activities and results of good practice. However, although both the responsible tourism guidelines and manual are freely available on DEAT's Web site (www.environment.gov. za), there is concern that little has been done to put them into practice.

At the 2nd Conference on Responsible Tourism in Declarations held in Kerala, India in 2008, it became clear that although there was a degree of awareness of responsible tourism among the private sector in South Africa, few enterprises were translating this into responsible tourism management activities. Frey and George (2008) state that this lack of responsible tourism management in South Africa is attributed to lethargy within the private sector, coupled with a lack of information about what businesses could do to implement responsible tourism. Clearly, transforming a 'business as usual' tourism industry into a responsible one not only requires market demand, but also tools and mechanisms to assist the private sector in modifying their practices. In the future, improvements might be more forthcoming by using policy and regulatory 'sticks' and market demand 'carrots' coupled with widely available information and assistance for the private sector to enact corporate social responsibility.

Strengthening the principles of responsible tourism outlined in the Cape Town Declaration, the Kerala Declaration recognised that "Responsible Tourism is not a product; it is an approach and which can be used by travellers and holidaymakers, tour operators, accommodation and transport providers, visitor attraction managers, planning authorities, national, regional/ provincial and local government. An integrated approach is required, involving many stakeholders in any place or space which attracts tourists" (Kerala, 2008: 1).

ENVIRONMENTAL PERFORMANCE OF TOURISM ENTERPRISES

The level of good environmental performance among tourism enterprises in southern Africa is difficult to establish comprehensively, due to the lack of systematic surveys within the tourism industry. However, with the growth of tourism certification in South Africa, it is possible to make some inferences for part of the continent. This chapter looks at three main areas where environmental performance has been evaluated: (1) environmental performance in nature-based tourism, (2) tourism certification systems, and (3) market demand for responsible tourism products.

NATURE-BASED TOURISM ENTERPRISES

Nature-based tourism, and particularly wildlife tourism, is a dominant part of the tourism sector in southern Africa. The extent of nature-based tourism in Africa is difficult to measure, because of often simplistic ways that governments conduct departure surveys. However, Scholes and Biggs (2004) compiled an overview of nature-tourism arrivals and revenues for the continent, where data was available (see Table 10.1):

Table 10.1   Measured and Estimated Nature-Based Tourism Numbers and Revenue in 2000

Country	Nature tourism arrivals (thousands)	Income from nature tourism (US$ millions)
Angola	0.9	0.3
Botswana	472.9	131.3
Gabon	28.0	1.3
Kenya	754.6	250.7
Lesotho	53.8	5.5
Malawi	109.4	13
Mozambique	42.0	8.4
Namibia	360.0	247.6
Rwanda	1.7	2.7
South Africa	4,634.5	2,298.8
Swaziland	243.9	27.0
Tanzania	203.7	299.9
Uganda	120.8	119.2
Zambia	459.2	72.8
Zimbabwe	1,149.4	143.5
Totals	8,974.0	3,622.0

Source: Adapted from Scholes and Biggs (2004).

The data demonstrate the dominance of South Africa, accounting for nearly half the recorded nature tourists on the continent, and over 60 per cent of its revenue. The dominance of this form of tourism in South Africa is illustrated clearly in the province of KwaZulu-Natal. KwaZulu-Natal's tourism market in 2005 consisted of 1.4 million tourists (South African Tourism, 2006), and an estimate that 68 per cent of foreign visitors to the province visited natural attractions (TKZN, 2006).

It is interesting to examine in more detail what specific nature-based tourism enterprises are doing to improve their environmental performance. Between 2000 and 2001, the author assessed the economic, social, and environmental impacts four nature-based tourism enterprises in South Africa, and evaluated their sustainability using the Sustainable Nature-based Tourism Assessment Toolkit (Spenceley, 2003). Ngala, Pretoriuskop, Jackalberry, and Sabi Sabi all operated photographic safari tourism as their core business, and did so within lowveld savannah habitats where fauna including elephant, rhino, buffalo, lion, and leopard could be found. In all four cases, the enterprises were located within a protected area and had a rural community as an immediate neighbour on one border. The enterprises were assessed in terms of energy use, water consumption, waste disposal, and purchasing activities. Ngala and Sabi Sabi were in the process of developing internal environmental management systems, but neither Pretoriuskop nor Jackalberry had begun to consider their environmental performance in a systematic way (Spenceley, 2005a).

Energy Use

Three of the enterprises used electricity from the national grid to supply the majority of their energy needs. Since the electricity in South Africa is largely generated at coal-burning power stations, the associated pollutants were calculated for each enterprise and related to the number of commercial bed/nights (see Table 10.2). This indicated that Pretoriuskop and Sabi Sabi consumed roughly the same amounts of electricity in relation to the number of commercial bed/nights, while Jackalberry used over five times their comparative consumption. In addition to electricity, the enterprises used diesel and petrol for vehicles, paraffin for lighting, gas and charcoal for cooking, and wood for ambient fires. Some renewable energy was used

Table 10. 2   Enterprise Resource Consumption Estimates

	Ngala	Pretoriuskop	Jackalberry	Sabi Sabi
Energy consumption estimates				
	Diesel generator used 255–292 kilolitres diesel p/a or ~16–19 litres per bed/night	~2,118 MWh grid electricity p/a or 17 kWh per bed/night	~370 MWh grid electricity p/a or 101 kWh per bed/night	~561 MWh grid electricity p/a or 16.7 kWh per bed/night
		Associated annual pollutant creation of ~1,800 tonnes CO_2, 17 tonnes SO_2, and 17.5 tonnes NO_x.	Associated annual pollutant creation of ~330 tonnes CO_2, 3 tonnes SO_2, and 1.4 tonnes NO_x	Associated annual pollutant creation of ~477 tonnes CO_2, 4.4 tonnes SO_2, and 2 tonnes NO_x.
Water consumption estimates				
	~ 31,280 m³ p/a or 2.0 m³ per bed/night	~ 44,640 m³ p/a or 0.4 m³ per bed/night	~ 4,380 m³ used p/a or 1.2 m³ per bed/night	~ 54,000 m³ p/a or 1.6 m³ per bed/night
	Of 83.3 million m³ falling on the reserve p/a this equated to ~0.04% of available water	Of 447.6 million m³ falling on region p/a, this equated to 0.008% of available water	Of 28.4 million m³ falling on reserve p/a, this equated to ~0.02% of available water	Of 20.8 million m³ falling on reserve p/a, this equated to ~0.03% of available water

Source: Spenceley (2003a).

at Pretoriuskop, Jackalberry, and Sabi Sabi in order to electrify wildlife fences. However, Ngala had discarded solar power as an option due to the amount of power required to operate the camp, and used a diesel generator (Spenceley, 2005a).

There was limited use of natural light through architectural design and construction at the enterprises. All four establishments used mixed watt-age incandescent light bulbs, although one of the three bush lodges located at Sabi Sabi had installed low-energy bulbs throughout. Office areas were generally lit by lower-wattage fluorescent strip lighting, and there were a few low-energy bulbs in place at Ngala, Pretoriuskop, and Jackalberry. However, two of the enterprises noted that although they had attempted to use low-energy bulbs, their fluctuating power supplies caused the expensive bulbs to fail relatively quickly. One of the enterprises left lights constantly on in guest accommodation for aesthetic reasons and so wasted both electricity and money (Spenceley, 2005a).

Laundry services took place at Ngala, Pretoriuskop, and Jackalberry lodges, while Sabi Sabi outsourced laundry to a local subcontractor. The private-sector enterprises changed linen daily and would wash towels between once and four times a day. Although the management of one enterprise stipulated that its policy was to change linen every two days, housekeeping staff actually changed all linen daily regardless. Active use of energetically expensive appliances and isolated use of washing lines for 'free' drying were observed. Pretoriuskop made communal laundry equipment available to self-drive tourists, and enterprise staff changed accommodation linen every other day, or when new guests arrived. Hot-water geysers at the enterprises were set at between 50°C and 60°C throughout the enterprises, although they need only be set to 40°C. Power was used to pump water from groundwater through boreholes at Ngala and Sabi Sabi, and was extracted from rivers in the cases of Pretoriuskop and Sabi Sabi. Pretoriuskop needed to pump its water from a river over thirty-seven kilometres away, which required a great deal of energy (Spenceley, 2005a).

Pretoriuskop sold petrol, diesel, wood, and charcoal to self-drive tourists. However, Ngala collected indigenous deadwood from the reserve on a regular basis to stock fires. All four enterprises used rechargeable batteries in radios used by staff (Spenceley, 2005a). None of the enterprises evaluated the number of 'air miles' used by guests to reach the tourist enterprise, nor did they try to offset the associated carbon-dioxide emissions through any carbon-neutral schemes (Spenceley, 2005a).

Water Consumption

None of the enterprises practised any form of water conservation, either through limiting use, setting guidelines or targets to reduce consumption, or practising environmental awareness for staff and guests (Spenceley,

2005a). In general, the enterprises had installed nine-litre toilet cisterns, which were sometimes set to lower flush volumes (e.g., six litres in the case of Jackalberry), but no dual-flush systems were present. None of the faucets or showerheads at the enterprises had low-flow water saving attachments. Two of the enterprises noted that the high levels of calcium carbonate in the water led to serious 'furring' of pipes and water-saving devices, and that they were therefore impractical to use. All rooms at Ngala and Sabi Sabi had baths in guest rooms, while they were fitted in only isolated suites at Pretoriuskop and Jackalberry (Spenceley, 2005a).

The lawns and plants in landscaping schemes around the enterprises were watered regularly. The best water-saving system for irrigation was found at Jackalberry, where sprinklers were used for two hours in the late afternoon (to avoid evaporation) on six cycles of fifteen minutes (to improve infiltration). Sabi Sabi only permitted lawns to be watered once a week and all enterprises promoted the use of indigenous, low-water-consumption species in their plantings (Spenceley, 2005a).

Only Pretoriuskop Camp formally monitored the volumes of water it pumped from river source. Although water meters were installed on some of the boreholes at one of the enterprises, not all were functioning. Meter readings had been taken for a period of time but this activity was short lived. To monitor water consumption, benchmarks were established based on the volume of water used by an enterprise and equated to the amount of precipitation on the enterprise property and the number of commercial beds (see Table 10.2). The public-sector enterprise had the lowest estimated consumption per bed night, while it appeared that Ngala had the highest relative level of use (Spenceley, 2005a).

Solid Waste

All of the enterprises operated recycling schemes and separated their waste glass, steel, and tin. Considerable investment had been made in the cases of Ngala and Sabi Sabi to set up recycling centres that were wildlife-proof. Ngala is located within the wider Timbavati Private Nature Reserve. The reserve policy dictated that all solid waste should be removed from the reserve. However, the external recycling plant used by Ngala had deteriorated, removing any incentive for the enterprise to manage waste in this way. The remoteness of Ngala meant that transport costs to remove waste were not covered by revenue generated from the sale of recyclables. Local farmers in Welverdiend and Huntingdon collected food waste from Ngala and Sabi Sabi, respectively, for use as fodder for their pigs. Waste oil was stored and collected for recycling at Ngala, Pretoriuskop, and Sabi Sabi (Spenceley, 2005a). Each of the enterprises had an incinerator to dispose of additional card and plastic waste, but none of these had air filters attached, nor was any air-quality monitoring implemented. Landfill pits within the protected areas were covered over with topsoil and left to re-vegetate after use (Spenceley, 2005a).

Wet Waste

Ngala, Pretoriuskop, and Sabi Sabi had constructed wetland wastewater purification systems in different designs to treat grey- and black-water waste. The reed beds at Pretoriuskop were the most heavily engineered, with a series of six evaporation ponds and two reed beds constructed. Septic tanks and wetlands at Sabi Sabi had been carefully designed to treat wastewater to such an extent that it could effectively be recycled back to the environment. Monthly water quality testing at Pretoriuskop and Sabi Sabi permitted the release of treated water back into natural wetlands. The artificial wetland at Ngala lay in a poor state of repair during the assessment, and electric fencing that had been used to keep wildlife out had been damaged by elephants. Sabi Sabi purchased biodegradable detergents and soaps in order that chemicals would not adversely impact on the natural purification process. Jackalberry had the weakest sewage treatment system comprising a series of French drains (or soak-aways), which due to the geology of the area were not draining effectively (Spenceley, 2005a).

Purchasing

The enterprises used their purchasing power to buy some local and environmentally friendly products. Biodegradable soaps and detergents were preferentially purchased at Ngala, Pretoriuskop, and Sabi Sabi, while Pretoriuskop ensured that KNP's nature conservation department approved all chemical products used by staff. Ngala also purchased paper that had either been produced from sustainable forests or was recycled (Spenceley, 2005a).

Since the assessments took place in 2000 and 2001, the enterprises have changed some of their environmental management processes. For example, Ngala now has a power line installed to connect the camp to the national electricity grid instead of using a diesel generator, and Sabi Sabi has received tourism certification through the Fair Trade in Tourism South Africa (FTTSA) awards scheme.

These four case studies can be considered as indicative of the type of practices undertaken by responsible nature-based tourism enterprises in southern Africa. Their relevance and implications of environmental certification programs and the wider role of environmental management systems in the region are discussed next.

TOURISM CERTIFICATION

The general aim of tourism certification is to foster responsible environmental, social, and cultural behaviour and provide a quality product to consumers. Certification is defined as a " . . . procedure that audits and gives written assurance that a facility, product, process, service, or management system meets specific standards. It awards a logo or seal to those that meet or exceed baseline criteria prescribed by the programme" (Honey, 2002: 4). Certification provides a mechanism through which enterprises can achieve voluntary standards of performance that meet or exceed baseline standards or legislation. While many schemes focus mainly on accrediting environmentally good practice and biodiversity conservation (e.g., Green Globe 21; ISO14001; the Nature and Ecotourism Accreditation Program [NEAP]), some schemes promote a pro-poor approach, by rewarding enterprises that are committed to employ and training local people, and purchasing local goods and services; supporting local small, medium, and micro enterprises (SMMEs); encouraging local participation in decision making; and improving local access to basic infrastructure (Roe, Harris, & de Andrade, 2003). This chapter considers the former: environmentally orientated certification.

CERTIFICATION SCHEMES GLOBALLY

Globally, the development of certification of ecolabels has been irregular between different countries, and different sectors of the tourism industry (Hillary, 1993). There are few programmes in low-income countries and 65 per cent of the approximately seven thousand certified tourism products in the world are located in Europe (Dodds & Joppe, 2005), where there were sixty environmental certificates and awards operating by 2001 (Hamele, 2002). Environmental certification has allowed companies to reduce costs (e.g., water, waste, and energy savings) (Dodds & Joppe, 2005). Enterprises can also benefit from certification through improvements in performance, financial benefits, improved employee morale, and enhanced corporate image (Chafe & Honey, 2005; Font & Tribe, 2001). However, many enterprises have not achieved the market differentials that they had anticipated (Chafe & Honey, 2005).

In a review of the potential for ecolabeling in developing countries, Sasidharan et al. (2002) report a growing concern that the small-scale tourism enterprises would be ill-equipped to conform to the environmental standards and criteria circumscribed by international ecolabeling schemes originating in developed nations. However, whilst international certification schemes such as Green Globe 21, Blue Flag, and ISO14001 are clearly operating in developing countries on the African continent, two 'homegrown' systems are reviewed next.

SOUTH AFRICAN CERTIFICATION SYSTEMS

There are two main environmentally focussed certification schemes operating in South Africa: (1) Fair Trade in Tourism South Africa and (2) Heritage that were reviewed by Spenceley (2005b).

1. Fair Trade in Tourism South Africa

Fair Trade in Tourism South Africa (FTTSA) was launched in 2002 as an independent initiative of the IUCN (the World Conservation Union) that aims to encourage equitable and sustainable tourism growth and development in South Africa. FTTSA does this by promoting the concept of fair trade in tourism, and by marketing fair and responsible tourism businesses using the "Fair Trade in Tourism" Trademark. This trademark is an independent symbol of fairness in tourism, which is monitored by FTTSA staff to maximise its effectiveness as a marketing tool for all trademark users (Seif, 2002). Commercial tourism products can apply for the trademark if they are (Seif, 2002):

- tourism resources (i.e., attractions and places of interest);
- tourism facilities (i.e., accommodation, conference, restaurant, entertainment); or
- tourism services (i.e., transport, tour guides, tour operators, ground handlers, travel agents).

The main criteria for being awarded the trademark are that products meet the six FTTSA principles (Seif, 2002): fair share, democracy, respect, reliability, transparency, and sustainability. The principles include the need for enterprises to practice responsible use of resources, while respecting conservation of the environment.

2. Heritage Ecotourism Rating Scheme, South Africa

Qualitour is a private South African company that launched the Heritage Ecotourism Rating Program in 2001. The program is linked with Green Globe (see www.heritagesa.co.za) and is partnered with AJA South Africa, the registered Green Globe auditors for the region. The Heritage program is designed to offer certification to businesses throughout the tourism industry in South Africa based on the International Hotels Environment Initiative, as the company believes that Green Globe 21 is not wholly suitable to South African realities. However, all enterprises enrolled with the Heritage program automatically receive Green Globe affiliate status, while qualification for Green Globe certification takes longer (Koch et al., 2002). The sectors of the tourism market covered by the scheme are accommodation, nature/wildlife reserve, tour operators, restaurants, tourist attractions, conference centres, and tourism service providers (Qualitour, undated).

Companies apply for the Heritage scheme and Qualitour responds by undertaking an audit of their operations. The evaluations cover sixty-four elements that are each given a weighted score (e.g., community and resource use issues weighted heavier than marketing). If enterprises score 50.1 per cent or more, they are accepted onto the scheme into the Silver class. Enterprises are then provided with assistance with action plans, work plans, and an environmental manual. Should they reach 75 per cent compliance, they receive the Gold award, and at 91 per cent they move on to the Platinum level (Pers. com. G. McManus, 2005). The system is used mainly by hotels across southern Africa, and by February 2008 there were forty-two accredited enterprises in Botswana (1), Lesotho (2), Namibia (1), South Africa (33), Swaziland (3), and Zambia (2). These included nature-based tourism enterprises such as Djuma Game reserve and Lesheba Wilderness.

To summarise, South Africa has two certification systems that have been operating for six years and have only certified fifty tourism enterprises between them. Given that there are between ten thousand and nineteen thousand enterprises providing accommodation in the country (DEAT & DTI, 2004: no accurate statistics are available), this is an almost insignificant proportion of the industry.

DEMAND FOR ENVIRONMENTALLY CERTIFIED AND RESPONSIBLE TOURISM PRODUCTS

Consumer studies have found increasing levels of awareness and demand among tourists for environmentally and socially responsible tourism, particularly in the UK, the United States, and Germany (Goodwin & Francis, 2003; Martin & Stubbs, 1995, 1997; Mintel, 2001; Müller & Landes, 2000; Stueve, Cook, & Drew, 2002; Tearfund, 2001). Historically, the lack of responsibility shown by tour operators towards environmental and cultural resources in destinations has been attributed to the lack of ownership and control over ground operations (Ashworth & Goodall, 1990), coupled with intense competition between tour operators and low profit margins (Evans & Stabler, 1995). However, evidence suggests that tour operators are increasingly requiring that their ground handlers report on their environmental performance (e.g., the Association of Independent Tour Operators). In 2001 a survey was published by Tearfund on the responsible business practices reported by sixty-five UK-based tour operators (Tearfund, 2001). This survey revealed that most tour operators had examples of where their operations were making a positive difference to the lives of local people. At that time, the report noted that responsible and ethical tourism issues were not mainstream, but the move was certainly in that direction (Gordon, 2001).

However, there has been very little market research in southern Africa to establish the level of demand for responsible tourism and environmentally sound practices. In 2006 the International Centre for Responsible Tourism attempted to replicate the Tearfund study in South Africa. The objective was to evaluate the extent to which South African tour operators were practicing responsible tourism activities, given the context of a country that released responsible tourism guidelines as national policy in 2002.

From an invited sample of one hundred South African tour operators attending Indaba 2006 (the largest annual tourism trade exhibition in Africa), twenty South African tour operators participated in the study by completing a questionnaire on issues regarding local benefits, donations, partnerships, impacts on the natural and cultural environment, training, policies, and tourist demand for responsible tourism (Spenceley, 2007). Operators were asked what kind of characteristics their suppliers had, and a high proportion were reported to be environmentally friendly (average of 82.3%), locally based (78.1%), and socially responsible (75%). Nine operators commented on the use of fair-trade products, who on average used 25 per cent FTTSA-certified products in their tours (see Table 10.3) (Spenceley, 2007).

One operator commented:

> . . . where possible and applicable we use accommodations & excursions accredited by Fairtrade in Tourism and or NACOBTA [Namibia Community Based Tourism Association]. If these are not available we ask for responsible tourism guidelines implemented & we promote sustainable tourism.

However, the operators were not yet experiencing significant demand from tourists for responsible products. A quarter indicated that their clients requested information about their corporate social responsibility practices; three operators said that this gave them market advantage over other companies (Spenceley, 2007). In a subsequent study to investigate adoption of responsible tourism practices, Frey (2007) e-mailed a questionnaire to 1,700 tourism businesses in the Greater Cape Town region. She achieved a response rate of 14 per cent (244 returns). Frey (2007) found that a high proportion of the businesses considered an ethical and responsible approach to business as very important (see Table 10.4).

Table 10.3 Proportion of Responsible Suppliers Used by Tour Operators

Type of supplier	Average (%)	Min (%)	Max (%)	No. responses
Environmentally friendly	82.3	30	100	11
Locally based	78.1	10	100	16
Socially responsible	75.0	0	100	10
Star-graded	69.6	0	100	14
Approved by an environmental body	41.0	0	90	10
Approved by Fair Trade in Tourism South Africa	25.2	0	100	9
Have their procurement rated by a BEE rating agency	15.8	0	40	6

Table 10.4   Relative Importance of Responsible Tourism to Tourism Enterprises in Cape Town

Scale Item	Strongly Agree & Agree (%)
Being ethical and responsible is the most important thing a business can do	94
Responsible management is essential to long-term profitability	94
Business planning and goal setting should include discussions of responsible management	92
We think responsible tourism management is a useful marketing tool	81
Our employees are proud to work for a socially responsible business	73
We think responsible tourism management improves our staff performance	67
Business has a social responsibility beyond making a profit	62

Source: Adapted from Frey and George (2008).

The data from Spenceley (2007) and Frey (2007) indicate a low level of interest in environmentally responsible tourism, simply by considering the number of participants in each survey.

CONCLUSIONS

The foregoing discussion illustrates that there are sound policies for environmentally responsible tourism in southern Africa. However, uptake by the industry of environmental management systems and certification programs is fragmented. The proportion of the industry formally and transparently reporting on their environmental practices is a tiny proportion of enterprises in the industry, which supports findings elsewhere (Dobbs & Joppe, 2005). Clearly, having strong policies is not sufficient to influence the private sector in this region. Legislation as a 'stick' and consumer demand as a 'carrot' might be persuasive in the future. In an interesting turn, it appears that current South African 'crises' with grid electricity supply, with frequent power cuts, have led to increased interest nationally in renewable energies (both within and outside the tourism sector). However, the Southern African Tourism Services Association (SATSA) states that:

> Solar power that does not feed off the national grid is the answer, but with limited components in the country, tourism concerns have no options but to install generators, at least in the short term. (cited by Coleman, 2008)

Newer facilities are reportedly being built with high efficiency levels, and using sustainable resource principles (Colman, 2008). Presumably when solar panels become more available (in response to consumer demand) the level of use of renewables will increase nationally. This will be one step towards addressing environmental sustainability in tourism.

ACKNOWLEDGMENTS

Many thanks to the managers and staff of Ngala, Pretoriuskop, Jackalberry Lodge, and Sabi Sabi; members of the rural communities who agreed to participate; to Professor Harold Goodwin at the International Centre for Responsible Tourism; and to The Leverhulme Trust, who generously funded this research, which was in part used to towards a doctorate from the University of Greenwich.

REFERENCES

Ashworth, G. & Goodall, B., 1990. *Marketing tourism places.* London: Routledge.
Cape Town, 2002. The Cape Town Declaration of Responsible Tourism in Destinations, August 2002. Available at: www.environment.gov.za/sustdev/documents/pdf/The%20Cape%20Town%20Declaration.pdf [accessed 6 August 2008].
Chafe, Z. & Honey, M., 2005. *Consumer demand and operator support for socially and environmentally responsible tourism.* Center on Ecotourism and Sustainable Development (CESD)/The International Ecotourism Society (TIES). Working Paper No. 104, April 2005.
Colman, M., 2008. A sustainable outlook, M&G business tourism. *Mail & Guardian*, February 22 to 28, p.11.
Commission on Sustainable Development (CSD), 1999. *Report on the seventh session.* 1 May and 27 July 1998, and 19–30 April 1999, Economic and Social Council Official Records, 199, Supplement No. 9, United Nations, New York, 1999. Copyright © United Nations Division for Sustainable Development 02/09/1999.
Department of Environmental Affairs and Tourism, 1996. *The development and promotion of tourism in South Africa.* White Paper, Government of South Africa: Pretoria. Available at: http://www.environment.gov.za/PolLeg/White-Papers/tourism96.htm [accessed 6 August 2008].
Department of Environmental Affairs and Tourism (DEAT), 2002. *Guidelines for responsible tourism development.* Pretoria: Department of Environmental Affairs and Tourism.
Department of Environmental Affairs and Tourism (DEAT) and the Department of Trade and Industry, 2004. Global competitiveness study—integrated presentation. August 2004, Monitor Group, L.P and South African Tourism: Pretoria. Available at: http://www.southafrica.net/satourism/research/viewResearchDocument.cfm?ResearchDocumentID=310 [accessed 6 August 2008].
Dodds, R. & Joppe, M., 2005. *CSR in the tourism industry? The status of and potential for certification, codes of conduct and guidelines.* Study prepared

for the CSR Practice Foreign Investment Advisory Service Investment Climate Department, June.

Evans, N.G. & Stabler, M.J., 1995. A future for the package tour operator in the 21st century? *Tourism Economics*, 1(3), p.245–263.

Font, X. & Tribe, J., 2001. Promoting green tourism: the future of environmental awards. *International Journal of Tourism Research*, 3, p.9–21.

Frey, N., 2007. *The effect of responsible tourism management practices on business performance in an emerging market.* Dissertation presented for a master's in marketing at the School of Management Studies, University of Cape Town, September.

Frey, N. & George, R., 2008.Responsible tourism and the tourism industry: a demand and supply perspective. In A. Spenceley ed., *Responsible tourism: critical issues for conservation and development*. London: Earthscan.

Gadebe, T., 2005. Huge tourism potential for SADC, 26 October 2005, *BuaNews*. Available at: http://www.southafrica.info/doing_business/economy/key_sectors/sadc-tourism-261005.htm [accessed 12 February 2008].

Goodwin, H. & Francis, J., 2003. Ethical and responsible tourism: consumer trends in the UK. *Journal of Vacation Marketing*, 9(3), p.271–84.

Hamele, H., 2002. Eco-labels for tourism in Europe: moving the market toward more sustainable practices. In M. Honey ed., *Ecotourism and certification: setting standards in practice*. Washington, DC: Island Press, p.187–210.

Hillary, R., 1993. *The eco-management and audit scheme: a practical guide.* Letchworth, UK: Technical Communications (Publishing Ltd.).

Honey, M. ed., 2002. *Ecotourism and certification: setting standards in practice.* Washington, DC: Island Press.

Kerala, 2008. *Kerala declaration on responsible tourism in destinations.* Available at: www.icrtindia.org/kd.htm [accessed 27 March 2008].

Koch, E., Massyn, P.J.& Spenceley, A., 2002. Getting started: the experiences of South Africa and Kenya. In M. Honey ed., *Ecotourism and certification: setting standards in practice*. Washington, DC: Island Press, p.237–63.

Martin, A. & Stubbs, R., 1995 & 1997. *Future development in tourism.* MORI–Mori 1995/7 research.

McManus, G., 2005. Heritage Program. Personal Communication.

Mintel, 2001. *Ethical tourism.* London © International Group Limited, October.

Mukogo, R., Dieke, P.U.C., Razafy, R.J. & Nyakunu, E.T., 2004. *New partnership for Africa's development (NEPAD) tourism action plan: phase one: preliminary report on the tourism baseline study.* Available at: www.satourismproducts.com/downloads/NEPADTourism.pdf [accessed 12 February 2008].

Müller, H.R. & Landes, A., 2000. *Tourismus und Umweltverhalten. Befragung zum Reiseverhalten.* Forschungsinstitut für Freizeit und Tourismus (FIF), Hans Imholz-Stiftung, Switzerland Travel Writers & Tourism Journalists Club Zürich (STW). Bern März.

NEPAD, 2001. New partnership for Africa's development . Buja, Nigeria, October 2001. Available at: http://www.nepad.org/2005/files/inbrief.php [accessed 14 February 2008].

Qualitour, Undated. *Application for membership.* Heritage Environmental Rating Scheme. Johannesburg, South Africa.

Roe, D., Harris, C. & de Andrade, J., 2003. *Addressing poverty issues in tourism standards: a review of experience.* PPT Working Paper No. 14, London, February.

Sasidharan, V., Sirakaya, E. & Kerstetter, D., 2002. Developing countries and tourism ecolabels. *Tourism Management*, 23, p.161–74.

Scholes, R.J. & Biggs, R., 2004. *Ecosystem services in Southern Africa: a regional assessment.* Pretoria: Millennium Ecosystem Assessment, CSIR.

Seif, J., 2002. *Trademark users' guide*. Fair Trade in Tourism South Africa, IUCN.

South African Tourism, 2006. *Indaba 2006 factsheet: 2005 tourism arrivals*. Pretoria: South African Tourism.

Spenceley, A., 2003. *Managing sustainable nature-based tourism in southern Africa: a practical assessment tool*. Doctoral thesis, University of Greenwich.

Spenceley, A., 2005a. Nature-based tourism and environmental sustainability in South Africa. *Journal of Sustainable Tourism*, 13(2), p.136–70.

Spenceley, A., 2005b. *Tourism certification initiatives in Africa*. Report to the International Ecotourism Society, 20 January. Available at: www.anna.spenceley.co.uk [accessed May 2006].

Spenceley, A., 2007. *Responsible tourism practices by South African tour operators: survey results from participants at the 2006 Tourism Indaba*. Unpublished report to the International Centre for Responsible Tourism, Durban, South Africa.

Spenceley, A. et al. (2002). *Responsible tourism manual for South Africa*. Department for Environmental Affairs and Tourism, Pretoria, July.

Stueve, A.M., Cook, S.D. & Drew, D., 2002. *The geotourism study: excerpts from the phase 1 executive summary*. National Geographic Traveller/Travel Industry Association of America.

Tearfund, 2001. *Guide to tourism: Don't forget your ethics*. Teddington, UK: Tearfund.

Tourism KwaZulu-Natal (TKZN), 2006. *Some useful statistics 2006*. Tourism KwaZulu Natal, Tourism Information Services, South Africa.

World Travel and Tourism Council (WTTC), 2007. Sub-Saharan Africa: travel and tourism. Navigating the path ahead. The 2007 Travel & Tourism Economic Research. WTTC/Accenture. Available at: *http://wttc.travel/download. php?file=http://www.wttc.travel/bin/pdf/original_pdf_file/sub-saharanafrica. pdf* [accessed 12 February 2008].

11 Turkey's Tourism Policy and Environmental Performance of Tourism Enterprises

Nazmiye Erdogan

INTRODUCTION

Issues surrounding environmental degradation rapidly increased in the late 1970s in Turkey, as in many other countries. Growing realization of this from the early 1990s prompted important changes in environmental consciousness, attitudes, and behaviour of Turkish people, but any corresponding increase in environmental awareness of business is yet to emerge fully. Hence, it is useful to assess the developing nature of Turkish policy and business practices in the tourism sector to establish the background context for current policy, practitioners, and interested parties who are more attuned to environmental impacts. In establishing a close connection with environment and development, the World Commission of Environment and Development has declared that sustainable development is development that meets the needs of the present without compromising the ability of future generations to meet their own needs. This notion of sustainability has grown in acceptance by governments, NGOs, and many environmentalists since the 1992 "Rio Conference" on the environment. The proponents of sustainability argue that natural, thus invariably tourism, resources should be used in such a way that future generations will also be able to benefit from these resources. This has come to be generally supported and promoted by national, regional, and international organisations, as well as by legal provisions and agreements. Also, government and tourism agencies, complemented latterly by the initiatives of various professional bodies, have been turning their attention to aspects of the environmental performance of tourism enterprises (Leslie, 2007). Turkey is no exception, and in reflecting the basic premise of Agenda 21, a number of basic principles for sustainable and economically successful tourism have been proposed (Tosun, 2001). In 1989, the Hague Declaration on Tourism focused on the place of tourism in economic and social development. It is regarded as a viable tool for economic development that takes into account environmental conservation. Subsequently, the focus of activity has shifted to the global politics of sustainability as green geopolitics supported by the United States and the European Union (Roe et al., 2003).

Tourism continues to be a steadily growing sector in the world economy, with developing countries seeing tourism as an important source of revenue.

The major trend, especially since the mid-1980s, has been to expand mass tourism and also to promote diversification from mass tourism towards various types of nature-based tourism, including ecotourism (Rein, 2004). Mass tourism has become the second most important economic activity in Turkey. International tourist numbers have been increasing steadily. According to the Turkish Statistical Institute, in 1994 there were 6.6 million visitors, generating revenues in excess of $4.3 million, which had almost quadrupled by 2007 to 23.3 million and an estimated revenue of $13.9 million. Further exemplifying this dynamic growth in tourism is that foreign exchange receipts from tourism as percentage of gross national product were 0.7 per cent in 1982 rising to 4.2 per cent in 2006. The same period witnessed an approximate eightfold increase in bed spaces provided by licensed accommodation operations. This rise in both tourist numbers and tourism income has led to an increasing focus on the development of policy initiatives in Turkey.

NATIONAL POLICY INITIATIVES

Tourism policy initiatives in terms of institutions, the establishment of legal provisions, and funding started with the Travellers' Association in 1923; subsequently the Touring and Automobile Club in 1930 (Nohutcu, 2002). However, the real interest in tourism by the government started in 1950s when the government decided to establish the Pension Fund in order to build tourism facilities as model investments for the private sector. The Istanbul Hilton, Tarabya, Izmir Buyuk Efes, and Buyuk Ankara Hotels were built through this fund and leased to foreign investors (Tezcan, 2004). In 1953, The Encouragement of Tourism Industry Law 6086 was enacted in order to encourage and regulate tourism facilities and activities. Two years later, the Tourism Bank was founded to promote the development of domestic and international tourism, to establish travel agencies and organise tours, to develop relations with all tourism institutions, to help in the development of new capacity in tourism, and to provide credits for private-sector investment in tourism.

The First Five Year Development Plan (1963–1968) improved the emerging tourism policy. The state undertook the role to establish and improve the infrastructure, e.g., transportation and communication, to encourage investments in areas having high tourism potential, and to intensify tourism activities in the west, southwest, and Antalya. In 1972, Law 1618 was enacted in order to organise travel agency operations and establish the Union of Travel Agents (TURSAB), a nonprofit organisation, to represent travel agents, maintain professional ethics, and assist the ministry on tourism promotions. The Third Five-Year Development Plan (1973–1977) enhanced the involvement of the private sector in mass tourism. It also instituted the subsidy system for "social tourism" (subsidy tourism) for citizens who could not afford the cost of a holiday. The level of assistance/subsidy was determined through a combination of government departments, local authorities, employers, trade unions, and welfare organisations.

Later, in 1982, the Tourism Encouragement Act was enacted in order to encourage both domestic and foreign investment companies to participate more effectively in the development of this sector. Under this law, tourism enterprises are required to be certified by the ministry in order to benefit from the incentives and rights prescribed in the legislation. However, the focus on developing mass markets started creating serious environmental problems, catalysing concern for environmental protection in the 1980s (Erdogan, 2003). This led to the Ministry of Tourism establishing a set of principles including attention to acceptable use of natural and cultural resources, sustainable tourism development in high potential tourist areas, creation of efficient tourism sector with high international competitiveness, tourism-related constructions to harmonise with natural landscape, continuous restoration and maintenance of natural and cultural resources, and protection of tourists and hosts against adverse environmental effects. Subsequent government plans reinforced these objectives, in particular the Sixth, Seventh, and Eighth Five Year Development Plans were concerned with sustainable tourism and environmental protection. The Eighth Five Year Development Plan shifted the emphasis towards improving quality and environmental sustainability and achieving a more balanced approach in spreading the beneficial effects of tourism, particularly to lesser developed areas.

The emergence of international policy initiatives and participation of Turkey in these wider policy contexts led to a questioning of tourism activities and their environmental outcomes, generating a range of global, regional, and national initiatives (Tosun & Fyall, 2005). Policy developments in Turkey in general also reflect manifestations of efforts to integrate such international initiatives across the political, cultural, and economic spectrum; including tourism and environmental protection initiatives. As an EU candidate country, involved in accession negotiations with the EU, Turkey has started the necessary initiatives to harmonise its tourism legislation with the EU. The Tourism Investors' Association undertook a review of tourism legislation leading to the reorganisation of the whole regulatory framework for the tourism sector. In 1999, Turkey signed up to the General Agreement on Trade in Services (GATS). This has a number of implications for tourism: foreign personnel in hotels and restaurants may not exceed 10 per cent of the local workforce; foreign tour operators are not allowed to organise tours abroad for Turkish residents. The only restriction to marketing and selling is the requirement for foreign suppliers to establish themselves in Turkey. A further factor is that foreigners can buy property in Turkey.

The changing nature of tourism markets and consideration about the future prospects of the country has forced Turkey to make serious changes in tourism policies and tourism activities. In order to better integrate environmental considerations in tourism policies, Turkey has progressively put in place a legislative and regulatory framework aimed at better organising tourism development and protecting sensitive areas. The "Tourism Vision of Turkey 2010" in 2004 and "Tourism Strategies 2023" in 2007 were developed in order to expand further the tourism policies that promote the industry framework. The 2010 Tourism Vision focuses on environmental sustainability and expansion of tourism activities. The main priority is investment in the infrastructure, including improved water and sanitation systems and waste management systems. The Tourism Strategy 2023 clearly acknowledges the prevailing problems, i.e., "Developments towards mass tourism activities and particularistic approaches to tourism planning in Turkey have led to Deficient Infrastructure and environmental problems" (Turkish Ministry of Culture and Tourism, 2007: 11).

Further, under the "objectives for the year 2023," the main strategic direction is: Provisions shall be made for establishment of participative mechanisms such as Local Agenda 21, with the local councils becoming functional in a given neighbourhood (p. 14). Also, it states that an effective policy " . . . should reroute all tourism investments toward reducing the imbalances of welfare and development imbalances throughout the country and treat them with an approach that safeguards, conserves and improves the natural, historical, cultural and social environment. . . ." and should " . . . conserve and use natural resources in the most economically and ecologically sustainable way" (p. 16).

Overall, whilst development of legal provisions and associated policy is well founded, the development of environmental policy and the daily practices found in the tourism sector lag behind these legal requirements and policy objectives. Furthermore, there is a lack of enforcement of legal requirements which exacerbates the situation. Thus, Turkey is in need of finding ways to enforce the laws properly and tourism enterprises need to develop honest social responsibility and environmental sensitivity.

STRUCTURAL CHARACTERISTICS OF THE TOURISM SECTOR

The structure of the tourism sector is a complicated one since it includes many interrelated parts that encompass almost every industrial, economic, cultural, and political administrative structure. Furthermore, it is difficult to specify and define a distinct tourism industry, because there are many different products and services involved, with numerous sectors and services catering to meet the needs of tourists. However, the tourism industry is dominated by major players, including those organisations directly involved in the business of tourism. As such, the tourist product is defined as a package tour. Hence, the study of tourism enterprises and their environmental performance in Turkey primarily includes government policy, legislation, structure, and activities of tourism organisations (mainly travel agencies, tour operators, and tourist accommodations). The travel agencies in Turkey are regulated by the Law 1618 enacted in 1972. Each enterprise must be certified by the Ministry of Culture and Tourism. According to the regulations, these agencies are divided into three categories: A Group, B Group, and C Group Agencies. There were 5,184 travel agencies in 2007 (Table 11.1).

Table 11.1   Number of Agencies by Groups (TÜRSAB, 2007)

Type of license	Head office	Branch	N	%
A Group	3,413	1,189	4,602	88.8
B Group	191	21	212	4.1
C Group	370	—	370	7.1
Total	3,974	1,210	5,184	100

Tourist accommodation operations, whilst evidencing the diversity to be found in many countries, are predominantly accounted for by the hotel sector (see Table 11.2).

Table 11.2   Distribution of Tourism Licensed Accommodations (TÜRSAB, 2007)

Type	Class	Tourism Investment Licensed N	Tourism Operation Licensed N	Total
Hotels	5 Stars	153	216	369
	4 Stars	213	416	629
	3 Stars	183	587	770
	2 Stars	116	679	795
	1 Star	34	107	141
	Total	699	2,005	2,704
Holiday Villages	1st Class	27	73	100
	2nd Class	14	24	38
	Total	41	97	138
Motels		5	20	25
Boarding houses		43	75	118
Campings		5	8	13
Inns		1	4	5
Apart Hotels		19	107	126
Special Licensed Establishments		22	148	170
Golf Facilities with Accommodation		5	2	7
Training and Practice Establishments		1	3	4
Tourism Complex		6	2	8
Boutique Hotel		16	2	18
B Type Holiday Site		3	1	4
Mountain House		1	1	2
Rural Tourism Establishment		2	—	2
Total		869	2,475	3,344

There were almost 400,000 beds in over 2,000 enterprises certified by the Ministry of Tourism and another 350,000 beds in some 8,000 enterprises certified by municipalities. In the past decade, the number of beds has almost doubled to about 750,000. It is necessary to note that tourism statistics provided by the Turkish Statistical Institute and Ministry of Tourism and Culture do not include many small accommodations (e.g., thousands of boarding houses) that have no license from the ministry and/ or municipality. The structure of the sector shows two main organisational traits: there is a multitude of small enterprises and comparatively few major players, which have developed vertical and horizontal integrations. These latter organisations include multinational companies which have their offices and operations in every major destination in Turkey. There are quite powerful hotel and vacation village chains in the integrated structure of the Turkish tourism industry. There are also large national independent hotel and vacation village chains, of which a few operate hotels in other Mediterranean, Balkan, and Turkic countries. This expansion into key European generating markets is a major development in the internationalisation of a number of firms based in Turkey. In contrast, the development of the many domestic small tourism enterprises has mostly stalled.

INDICATORS OF ENVIRONMENTAL PERFORMANCE

Initiatives and developments which aim to address and promote improvement in the environmental performance of tourism enterprises in Turkey have been partly influenced by steps taken for integration to the EU and other international environmental policies. But they also arise from policies relating to tourism, as noted earlier. This combination leads to identifying a comprehensive set of indicators against which to consider the environmental performance of tourism enterprises, predominantly the hotel sector, in Turkey. These are summarised as follows.

Ensuring New Developments Meet Regulatory Requirements

The European Commission has made it a requirement of Turkey's accession to the European Union that the Environmental Impact Assessment (EIA) Directive of the EU is adopted. Legal provision for this is provided by the Environment Act, aided by the EIA Regulation, with temporary provisions (Ahmad & Wood, 2002). According to the EIA Regulation, hotels with fifty or more guest rooms must prepare an EIA pre-report and accommodation with over five hundred rooms, e.g., holiday villages, tourism complexes have to provide a full EIA report. Since 1994, 104 accommodation operations have received EIA approval from the authorities (http://www.cevreorman.gov.tr/). However, the majority of hotels in Turkey do not meet this legal requirement; for instance, only 20 per cent of hotels in Ankara have produced an EIA report. Hence, enforcement of currently applicable environmental legislation is seen to be of paramount importance under the prevailing conditions in Turkey.

Architecture and Landscape Planning

The large-scale and unplanned rapid growth of tourism has brought negative impacts on urban areas with rich cultural, heritage, and other appeals. New tourism accommodations and establishments have changed the original setting of many small towns designated exclusively for tourism, particularly in coastal and some central parts of Turkey. Basically, the way that tourism developments are constructed is capable of destroying the natural resources. A significant factor here is the need to pay due consideration to building design and landscape planning, especially in protected areas, coupled with the necessary coordination and control. The lack of such an approach is manifest in the national parks wherein uncontrolled developments have negatively impacted on both visual amenity value and the flora and fauna. These national parks are protected yet under constant threat of misuse from a host of various parties, including tourism developments. According to National Parks Act (No. 2873), all developments must be compatible with the environment, including, as appropriate, sewage management; native plants disturbed from the site and surrounding area must be relocated as an integral part of plans for landscaping and landscape restoration. The importance of hotel architecture and landscape design is more clearly recognised today and are significant criteria in Turkey's certification scheme known as the Pine Award (see following). The indicators included relate to planning that does not spoil natural and historical environments, hotel architecture in harmony with the environment, landscape planning, and using local materials in construction.

However, and whilst there are some excellent examples such as Club Aquamarine Holiday Village, Champion Holiday Village, and Myndos Hotel, Turkey's tourism accommodation mostly lacks environmentally friendly architectural and landscape design. There is a clear need for better and more effective building regulations and development controls to ensure that buildings and landscape designs are in harmony with the environment.

Certification and Ecolabelling

Awards, and particularly ecolabel accreditation schemes, have been viewed as promising self-regulatory mechanisms for improving the sector's environmental performance (Warnken et al., 2005; Sasidharan et al., 2002). Ecolabels have also been used to encourage the development of less-damaging, more environmentally friendly hotels as well as potential tools to educate and influence customer behaviour. Ecolabelling started in Europe in 1985 with the Blue Flag Award, granted by the Foundation for Environmental Education in Europe (FEEE), for beaches and marinas where environmental protection is a high priority. In 2007, 235 beaches and fourteen marinas received Blue Flag status, ranking Turkey fifth among forty-one countries. Ecolabelling developed significantly in the latter half of the 1990s and has been adopted by the tourism sector to promote a clean and green image. Today there are many ecolabels; for instance, the World Tourism Organisation identified fifty-nine ecolabelling or certification schemes by the start of this century (WTO, 2002). Also, various environmental assessment methods have been introduced to evaluate the environmental performance of hotels such as Green Globe 21 (GG21), which includes a set benchmarks specific to hotels, ECOTEL, Green Leaf, the EU Ecolabel in Europe, Energy Star in the United States, ISO 14000, and so on.

GG21 is a global certification programme developed by the World Travel and Tourism Council in 1998 to address sustainable development issues in the tourism industry. A few hotels have gained environmental management awards such as GG21 and Green Hotelier status. For instance, the 1998 Green Hotelier and Restaurateur of the Year award winner was Ibrahim Birkan, general manager of Club Alda, which has long been recognized in Turkey for its green operations and high environmental standards. The environmental programme started from the outset with the building of the hotel and was managed without destroying even a single tree. Its commitment continues; the installation of a new biologically treated water distribution system has reduced water use for grounds maintenance by over 50 per cent. It is the first resort in Turkey to use solar energy, which now accounts for 45 per cent of the hotel's hot-water requirements. However, the majority of hotels (approx. 90%) have not received environmental awards (Erdogan & Baris, 2007)

A far more widely recognised accreditation system for environmental management is ISO 14001. The goal of ISO 14001 is to support and recognise environmental protection and pollution prevention through the implementation of continuous improvement initiatives in a rigorous management framework. Such international standards can help hotels to establish environmental protection programmes and integrate them into a coherent framework, thereby enhancing relationships with government agencies, consumer groups, communities, and environmentally conscious investors and tourists (Chan & Wong, 2006; Font, 2002). Very few enterprises, for example, Iberotel Sarigerme Park, have gained ISO 14001 certification as few enterprises would meet the requirements on environmental policy, planning, and management activities (Erdogan & Baris, 2007).

TUI, the largest tour operator in Europe, has incorporated environmental and socioeconomic criteria as part of its purchasing policy based on the assessment of suppliers against an environmental checklist. The Iberotel Sarigerme Park Hotel has received the TUI Environmental Championship award annually since 1997; other TUI Environmental Champions (in 2005 and 2007) are Robinson's Clubs–Camyuva, Pamfilya, and Select Maris.

Club Asteria Belek was awarded the "Friend of Environment" Three Pine award (see following) and achieved Blue Flag status. There is just one travel agency which is a member of Tour Operators' Initiative for Sustainable Tourism Development (TOI)–Vasco; which is also the first travel agency certified with the TS-EN ISO 1999 and TS-EN-ISO 14001 by the Turkish Standards Institute.

In recognising the need for improving the environmental performance of the sector generally, the Turkish Ministry of Culture and Tourism started an environmental sensitivity campaign in 1992 to encourage tourism enterprises to contribute to environmental protection and conservation in their daily practices. The defined criteria include: harmony of the facility with nature, the choice of materials used in construction, the selection and use of landscape elements, isolation measures taken against noise, the quality and quantity of materials used for decoration of the facility, the measures and arrangements taken for energy and water conservation, the measures taken for fire prevention, the arrangements for waste management, wastewater treatment and reuse, kitchen and service materials used, the quality and quantity of consumables (e.g., detergents, disinfectants, and shampoos), environmental education materials (e.g., brochures and posters) for visitors, and environmental training of the staff. This is a voluntary certification programme for hotels whereby an enterprise that meets the requisite criteria can apply for accreditation. If successful, a "Friend of the Environment" certificate, known as the Pine Award, will be awarded. More than thirty hotels, mostly situated along the Mediterranean seashore, and predominantly five- and four-star establishments, have gained the Pine Award. However, the scheme is not well known; for example, few hotel managers in Ankara had heard about or were interested in the Pine Award (Erdogan & Baris, 2007).

Energy Use and Renewable Energy Management

Turkey is in the process of developing energy policies aligned with the requirements of the EU. To date, it has met the EU requirements in terms of adopting regulations on the energy labelling of fridges/freezers and ballast for fluorescent lighting. All five-star hotels in Turkey have effective energy management policies which aim to reduce costs and incorporate the use of energy-saving materials. In Ankara, it was found that most four- and five-star designated hotels do pay attention to the cost of energy use and seek to reduce such costs and use energy-saving materials. Energy-saving light bulbs were widely used in guest rooms, but the use of photocell lighting in washrooms was slightly above 40 per cent in Ankara hotels (Erdogan & Baris, 2007). However, it is hard to find any hotel with less than a five- or four-star designation that has introduced an efficient energy-saving practice. To date no evidence has been found of enterprises using renewable energy supplies such as wind turbines.

Water and Wastewater Management

It is generally recognised that water and waste management are important components of an overall environmental management program. Water consumption depends on the type, size, standards, and range of facilities and services; and is also subject to the climate and irrigation needs, and on existing water conservation practices. Water conservation is an issue, which is exacerbated in some areas due to excessive groundwater extraction partly as a result of the seasonal nature and geographical concentration of tourism. This high level of groundwater extraction needs to be urgently controlled. Overall, water use is a key issue of concern in many tourist areas.

In many destinations around the world, rapid mass tourism development has overloaded local sewage treatment and disposal infrastructure. Based upon his coastal studies, Tosun reports that "Environmental pollution has become an important problem at these popular local tourist destinations due to the lack of measures to cope with the generation of new or increased waste residues. Sewage disposal systems were installed solely according to local residents" (2001: 95). The carrying capacity of sewage disposal systems has been exceeded due to the rapid increase in the number of hotels and construction of second homes across Turkey. Moreover, since there has been a lack of control and regulation that could have prevented hoteliers from polluting the environment, particularly at the initial stage of development, it is possible that non-solid waste finds its way into natural water supplies and so causes the pollution of underground and surface water. This is despite the fact that regulation on water pollution control was brought into force in 1988 (subsequently modified in 2004) which defines the principles of pollution control for water sources. Enforcement is weak.

This situation is not helped by the limited number of wastewater treatment plants; 3,000 of the 3,225 municipalities do not have a waste treatment system—well below the requirements expected by the EU. In many tourist destinations and adjacent residential areas, wastewater treatment is insufficient or nonexistent. Wastewater treatment is therefore often limited to a few four- and five-star hotels. Large untreated volumes of wastewater run off into coastal waters, rivers, and lakes, potentially putting fragile freshwater and marine ecosystems at risk. According to research by Turkish Marine Environment Protection Association of 131 hotels, 80 per cent of hotels dump their waste in the sea; most hotels dump their used oil in the sea; 26 per cent have their own wastewater treatment systems; 13 per cent have a primitive septic system with no tanks; and 62 per cent have their septic system connected to the municipal system. Clearly, tourism enterprises need to participate in the voluntary monitoring of environmental pollution, promote the efficient use and cleaning of water and the recycling of used water.

Solid Waste Management and Recycling

Waste management and recycling are also criteria of the Pine Award. As with wastewater, infrastructure for solid waste management and recycling is improving but still poor. Infrastructure for tourism-related solid waste seems to be inadequate and recycling rates are very low, particularly in terms of the standards expected by the EU. However, the establishment of treatment plants, recycling companies, waste products, modern landfill and waste management facilities are steadily growing in number. Waste collection and disposal inevitably require the establishment of relations with the municipal government and with recycling firms. According to Municipal Law 1580, the municipal government collects waste and transports it to the disposal location. According to the Turkish National Environmental Action Plan, 18 per cent of restaurant waste and 25 per cent of hotel waste are recycled. Private recycling firms collect the recyclable waste from the source. A study by Erdogan and Baris (2007) of hotels in Ankara found that nearly one-third of the hotels (30%) sort their waste to extract recyclable material; approximately a third do some sorting and nearly 40 per cent do no sorting at all. Waste sorting was most common for the larger hotels: 43 per cent, 35 per cent, and 19 per cent of five-star, four-star, and three-star hotels, respectively. This tendency is reversed when they were asked whether they would sort their waste if the municipal government organised the collection: 67 per cent for five-star, 90 per cent for four-star, and 73 per cent for three-star hotels. The majority of hotels (92%) reported that they do not compost organic and food wastes. Not surprising, perhaps, given the very limited number of available composting sites; for example, Antalya has two composting centres and one modern landfill system in Kemer and Manavgat. During the interviews, the hotel managers were asked what kinds of waste were sorted. It was found that sorting was inadequate, with no predefined system for waste separation. On the other hand, the Radisson SAS Hotel (five stars) has three different containers to collect glass, plastic bottles, and paper. The Capital Hotel (three stars) collects paper, aluminium, and metal and sells them (Erdogan & Baris, 2007).

Ecofriendly and Responsible Purchasing

Studies in Turkey have found that hotels generally fail to meet the basic requirements of an environmentally sensitive purchasing policy that emphasises recyclable and reusable goods, energy-saving equipment, reduced use of detergents, and buying suitable containers for effective waste and pollution prevention (Erdogan & Baris, 2007). Invariably it is those hotels with five-, and though less so, four-star designations which do pay attention (albeit variable) to recyclables (63%), reusability (83%), energy efficiency (97%), and oxygen detergent (87%) in their purchases as Ozgen 's (2006) study in Izmir found

Environmental Education and Communication

The willingness and ability of facility management and staff to adopt greater environmental awareness and responsibility is crucial in striving towards a higher degree of sustainability in the tourism sector. Influencing the behaviour of guests through promoting perceived environmentally friendly behaviours has been recognised as another dimension of the environmental performance of operations (Leslie, 2007). There is a general lack of environmental awareness and concern, albeit some hotels give a high priority to the environment (Erdogan & Baris, 2007). Many studies indicate that there is an increase in consumer awareness of environmental issues and hotel managers are facing increased societal pressure to take action on environmental issues. Yet, there is a lack of environmental awareness and interest in sustainability issues. Few hotel activities are satisfactory in terms of environmental concerns. For instance, in Ankara in addition to showing little concern about environmental issues, most hotel managers lack knowledge of environmental management systems, the existence of recycling firms, energy management systems and environmental award programmes, and have little interest in belonging to environmental organisations. In order to achieve meaningful improvement, hotel managers must obtain adequate knowledge and develop appropriate concern for environmental issues. There is also a lack of interest in environmental education. In Ankara, for example, 27 per cent of hotels provide environmental education brochures for customers and 15 per cent provide environmental training for their employees; participation in environmental seminars and membership of environmental organisations (10%) were also found to be very low (Erdogan & Baris, 2007). The latter, partly at least, is accounted for by the limited number of environmental groups at the local level; seemingly there is less interest in such participation on the part of owners/managers of accommodation enterprises. There are also limited opportunities for enterprises to become involved in environmental initiatives, though it is noted that the World Wide Fund for Nature in Turkey is active in the field of responsible tourism and some of the larger hotels are active in community and environmental initiatives.

Using Local Goods and Benefiting Communities

Socioeconomic issues are increasingly being addressed in tourism standards, particularly in terms of the importance of local employment, local sourcing of goods and services, and participation in planning and decision making. The Certificate of Sustainable Tourism (CST), Smart Voyager (SV), Fair Trade Tourism South Africa (FTTSA), and Green Deal (GD) all consider local employment a priority, or even a nonnegotiable element of the scheme (Roe et al., 2003). Further, GG21 states that although a hotel should employ local people, this is a flexible element of the scheme's requirements; while all the schemes ask that 'where possible' hotels and enterprises use locally produced goods and services (Roe et al., 2003). These are all important aspects of the environmental performance of any tourism enterprise (Leslie, 2007). As yet, there are no government-set conditions and industry practices geared toward investing in specific geographical areas, with specific criteria for the use of local goods or services, employing local people and encouraging local financing. In Ankara, 26 per cent of hotels were identified as having an above-average consideration for the environment and localism in their purchasing activities (Erdogan & Baris, 2007). Yet a range of local goods are invariably available in every tourism location. However, there is a serious lack of interest in everything local in daily tourism activities, since most supplies consist of the popular goods of international and large national corporations.

CONCLUSION

Turkey has three core forms of tourism—nature-based (ecotourism), coastal (beach tourism), and heritage (cultural tourism), which are often developed within sensitive ecosystems (Erdogan, 2003). Thus the development and promotion of tourism is based primarily on the appeal of natural resources and maintaining the quality and condition of these resources is essential to tourism. Yet, whilst it is manifest that there has been progress towards addressing negative impacts on the part of the government, the facts of the matter are that there is a schism between the policy and daily practices of the tourism sector and the regulatory system that has developed, which aims to protect the very resources on which tourism is so dependent. Some of the prevailing environmental outcomes of tourism development to date include the degradation of ecosystems in national parks, forests, preserves and wetlands, depletion of grazing lands and water resources, loss of vegetation coverage, soil erosion, tree damage, root exposure, habitat fragmentation, degradation and destruction, introduction of exotic species, decline and extinction of wildlife species, and problems arising from intensive water extraction and effluent solid waste disposal. These outcomes to varying extents have arisen due to the rapid expansion of tourism supply within which context tourism enterprises are the major providers. In the wider context, progress has been made in the supply of drinking water and wastewater treatment services in tourist areas. In contrast, little progress is to be seen in the field of air quality, waste management, sanitary infrastructure, water quality, nature protection, industrial pollution, risk management, and proper monitoring and application of rules and regulations. It has been noted that environmental protection is becoming a key principle of Turkey's tourism policy. However, there is a need for wider acceptance of social and business responsibility with regard to the sensitive use of the country's natural resources and cultural heritage on the part of the owners/managers of tourism enterprises.

Few enterprises, predominantly those with the managerial personnel and financial resources, e.g., five-star hotels, have addressed their environmental performance and developed an environmental policy. The substantial majority of small-scale tourism enterprises and other comparatively resource-deficient parties or stakeholders currently have little or no involvement in environmental management activity. Despite some promising changes and expectations, there is a general lack of environmental knowledge and genuine concern for better environmental management and performance on the part of tourism enterprises. These shortcomings all too clearly emerge from the summary of a range of indicators of their environmental performance despite the existence of legal provisions suggesting to the contrary, which, as noted, are all too often not effectively enforced.

Environmental plans, policies and activities, enforcement of legal provisions, interest in environmental organisations and professional associations, waste minimisation and waste management and energy consumption generally lack attributes relevant to environmental protection and conservation. Furthermore, the managers mostly lack the necessary environmental knowledge and interest to meet the basic objectives of social and environmental responsibility. To help address these issues, tourism sector/establishments should:

- introduce measures to promote greater energy conservation and energy efficiency;
- improve the evaluation and control of the environmental impact of small and medium-sized enterprises;
- adopt tourism and environment indicators to evaluate their performance in carrying out action plans;
- ensure that environmental concerns are fully integrated in tourism development strategies;
- actively support the national strategic action plan which aims for progress towards sustainable development in the promotion and delivery of tourism products and services;
- expand the use of economic instruments to better internalise tourism's environmental costs and increase its financial contribution to environmental protection.

Overall, it is necessary to develop an integrated system of policy and practice that involves not only the managers and staff of tourism enterprises but also all parties concerned with environmental protection and sustainability. Furthermore, there is a need to re-evaluate policy at both national and local level and, in the process, bring into consideration the policies, practices, and training activities of the enterprises involved in the provision and delivery of tourism products and services. Mechanisms for permanent dialogue among tourism authorities, local public authorities, and the tourism sector are also required to reinforce the integration of environmental concerns in tourism policies and practices.

REFERENCES

Ahmad, B. & Wood, C., 2002. A comparative evaluation of the EIA systems in Egypt, Turkey, and Tunisia. *Environmental Impact Assessment Review*, 22, p.213–34.

Blue Flag Award: Available at: http://www.blueflag.org/App_criteria.asp [accessed 20 March, 2008].

Chan, S.W.E. & Wong, C.K.S., 2006. Motivations for ISO 14001 in the hotel industry. *Tourism Management*, 27(3), p.481–92.

Erdogan, N., 2003. *Ecotourism and environment*. Ankara: Erk.

Erdogan, N. & Baris, E., 2007. Environmental protection programs and conservation practices of hotels in Ankara, Turkey. *Tourism Management*, 28(2), p.604–14.

Font, X., 2002. Environmental certification in tourism and hospitality: progress, process and prospects. *Tourism Management*, 23(3), p.197–205.

Green Globe 21: Available at: http://www.greenglobe.org/ [accessed 4 July, 2008].

IH & RA Environmental Award: Available at: http://www.ih-ra.com/awards/ [accessed 15, February 2008].

Leslie, D., 2007. The missing component in the 'greening' of tourism: The environmental performance of the self-catering accommodation sector. *International Journal of Hospitality Management*, 26(2), p.310–22.

National Parks Act No. 2873, 2008. Republic of Turkey Ministry of Environment and Forestry. Available at: www.cevreorman.gov.tr/ [accessed 27, February, 2008].

Nohutcu, A., 2002. *Evaluation of public policymaking within the dynamics of governance in the field of tourism: the Turkish case*. Unpublished Ph.D. thesis, Ankara: The Graduate School of Social Sciences of METU, 2002.

Ozgen, I., 2006. *Waste management in large scale hotel establishments and a case study at Iber Hotel Sarigerme Park Resort*. Unpublished Ph.D. thesis, Izmir, 9 Eylul University.

Rein, H., 2004. *Ecotourism as market: demands and successes*. II International Tourism Environment and Culture Symposium, Izmir, p.67–89.

Turkish Ministry of Culture and Tourism, 2007. *Tourism strategy of Turkey—2023*. Available at: http://www.kulturturizm.gov.tr/genel/text/eng/TST2023.pdf [accessed 12 March, 2008].

Roe, D., Harris, C. & Andrade J., 2003. *Addressing poverty issues in tourism standards: a review of experience*. PPT Working Paper No. 14. Available at: http://www.propoortourism.org.uk/ 14_Standards.pdf [accessed 25, January, 2008].

Sasidharan, V., E. Sirakaya & Kerstetter, D., 2002. Developing countries and tourism ecolabels. *Tourism Management*, 23(2), p.161–74.

Tezcan, B., 2004. *Developing alternative modes of tourism in Turkey*. Unpublished master's thesis, Ankara: The Graduate School of Social Sciences of METU.

Tosun, C., 2001. Challenges of sustainable tourism development in the developing world: the case of Turkey. *Tourism Management*, 22(3), p.289–303.

Tosun, C. & Fyall, A., 2005. Making tourism sustainable: prospects and pitfalls. In F. Adaman & M. Arsel eds., *Environmentalism in Turkey: between democracy and development*. Burlington, VT: Ashgate Publishing, p.249–62 [accessed 25, March 2008].

TURSAB, 2007. Available at: http://www.tursab.org.tr/content/english/home/.

Warnken, J., Bradley, M. & Guilding, C., 2005. Eco-resorts vs. mainstream accommodation providers: an investigation of the viability of benchmarking environmental performance. *Tourism Management*, 26(3), p.367–79.

WTO, 2002. *Voluntary initiatives in tourism*. Madrid: World Tourism Organisation.

WWF, 2001. *Preliminary assessment of the environmental and social effects of trade in tourism*. WWF international discussion, Gland, Switzerland.

12 Environmental Performance and Tourism Enterprises in the UK
Progress towards Sustainability?

David Leslie

INTRODUCTION

Tourism services are as susceptible as any other business activity to the imperatives of contemporary environmentalism, which most simply expressed means 'going green': " . . . an approach which reflects much greater awareness of the interconnectedness of the economic, the physical and social dimensions of the environment rather than just the physical or natural e.g. pollution and damage" (Leslie, 2005: 251). Through the processes involved in the provision of products and services, which are largely fossil-fuel dependent (Kelly & Williams, 2007; Mintel, 2007), tourism enterprises generate pollution and waste, thereby placing additional burdens on the locality, the infrastructure, and wider environment to handle these by-products. At the same time, they generate employment opportunities and socio-cultural benefits for many people within the host community and possibly support environmental initiatives (see Blanco et al., 2008). However, the provision of tourism supply is dominated by small and medium-size enterprises (SME) within which category the majority of enterprises are "micro-businesses," i.e., less than ten employees. At the individual level these enterprises might be seen to be missing in environmental terms. But aggregated, their energy consumption and waste become substantial and thus tourism per se is a major polluter, and largely unregulated (Leslie, 2006). It is not difficult to concur with Blair and Hitchcock (2001) that, in comparison with most other sectors of consumer services, tourism overall has the most substantial negative impacts.

Attention to the environmental impacts of the operations of tourism enterprises emerged at the end of the 1980s, primarily catalysed by the Bruntland Report and the advocacy of sustainable development. Throughout the 1990s to date, government agencies and local authorities, directly or indirectly involved in tourism, have been promoting attention to many aspects of the environmental performance of tourism enterprises, complemented by the initiatives of various professional bodies (Leslie, 2001, 2005). An ongoing process which is still informed by the government's tourism policy: "A wise growth strategy for tourism . . . which integrates the economic, social and environmental implications of tourism and which spreads the benefits throughout society as widely as possible" (DCMS, 1999: 48). Further action plans and initiatives have reaffirmed this "message," a message recognised by the UNEP (2002) and in terms of the UK, more significantly by the European Union (EU).

Coupled with a plethora of non-sectoral specific policies and directives germane to sustainability not only reinforces the advocacy of environmental management systems (EMS) and related practices but also the need to attend to the wider aspects involved in maximising the role and contribution of tourism enterprises within their own locality, in effect, their connections with the community and the economy—the wider environment and hence sustainability. Thus the environmental performance (EP) of enterprises involved in tourism supply is therefore very much a part of today's international agenda and the quest for sustainable development. This brings into focus the principles of sustainable development and a problem, which is a lack of clarity and definition given it is still a contested concept (Butler, 1994). Thus to move forward the focus shifts to the objectives of SD, which are encapsulated in the following:

- social progress which recognises the needs of everyone;
- effective protection of the environment;
- prudent use of natural resources;
- maintenance of high and stable levels of economic growth and employment (SDC, 1999: 1).

In combination, these objectives demand more than just consideration of tourism's impact within destination locales but also the extent, and within which the equity, of the interrelationships between tourism enterprises and the local/regional economy, communities, and the environment. In the process, the aims of making progress towards the 'sustainability' of tourism enterprises, which is not in itself without problems (see Ko, 2005), can be promoted. As noted earlier, and in preceding discussions, enterprises in the UK have been encouraged through policy and government agencies, local government, and professional bodies to address their environmental performance for well over a decade. This attention was also evident in the promotion of Environmental Management Systems (EMS), e.g., BS 7750, ISO 14001 and the EU's Community EMS. Also of note is the International Hotels Environment Initiative (IHEI), which was promoted in the UK initially by Intercontinental Hotels and subsequently the WTTC. The IHEI is very much aimed at hotels and mainly adopted by national/international groups and gained little attention on the part of small operations or other categories of tourism enterprise. However, a perceived need for a system specifically for tourism enterprises led to the development and promotion of the Green Audit Kit and subsequently Scotland's Green Tourism Business Scheme (GTBS) (www.green-business.co.uk) as well as a number of other localised initiatives (see Leslie, 2001, 2002), of which the GTBS has been the most successful and is now the basis of a major scheme throughout the UK. The key question is not only what progress may have been made in response to such advocacy but also what are the reasons for, and barriers to, any lack of progress. This was first addressed in a major study of tourism enterprises in the Lake District National Park (LDNP) of England (Leslie, 2001). The primary aim of the project was to identify and evaluate the level of awareness, attitudes, and perceptions of green issues, and associated practices, of owners/managers of tourism enterprises. Further, to establish key influential factors, which help or hinder the adoption of such practices.

METHODOLOGY

The methodology formulated involved surveying the main categories of tourism enterprise. First, a primary survey for serviced accommodation was designed, informed by Bell and Morse's (2000) work on sustainability indicators, based on an extensive set of environmental performance indicators. These were derived specifically for hotels in order to ensure comprehensive and detailed coverage of all aspects of a hotel's operations pertinent to its environmental performance. After an initial pilot stage and refinement of the questionnaire, the survey was then implemented by mail. This questionnaire was then tailored to meet the different and specific aspects of each of the other categories of tourism enterprise. Subsequently, more detailed investigations to explore in depth the approach and actual practices of owners/managers of tourism enterprises were undertaken. Participation was in response to an invitation to participate further in the study, which led to a total of fifty interviews. These took the form of extended personal interviews, in effect environmental audits. Subsequently, based on the same methodology though appropriately amended for the change in geographical context, an extensive survey of rural tourism enterprises in Scotland was undertaken (Leslie, 2005). Then, the opportunity arose to replicate the audit stage of the LDNP study; only this time urban tourism enterprises were audited using the same interview format and questions but for a few minor amendments because of their location in Scotland. Thus, a longitudinal study has been established with three sets of data, namely the LDNP survey and audits of rural enterprises (2001), rural enterprises in Scotland (2005), and now urban enterprises in Scotland.

A key point on this convenience sample of fifty urban/city-based tourism enterprises is that they were invited, without any prior consideration to environmental matters, to participate in support of students undertaking a final year module in tourism, sustainability, and environmental management. Their participation is more influenced by this criterion than those involved in the earlier research who opted to participate on the basis of the invitation and explanation of the aims, namely to survey the views and environmental management practices of owners/managers. As such, it is argued that these findings are more indicative of the performance of the sector as a whole whilst also providing the opportunity to compare and contrast urban with rural enterprises and gain insights into possible evidence of progress over the period of the study. Other factors which should be borne in mind when considering comparative analyses is the time difference between the two sets of audited enterprises, i.e., eight years, the substantial increases in utility costs witnessed over this period and, particularly the more likely given the latter, the higher proportion of national company enterprises in the urban sample compared with the LDNP audited enterprises. Also of note is that there was a particularly high response rate from relatively new market entrants in the LDNP study, which further indicates the interest of participants in the earlier studies. This was evident in the genuine interest demonstrated in the surveys, subsequent discussions, and especially in the audits for the LDNP study but rarely found in the urban study. A factor which is attributed to the difference in the way the samples were gained, i.e., by responding to the invitation to participate vis-à-vis a direct request to support a student project.

FINDINGS AND DISCUSSION

Given the constraints of space it is not possible to present here anything other than a limited range of the data gained from the audits undertaken of enterprises in the Glasgow/West of Scotland region. In the process the findings are compared with the equivalent data from the major survey of rural enterprises in Scotland and with the outcomes of the audited enterprises in the LDNP. As the preceding discussion and indeed chapters within these pages attest, it is the awareness, attitudes, and perceptions of the owners/managers of tourism enterprises which are often of most importance outwith those organisations, predominantly national and international companies, wherein policy is dictated by head office. The focus therefore is on a cross section of findings with the aim of establishing a comprehensive insight of these enterprises and their wider environmental performance. Attention is given to staff development, purchasing patterns involving local products, and recycling activity as well as aspects of environmental management and the attitudes and perceptions of the owners/managers. First, key details of the participant enterprises are identified.

The rural enterprise study comprised a much higher proportion of micro-businesses and conversely there is a substantially higher proportion of medium-sized enterprises and also operations which are part of a national group. The higher proportion of small and medium-size enterprises is further evident in the revenue figures: 64 per cent have a turnover in excess of £0.5 million whilst 10 per cent have less than £100,000. A further influential factor on staffing and turnover is that demand for most of these enterprises is not notably seasonal. Thus continuity of revenues and demand in combination support appointment of full-time permanent staff. This is further supported by the findings that over the last five years all but two of these enterprises reported an increase in profitability and an increase in staffing over the same period. Significantly, by far the majority of staff come from within the area (including the managers) and thus the local economy and the host community gain through the multiplier effect. Whilst this is equally true for rural areas, the demand for staff may often exceed local resources and thus staff are imported, leading to the need for staff accommodation; such a need may also arise due to difficulties of access. Thus some socioeconomic benefits are lost to the locality.

CONNECTIONS WITH LOCAL ECONOMY

In the context of sustainability it is important to establish connections between an enterprise and the local economy. Further to employment, as noted earlier, enterprises can seek to support diversity in the economy through their purchasing patterns, for example, locally produced produce and products. By their very locality, urban enterprises are possibly less likely to have available within their area a range of local products and produce which they could access. However, and particularly over the last five years, initiatives promoting purchase of local products and produce have significantly increased their availability in many areas, including urban centres (see Defra, 2007). This is confirmed by the findings in that the response to questions on the availability of a predefined range of popular items indicated that these were available. With few exceptions, all respondents indicated that they would prefer to 'buy local,' noting in some cases that this was not possible given their company policy. It was also established that actual purchasing of locally produced products and produce was, at best, limited. Reasons, drawn from the findings of the earlier studies, to account for this are presented in Table 12.1. Summing up, it appears that "control"

Table 12.1   Factors Discouraging Local Produce Purchasing

Factor	Mean Response	
	Rural	Urban
Cost, i.e., too expensive	3.26	3.74
Portion control, e.g., not preportioned	2.35	2.89
Quality control	4.22	3.92
Availability	3.91	3.89
Time, i.e., time to go and purchase	3.20	3.69
Hygiene/environmental health/regulations	4.07	4.02
Lack of awareness, i.e., of what is available	2.89	3.15

Note: Mean based on scale of 1=not significant to 5= very significant and cost are the major barriers to 'buy local.' Other points noted by interviewees as to why they might not make such purchases were: delivery, service, limited choice, not convenient, which reflect earlier findings and also Revell and Blackburn (2004).

Another way through which enterprises can contribute to the local area is through the purchase of local crafts and products which might be suitable for daily use in the operation or for decoration and also to display for sale. In this way they can encourage production, promote sales, and help diversification in the local economy. The urban enterprises were found to be less supportive of this than their rural counterparts in the LDNP. This may be partly accounted for by the high presence, and accessibility, of arts and crafts producers and outlets in the LDNP compared with Glasgow and urban areas in the west of Scotland.

Overall, these enterprises could do much more in regard to building connections with the local economy.

ENVIRONMENTAL PERFORMANCE (EP), ENERGY, AND WASTE MANAGEMENT

Attention to their EP by the urban enterprises was found to be comparatively higher than their rural counterparts (see Table 12.2). These higher percentage figures for Scotland compared with the LDNP sample (in England) were also evident in a UK-wide general survey of business and industry (EA, 2007). These differences may be partly accounted for by the fact that VisitScotland has been actively promoting an EMS—the Green Tourism Business Scheme (GBTS)—since the late 1990s, which they specifically say will also be a promotional tool. This bears out Tzschentke et al.'s (2008) study which found accreditation by programmes such as the GBTS is seen as a promotional tool. However, the evidence that this actually does influence customer choice is limited (Mintel, 2007; and see following).

Table 12.2   Environmental Performance

Question	Yes (%)	
	LDNP	Urban
Is the environmental performance of the operation monitored in any way?	24	38
Does the business have a written environmental policy?	12	16
Has an environmental performance audit been undertaken?	20	28
Is the environmental performance of the operation communicated to staff?	16	44

Further analysis of the data established that those enterprises with a written environmental policy and those who have undertaken an environmental audit were either sole traders or part of a national company. Apart from this, no correlations were found on the basis of type of enterprise. This is very similar to Kirk's (1998) study and supports the findings of other studies that motivation for the introduction of EM practices is either self-motivated or a function of corporate policy (see Tzschentke et al., 2004; Chan & Wong, 2006).

The enterprises with an environmental policy correlate with those participating in a green business scheme; not necessarily the formal accreditation system of VisitScotland but, and all single cases, Green Glasgow, Hospitable Climates, or, as considered by one interviewee, the Carbon Trust. As the findings indicate, the absence of a written policy does not mean there is no attention to managing the environmental performance. What we find is that the larger enterprises give some attention to energy consumption, for example, the use of room key cards to switch on the electric fittings. Also, approximately 50 per cent of the accommodation operators seek to encourage their customers to be environmentally friendly in some way—most often this is through encouraging guests to use bath towels again rather than be laundered daily. Both of which illustrate EM practices in reducing energy consumption; thus cost savings. Secondly, they indicate ways of drawing guests' attention to environmentally friendly practices and thereby potentially influence their behaviour; a factor recognised as another dimension of the EP of operations (EU, 2004). Even so, 90 per cent take no steps to communicate to customers what the enterprise might do regarding environmental management. In comparison, 30 per cent of the LDNP enterprises did seek to promote related practices to guests, including not changing towels daily, encouraging recycling, and the use of public transport.

The significant increases in energy costs witnessed over the last five years suggests increased attention is being given to such costs. However, this was not found to be the case in general. Three quarters of the urban enterprises do not have any form of energy policy, which is substantially lower than the LDNP enterprises at 62 per cent. Further evidence of the limited attention to managing resources is identified by the finding that few enterprises monitor water consumption whilst waste is monitored by approximately 50 per cent, but comparatively few undertake any analysis of this and do not know if it is decreasing. These findings show little evidence of progress being similar across the surveys and Warnken et al.'s (2005) and Scanlon's (2007) studies.

Staff also have a key role to play in managing resources, which is predominantly recognised by the larger operations, especially in the findings for urban enterprises. Even so, 76 per cent (74% in case of LDNP sample) provide no guidance to staff in ways of reducing consumption. Activities identified by those enterprises, which do encourage staff, include promoting the reuse of paper for notes etc., saving energy use on laundry, recycling and using fewer paper products, e.g., napkins.

A further indication of their approach to resource and waste management is that of attention given to the three Rs—reduce, reuse, and recycle. A simple indicator of this is reuse of paper: approximately 50 per cent of the urban enterprises reuse paper in some way compared with 87 per cent in LDNP. Also, 12 per cent (56% in case of LDNP) purchase some type of recycled product—mainly paper products. Across a range of waste materials, e.g., glass, cans, paper, which can potentially be recycled, little is done, which apart from glass and paper is similar to the LDNP. However, approximately half the enterprises, substantially higher than in the LDNP study, recycle cooking oil and toner cartridges. The former perhaps because of the comparative density of enterprises in urban settings and thus easier to collect large volumes and second, due to the potential to convert such oil waste to a bio-fuel whilst the latter is probably due to suppliers taking back used cartridges; which does suggest progress in these two areas. The limited activity across other areas is partly due to a lack of space for holding containers, access issues, and limited support from local government. Overall, these findings are very similar to the previous studies and indicate little progress despite the pressures on local government to increase recycling arising from EU regulations and encouragement of households to recycle waste materials. Also, it could be argued that this lack of recycling activity conflicts with the view that 75 per cent of people in the UK believe that if there was more recycling then this would have a positive impact on reducing the UK's carbon emissions (Defra, 2007). However, as Holmes et al. (2008) found, behaviour within the home environment does not translate into behaviour whilst away; arguably, it appears that the same principle is applicable in the work environment.

PERCEPTIONS AND ATTITUDES OF THE OWNERS/MANAGERS

The audits explored the owner/managers' attitudes to the impact of their enterprise, and tourism more generally, on the environment. The managers of the urban enterprises generally were found to be less interested and less committed than their rural counterparts. Also, the impact of tourism per se on the area was considered of substantially less interest. These differences between the two samples may be attributed to the very different environments within which they operate, from the renowned landscape of the Lake District to inner-city Glasgow. But also, this evident lack of interest has been found in other studies (Revell & Blackburn, 2004; Carlsen et al., 2001).

Further to inquiries into commitment, participants were invited to indicate their agreement (or otherwise) on a number of statements covering a range of environmental matters (see Table 12.3). There is little substantive difference between the LDNP and urban results, though the latter agree

Table 12.3   Perceptions of the Sector's Impact and Related Aspects

Statement	Mean	
	LDNP	Urban
The *** sector has an impact on the environment.	4.02	3.90
The *** sector's impact on the environment is significantly less than the manufacturing sector.	3.54	3.50
*** operators who claim to be 'green' are using it as a marketing ploy.	3.06	3.40
Most owners/managers do not have time to worry about the environment.	2.92	3.20
Customers are not interested in whether an operation is environmentally friendly.	2.56	2.51
It is not possible to be profitable and be environmentally friendly.	2.06	3.00

Note: "xxx" = category of enterprise, e.g., accommodation, inns, attractions. Mean: based on scale of 1 = 'Strongly disagree,' 5 = 'Strongly agree.'

more with the 'green' claims being used as a marketing ploy and also "do not have time to worry about the environment."

The "ranking" of "customers not being interested" correlates with those enterprises identified as giving no attention to promoting 'green' practices (similar to Revell & Blackburn, 2004). However, it is also contrary to the findings of other studies, for example, Fairweather et al. (2005) and Masau and Prideaux (2003), which did show that there is some degree of customer interest in green accredited accommodation; particularly on the part of international visitors. These findings generally mirror the earlier surveys, with the exception of customer interest with which more enterprises in the LDNP agreed; and the Environment Agency's (2007) survey of SME in general. This ambivalence towards customer interest correlates with responses to other enquiries (see following) and, overall, indicates limited support for the introduction of EM practices.

AWARENESS OF EM AND RELATED SYSTEMS

A knowledge of an EMS is not a prerequisite to introducing EM practices, though it can be a key indicator of the likely involvement in such schemes (see Tzschentke et al., 2008). However, such systems present greater scope for the incorporation of such practices into the business and hold the opportunity for accreditation which can then be used in promotion. Thus, the study sought to establish the managers' knowledge of a number of the more commonly cited systems. The findings are presented in Table 12.4. As

Table 12.4   Awareness of Selected 'Green' Initiatives

Initiative	Aware (%)	
	Rural	Urban
BS 7750	23	16
Ecolabelling	15	14
ISO14001	17	14
The Green Audit Kit	4	10
Green Globe	6	2
British Airways Environment Awards	7	8
Green Business Scheme	27	20
IHEI	4	4

apparent, the results are similar across the two samples and also compared with the LDNP data. The one significant variance across the range is the awareness of the Green Business Scheme. This is perhaps to be expected given that VisitScotland has been promoting the scheme for a decade and thus the expectation that members at least would be aware. Even so, it is noteworthy that within the rural sample, approximately 50 per cent are members of VisitScotland and thus a higher level of awareness might justifiably be expected. It also appears that knowledge is limited, at best, to a few schemes.

Further analysis of the data found no substantive variance on the basis of other factors, for example, length of career in the sector. In the case of the LDNP there was a clear bias to awareness on the part of newer entrants, which is partially due to the promotion and activities of the Tourism and Conservation Partnership and green seminars (see Leslie, 2001). By way of comparison, 80 per cent of the audit interviewees in the urban group had not attended any form of green seminar. Also, the latter group show little increase in awareness, which is contrary to the findings of the Environment Agency (2005).

Awareness, though, does not mean participation/adoption, and thus their involvement in any of these systems was subsequently explored (see Table 12.5). The evident lack of participation reinforces Sasidharan et al.'s more general view that " . . . environmental education of consumers and increasing environmental awareness does not stimulate environmentally responsible behaviour . . ." (2002: 172). The majority of those involved in a green business scheme (three of which are accounted for by Green Glasgow, a Carbon Trust and Hospitable Climates) are all enterprises which are part of a regional/national organisation, which, in terms of motivation, reflects Chan and Wong's (2006) study into motivations for ISO 14001 in the hotel sector which found this to be a

Table 12.5   Involvement in Selected 'Green' Initiatives

Initiative	YES (%)	
	Rural	Urban
Made in Cumbria/Made in Scotland	4	0
Business Environment Network	2	4
Green Business Scheme	11	12
IHEI	2	0

corporate function. This finding further affirms the view that what the multi-national and national companies are doing in terms of EMSs is not representative of tourism supply as a whole, as also evident from the Environment Agency's study (2005).

Involvement in other green initiatives was also found to be very limited amongst the urban group. However, 24 per cent were involved in local projects or community schemes of which two in some way relate to a conservation scheme, thus indicating some degree of further involvement with the local community.

Awareness of EMS, given the absence of general media attention, may be attributable to membership of one or more professional organisations. This was explored with the interviewees which identified that owners/managers in rural areas are more likely to be a member of a tourism or local community forum and conversely a business forum if in an urban area, e.g., chamber of commerce. Membership of VisitScotland is not considered important by approximately 50 per cent of the urban enterprises. However, this is also influenced by the fewer number of accommodation operations in the urban sample. Few respondents were members of any other tourism, community, or environmental forum. This is a clear indication of both their involvement in professional organisations and of their "green" credentials. On this basis it can be speculated that the majority of owners/managers are not interested in the environment per se.

INFLUENTIAL FACTORS AND BARRIERS

On the presumption that enterprises may not have introduced a formal EMS, respondents were invited to address what would influence them to consider introducing EM practices. Drawing on the outcomes of previous research, a range of factors were presented and they were asked to indicate how likely each factor would be an influence on the basis of ranking from 1 = least likely to 5 = most likely (see Table 12.6). The rural enterprises, whether in Scotland or the LDNP, were found to be very similar. However,

Table 12.6   Factors Potentially Influential to Addressing Environmental Performance

Factor	Most important(%)	
	Rural	Urban
Customer care	52	42
Cost savings	59	66
Health and safety	49	52
Care for the environment	48	18
Customer demand	39	34
Personal beliefs	35	12
Quality management	32	38
Public relations	29	30
Potential legislation	22	32
Industry standards	14	32
Competitors' actions	6	14

as the table shows, the urban group evidence substantial differences regarding the influence of "Care for the environment" and "Personal beliefs," considering these of little importance comparatively. In contrast, there is evidence of a bias towards cost savings, potential legislation, and industry standards amongst the urban sample. The importance given to cost savings reflects other studies (see Leslie, 2001; Bohdanowicz, 2005; Blanco et al., 2009) and is a factor recognised by those who participate in Scotland's GTBS (Tzschentke et al., 2008). That customer demand is perceived to be of comparative limited importance, on the one hand, supports Leidner's (2004) findings but is in contrast to other studies (as noted earlier).

Overall, these findings suggest a large degree of ambivalence with a clear bias to government regulation coupled with economic instruments. This bias, comparative with previous studies, is arguably a reflection of the lower proportion of micro-enterprises and owner-managed enterprises in the urban sample, in effect suggesting that larger organisations respond to external, particularly government, pressure rather than individual attitudes. This is reinforced through comparative analysis of the mean figures for the audited enterprises.

Whilst the foregoing findings are drawn from the surveys (including the audited enterprises), this area of enquiry was further explored in the audits. Interviewees were invited to indicate how significant a role they would predict each of these factors would play in advancing progress over the next five years. They were invited to grade their responses on the basis of '1 = minor influence' to '5 = major influence.' The findings, based on the

Table 12.7 Potential Factors of Influence

	Mean	
Question	LDNP	Urban
Government policy to adopt environmentally friendly practices.	3.58	3.65
National Park Authority/local government presents clear policy favouring such action.	3.22	3.29
Green consumerism.	2.98	2.84
Legislation requiring environmental audits.	2.92	3.60
Economic instruments, e.g., taxes.	2.86	3.60
Voluntary agreements and industry-led initiatives.	2.78	2.35
Business customers requesting environmental policy statements.	2.62	2.45
International/national role models.	2.48	3.02
Voluntary environmental reporting.	2.44	2.64

Mean: Based on '1 = minor influence' to `5 = major influence.'

mean response, are presented in Table 12.7 and correlate with their previous responses in the survey (see Table 12.6). There is little evidence of any general change in perspectives over the time span between the two sets, which brings into question whether, at least in terms of the perceptions of these owners/managers, there has been any progress.

"Government policy" is considered to be the most influential factor in encouraging the adoption of environmentally friendly management practices. Possibly reflecting more the reality of demand is that green consumerism is seen to be less influential than the foregoing factors and only slightly more so than legislation, which rather supports Mintel's (2007) study which found that in the main, tourists' priorities lie with good accommodation and facilities. Their research also showed that the number of tourists interested in more responsible tourism had dropped since 2003.

In concluding this area of investigation, each interviewee was presented with a range of statements relating to the progress of operators towards sustainability and invited to rate each statement on the basis of '1 = strongly disagree' to '5 = strongly agree.' The results, based on the mean response for each statement, are presented in Table 12.8. The responses clearly demonstrate that 'good housekeeping' cuts costs. Yet cost is often cited as a mitigating factor against the introduction of an EMS. Second ranked in agreement is that the primary determinant in tourists' decisions on choice of accommodation is price. The limited importance placed on guests' interest suggests the perception that they, i.e., customers are not really interested, an outcome evidencing little change from the findings of earlier studies (see Hobson & Essex, 2001; Leidner, 2004; Revell & Blackburn, 2004), though, as noted earlier, not all.

Table 12.8   Progress towards Sustainable Development

	Mean	
Question	*LDNP*	*Urban*
Commitment to "greening" the business is being used to gain competitive advantage.	2.34	2.60
Apart from a few notable examples, little progress has been made over the last five years.	3.26	3.43
Compared with five years ago, owners/managers have a better understanding of how to maintain financial performance while improving environmental and social performance.**	3.02	2.73
Anyone can introduce some environmentally friendly practices and claim to be green.	3.80	3.60
The "first steps" practices, e.g., reducing heating costs and waste all save on costs.	4.34	4.07
Once the "first steps" have been taken, there are a few, if any, cost savings.	2.80	2.53
By and large, the deciding factor for potential customers is the price of the accommodation	3.90	3.94
Operators should support local producers, even if the products cost a little more.	3.78	3.02
Environmental problems are threatening the future of the local tourism industry.	2.84	2.65
Guests are not really concerned about the environment.	2.82	3.07

**Those respondents who indicated their commitment to reducing negative environmental impacts were more likely to disagree with this statement.

BARRIERS

The foregoing findings are certainly subject to a number of external and internal influences on the business. First and foremost is the 'health' of the business and thus, it is argued, owners/managers will prioritise those factors which are seen to be most influential to their ongoing performance. Thus, the interviewees were presented with a range of factors and invited to grade these in terms of importance on the basis of 1 = not at all important to 5 = very important. The results, based on the mean responses, are presented in Table 12.9.

Whilst addressing customer complaints is considered most important, profitability and financial performance are also considered to be more than of "average" importance. Staff retention is notable for the importance given to it and this is further evident in the provision of in-house training (by 84%) and opportunities presented for staff development (72%). In contrast, the low level of importance given to environmental factors is further evident in that 25 per cent consider staff are not concerned about

Table 12.9 What is of Importance to the Owners?

Factor	Mean LDNP	Urban
Addressing customer complaints.	4.80	4.20
Maintenance/improvement of profitability.	4.46	4.46
Achievement of budget.	4.26	4.39
Staff retention.	3.04	4.07
Achieving environmental targets.	2.42	2.27
Environmental reporting.	2.22	2.41

the environmental performance of the operation whilst 50 per cent do not know whether they are or are not concerned, as also found by Revell and Blackburn (2004). In contrast, environmental management is considered to be of least importance. As well as correlating with the other findings, this also may explain why commitment is so limited. Secondly, why there is so little voluntary action and that government intervention is seen as the major influencing factor, which is further affirmed by the 34 per cent of interviewees, who do not consider that the practices identified within the audits should be more widely adopted. Overall, such outcomes are evident in other similar studies.

Further inquiries into what respondents considered to be barriers to progress evidenced recurrent themes (see Kirk, 1998; Leslie, 2001; Barnett, 2004; Chan, 2008) of costs (28%), constraints of lack of time (14%), and knowledge (8%), and in some cases "effort." A need for more information was also noted: 20 per cent of the urban enterprises (32% in the LDNP findings) and 50 per cent in the EA's (2007) general survey; the perception of customers and lack of exemplars were also noted as not being helpful. In response to further inquiry, it was often suggested that the latter should come from the local authority and/or VisitScotland. Throughout the interviews, respondents had the opportunity to identify any initiatives or support networks that might have been overlooked. Only those few already noted, e.g., Carbon Trust, were identified and no one made reference to readily accessible information sources and guidance such as the Business Environmental Training Initiative Plus or to the Environment Agency's "NetRegs" or other information.

CONCLUSION

This analysis and discussion of a range of outcomes from the three data sets covering a period of eight years evidence remarkable similarities across a spectrum of EM practices and as regards the attitudes and perceptions of the owners/managers of these enterprises. A major difference, though, between the enterprises in Scotland, whether rural or urban, and those in England's Lake District is that the Scottish enterprises were more likely to be involved in a green business scheme, e.g., GTBS, than the Lakeland enterprises, which were far more likely to be involved in a tourism conservation initiative, i.e., Tourism and Conservation Partnership. Not surprising, perhaps, given that both schemes are confined to the respective geographic contexts, as such reinforcing the view that for any EMS or environmental initiative to be successful to any degree it needs to be promoted directly to and adopted by the local/regional community. Even so, such schemes are found not to be that popular. A contributory factor to this outcome is that it is predominantly accommodation enterprises which participate in an EMS such as the GTBS rather than other categories of tourism enterprise, e.g., inns, restaurants, attractions, which is perhaps due to a perception on the latter's part that such schemes are seen as systems for hotels. However, as noted in the opening discussion, the EP of these enterprises is more than just whether they have introduced an EMS or related practices but also their business performance, employment, and connections with local/regional community and economy. This brings into focus the findings from the audited enterprises and particularly the urban group, thus opportunities to compare these findings with the earlier audits and consider any emergent differences which might indicate progress in the adoption of EM practices over the intervening period.

First, it is to be noted that the urban enterprises predominantly have been enjoying a minimum period of five years of improved business performance. This has not only been a period of substantial economic growth in the UK but also one that has witnessed significant increases in utility costs. Over this period all but a few of these enterprises have maintained or increased their staff. Even so, staff retention was considered significant compared with the LDNP group, which may in part at least be due to the higher proportion of enterprises employing more than ten persons. However, both groups indicated a similar problem with staffing—that of the availability of quality recruits, a factor which might be considered surprising given the expansion of further and higher education witnessed over the last decade. Other aspects of interrelationships with the local economy and community explored included the purchase of locally produced produce and products, which established a high level of support for the idea but little manifest in practice; as such similar to the LDNP. Reasons for such limited purchasing were given as cost, availability, quality, and consistency. Evidently, in many cases in both rural and urban enterprises local suppliers are often overlooked due to competition from, for example, regional/national suppliers, supermarkets, and wholesalers where the actual benefits, e.g., cost savings, of purchasing are more evident. Purchasers in general are less inclined to consider the longer term value and benefit of buying locally in terms of supporting the local community and favour short-term gain. Overall, these findings evidence no signs of progress despite the promotion of such within the tourism sector and, certainly in the last few years, more generally in society. This further reinforces the noted primary importance of profitability and achieving budget targets to the majority of these enterprises. Even so, there is no doubting the fact that these enterprises could, and in terms of sustainability should, be increasing their demand for locally produced produce and products.

Further indications of the attitudes of owners/managers are found in their approach to recycling waste materials. Both samples were found to recycle glass and paper to varying extents, but significant differences between the two sets were that the urban group is far more likely to recycle waste cooking oil and printer cartridges. These increases suggest some progress attributable to suppliers collecting used cartridges and the increasing demand for bio-fuel. However, both groups indicated similar problems with recycling other materials, e.g., storage, collection. The fact that the urban group presented similar comments is once again possibly surprising given the emphasis on this area for local authorities and waste removal companies.

A major aspect of the promotion of any accredited EMS is that of its value as a promotional tool in influencing consumer choice. Secondly, that EM practices are of interest to customers. Albeit that the findings of both groups are somewhat ambivalent, the conclusion drawn from the investigations into these areas is they perceive that customers are not really interested. They react to perceived needs and interests of their customers rather than being proactive and encouraging them to be more aware and 'environmentally friendly' in their behaviour. Again, these findings evidence little sign of progress in spite of all the advocacy of the "three Rs" in society witnessed in the last few years.

It could be argued that an EMS lies at the heart of an enterprise's environmental performance. Its very introduction provides clear signals of the owners/managers' attitudes and values. On such a basis, this aspect of the findings merits further consideration. In the case of the urban enterprises it was found that they are more likely to monitor their environmental performance, have a written environmental policy, undertake an environmental audit, and communicate this environmental performance to their staff in comparison with the LDNP audits by factors of approximately 50 per cent, 30 per cent, 30 per cent, and 180 per cent, respectively. On cursory consideration this suggests significant signs of progress. However, there are a number of factors that counteract such an interpretation. First, the size of the enterprise is often an influential factor in that the smaller the enterprise, the more likely there is to be an absence of formal procedures regarding these areas. For example, in the case of the LDNP sample, interviewees, whilst more likely to say no to a statement which might imply a formal procedure, they still, as one interviewee said, "have a regard for environment performance, including waste" (Leslie, 2001: 109). Second, the urban sample included a higher proportion of small-size (i.e., not micro) enterprises and thus their energy supply costs are higher which, given the increased costs of supply, suggests that they would pay more attention to this facet of their operation. This, in part, also accounts for the higher number of urban enterprises which communicate their environmental performance in some way(s) to staff; e.g., such communications in some cases were found to be based on the mantra of 'cut costs.' Overall, these findings, rather than indicating some degree of progress, rather confirm that the comparative larger enterprises are more attentive to resource costs than their smaller counterparts. In many cases this is understandable given that the latter would find it difficult to disaggregate, for example, the energy supply costs attributable to delivering their customer service from that of their own consumption in the case of the many tourism enterprises which are also the homes of the owner/manager. Furthermore, the government's introduction of an energy tax on consumption appears to have little effect in catalysing further developments in this area.

In total, whilst owners/managers consider that they are committed to their environmental performance in some way(s), this is overshadowed by greater attention being paid to attaining maximum financial returns. Findings from the attitudinal questions further affirm this conclusion whilst the results across all categories of supply are similar, evidencing a degree of cynicism and a large amount of ambivalence. Significantly, for those enterprises that have introduced EM practices, no common factors on basis of category or type of enterprise were found. But what does emerge from these audits is a common factor between those owners who do adopt such practices and further seek accreditation through a scheme such as the GTBS, which are similar attitudes and values. Alternatively, it is a function of company policy in the case of larger organisations, e.g., national. However, in such cases it may equally be argued that there is someone in a key position championing the introduction of an EMS. In the absence of such a person, the recurrent themes of cost, lack of awareness, and information serve to explain or justify a lack of adoption of EM practices.

Overall, the findings provide a valuable review of the current position of the environmental performance of tourism enterprises—their sustainability—and the incorporation of EM practices and systems. There are many owners who consider the environmental performance of their enterprise in some way(s) and who, along with potentially many other enterprises, may well respond positively to effective promotion of environmental management systems and initiatives designed to promote and further linkages with the economy, environment, and community, as long as such promotion is presented in the right way, i.e., positively with the "right message." But further encouragement and promotion is needed. As the Countryside Agency argued, ways must be developed " . . . to encourage new and existing tourism businesses to adopt socially and environmentally sustainable practice" (cited in Leslie, 2001: 305).

REFERENCES

Barnett, S., 2004. *Perceptions, understanding and awareness of Green Globe 21: the New Zealand experience.* State of the Art Conference II, Glasgow, July.

Bell, S. & Morse, S., 2000. *Sustainability indicators: measuring the immeasurable.* London: Earthscan.

Blair, A. & Hitchcock, D., 2001. *Environment and business.* London: Routledge.

Blanco, E., Rey-Macquieira, J. & Loxano, J., 2009. Economic incentives for tourism firms to undertake voluntary environmental management. *Tourism Management,* 30(1) pp. 112–22.

Bohdanowicz, P., 2005. European hoteliers' environmental attitudes. *Cornell Hotel and Restaurant Quarterly,* 46(2), p.188–204.

Butler, R., 1994. Alternative tourism: the thin edge of the wedge. In V. Smith & Eadington, W.R., eds., *Tourism alternatives problems and potentials in the development of tourism.* Chichester, UK: John Wiley.

Carlsen, J., Getz, D. & Ali-Knight, J., 2001. The environmental attitudes and practices of family business in the rural tourism and hospitality sectors. *Journal of Sustainable Tourism,* 9(4), p.281–97.

Chan, E.S.W., 2008. Barriers to EMS in the hotel industry. *International Journal of Hospitality Management,* 27(2) pp. 187–96..

Chan, S.W.E & Wong, C.K.S., 2006. Motivations for ISO 14001 in the hotel industry. *Tourism Management,* 27, p.481–92.

Chan, W.W., 2005. Partial analysis of the environmental costs generated by hotels in Hong Kong. *International Journal of Hospitality Management,* 24(4), p.517–31.

Connelly, J. & Smith, G., 2003. Politics and the environment: from theory to practice. 2nd ed. London: Routledge.

DCMS, 1999. *Tomorrow's tourism: a growth industry for the new millennium.* London: Department of Culture, Media and Sport.

Defra, 2007. *Survey of public attitudes and behaviours toward the environment.* London: Department for Environment, Food and Rural Affairs. August.

EA, 2007. *Business and industry—more small businesses taking environmental actions.* London: Environment Agency.

Environment Agency, 2005. *Environmental awareness is on the way up the SME agenda.* London: Environment Agency, UK Government.

Environment Agency, 2007. *Green business—the financial angle.* Available at: http://www.environment-agency.gov.uk/business/1768048/1768064/1768585/?lang=_e [accessed 11 March 2008].

EU, 2004. *Strategy for integrating the environment into industry.* Available at: europe.eu.int/scadplus/leg/en/lvb/128093.htm [accessed 5 November 2004].

Fairweather, J.R., Maslin, C. & Simmons, D.G., 2005. Environmental values and response to ecolabels among international visitors to New Zealand. *Journal of Sustainable Tourism,* 3(1), p.82–98.

Hillary, R., 2004. Environmental management systems and the smaller enterprise. *Cleaner Production,* 12, p.561–69.

Hobson, K. & ᵣₛex, S., 2001. Sustainable tourism: a view from accommodation businesses. *Service Industries Journal,* 21(4), p.133–46.

Holmes, K., Miller, G., Scarles, S. & Tribe, J., 2008. "I just don't think about it." Public attitudes towards sustainable leisure. In D. Leslie guest ed., *Leisure, consumerism and sustainable development: "mission impossible."* Brighton: Leisure Studies Newsletter 80, July, p.27–31.

Johnson, D. & Turner, C., 2003. *International business—themes and issues in the modern global economy.* London: Routledge.

Kelly, J. & Williams, P. W., 2007. Modelling tourism destination energy consumption and greenhouse gas emissions, Whistler, British Columbia, Canada. *Journal of Sustainable Tourism*, 15(1), p.67.

Kirk, D., 1998. Attitudes to environmental management held by a group of hotel managers in Edinburgh. *Hospitality Management*, 17, p.33–47.

Ko, T.G., 2005. . Development of a tourism sustainability assessment procedure: a conceptual approach. *Tourism Management*, 26(3), p.431–45.

Leidner, R., 2004. *The European tourism industry—a multi-sector with dynamic markets. Structures, developments and importance for Europe's economy.* Brussels: EC, Enterprise DG (Unit D.3) Publications.

Leslie, D., 2001. *Environmental audit of the tourism industry in the Lake District National Park.* Report for Friends of the Lake District/Council for the Protection of Rural England, Kendal.

Leslie, D., 2002. The influence of government agencies on the greening of tourism enterprises. *Tourism Today*, 2 (Summer), p.95–110.

Leslie, D., 2005. Rural tourism businesses and environmental management systems. In D. Hall, I. Kirkpatrick, & M. Mitchell eds., *Rural tourism—issues and impacts.* Aspects of Tourism Series 26, Clevedon, Channel View, p.228–49.

Leslie, D., 2006. Scottish rural tourism enterprises and the sustainability of their communities: a local Agenda 21 approach. In M. Augustyn & R. Thomas eds., *Tourism in the new Europe, perspectives on SME policies and practices.* Advances in Tourism Research Series. Oxford: Elsevier, p.89–108.

Masau, P. & Prideaux, B., 2003. Sustainable tourism: a role for Kenya's hotel industry. *Current Issues in Tourism*, 6(3), p.197–208.

Mintel, 2007. *Holiday lifestyles—responsible tourism in the UK*. Mintel International Group Limited. Available at: http://academic.mintel.com/sinatra/oxygen_academic/search_result [accessed 3 March 2008].

Revell, A. & Blackburn, R., 2004. *UK SMEs and their response to environmental issues.* Kingston: Kingston University, Small Business Research Centre. March.

Sasidharan, V., Sirakaya, E. & Kerstetter, D., 2002. Developing countries and tourism ecolabels. *Tourism Management*, 23, p.161–74.

Scanlon, N.L., 2007. An analysis and assessment of environmental operating practices in hotel and resort properties. *Hospitality Management*, 26, p.711–23.

SDC, 1999. *UK government's strategy for sustainable development.* London: UK Government Sustainable Development Commission.

Tzschentke, N. et al., 2004. Reasons for going green in serviced accommodation establishments. *International Journal of Contemporary Hospitality Management*, 16(2), p.116–24.

Tzschentke, N.A., Kirk, D. & Lynch, P.A., 2008. Going green: decisional factors in small hospitality operations. *International Journal of Hospitality Management*.,27, p.126–33.

UNEP, 2002. *Industry as a partner for sustainable development: tourism.* Paris: United Nations Environment Programme, Division of Technology, Industry and Economics.

Warnken, J., Bradley, M. & Guilding, C., 2005. Eco-resorts vs. mainstream accommodation providers: an investigation of the viability of benchmarking environmental performance. *Tourism Management*, 26(3), p.367–79.

Conclusion

The rise of the green agenda, combined with exhortations on the impact of climate change, has catalysed a raft of policy initiatives designed to address global pollution and promote the objectives of sustainable development. From the outset, this text aimed to establish a comprehensive view of the responses of tourism enterprises to this agenda across the world. However, it is impossible within one manageable text to cover all the policies, programmes, and initiatives to, and the actions of, tourism enterprises given such a scope. Thus a compromise was required to achieve a balance of articles which collectively cover the key dimensions of the environmental agenda and the implications, policy responses, and initiatives pertinent to tourism enterprises. This led to the formulation of the scope of the introduction and opening chapters, which built on and developed the key themes and issues running throughout this text.

The broad contextual background established through these opening chapters identified that the promotion of progression towards sustainable development has and continues to be a key catalyst in drawing attention to the environmental performance of tourism supply in broader terms rather than just the more manifest impacts of development on the physical environment. Therefore, it is not so much a matter of sustainable tourism but rather what measures are being taken to make it a less unsustainable form of consumption. In total, these early chapters provided an essential overarching discourse and context for the subsequent chapters on specific countries.

Progress towards sustainability in tourism requires an overall strategy, which aims to promote diversity and added value within the local economy. Thus the need for tourism enterprises to be analysed and evaluated in the context of the local economy, environment, and community. This supply side of tourism is dominated numerically by small and micro-businesses and accounts for the foundation of tourism in any destination in general. Furthermore, they are very much part of the local community and as such they hold tremendous potential to contribute towards achieving the balancing act between the three pillars of sustainability; especially through adopting and promoting environmental management practices which may then diffuse into the wider community (and vice versa). Thus, the focus of many chapters has been on micro and small/medium size enterprises. Often the enterprises discussed are in the accommodation sector, which still accounts by far for the majority of studies in this area. However, this has not been to the exclusion of larger operations, which in the case of hotels and resort complexes has affirmed that it is the larger scale enterprises which are more likely to have introduced environmental management practices, notably in the area of energy saving, i.e., cost reduction.

Collectively, these chapters illustrate differences in approach and response to the sustainability agenda. They combine well to present a detailed analysis of the progress (or otherwise) of tourism enterprises towards enhancing their environmental performance. It is clear that in every area, whilst appropriate responsive action is limited, there are tourism enterprises which have adopted environmental management practices, albeit such practices may be limited in scope. But each practice adopted is a positive step and a measure of progress towards sustainability by way of reducing their ecological footprint. There is still substantial scope for the tourism sector as a whole to increase its environmental performance across a whole range of sustainability indicators; such as:

- from energy management to waste management and recycling
- water management
- purchasing policies and practices and use of 'green' products
- support for other sectors of the local/regional economy
- community involvement
- conservation initiatives

Certainly, there are reservations on the part of some owners/managers on the need to address the environmental performance of their operations. However, there will always be reluctance on the part of some, or more likely the majority, of enterprises and organisations to change in advance of explicit need or direction. This "resistance" is all the more apparent in the context of sustainability. Yet international, intra-regional, and state organisations and agencies evidently have been seeking to address these issues and formulate appropriate polices, but manifestly there is lack of concerted action, which was notably advocated over a decade ago by the World Travel and Tourism Council (WTTC, 1996: 4).

In all of the foregoing examples, we can identify some form of tourism policy directly relating to the environment, often complemented by one or more ecolabel certification programmes; yet these are gaining limited support irrespective of whether they are well established or comparatively recent. Furthermore, there is a proliferation of such schemes, suggesting every region, every category of supply in every country requires their own scheme rather than seeking to adopt (and adapt if necessary) the same certification programme as elsewhere. There are exceptions in terms of more widely recognised and used schemes such as Green Globe, which has been heavily criticised, and the International Hotels Environment Initiative, which is hardly known outside of the Green Hotelier and major hotel companies.

Overall, whilst some progress is evident the predominant picture, as portrayed by Mastny, is that: " . . . while many industry efforts embrace a shift toward environmental sustainability, they are less willing to incorporate social and cultural needs, including addressing labour and employment issues, protecting cultures, and maximising linkages with local economies and communities" (Mastny, 2002: 120). In this sense the findings are not unexpected and effectively demonstrate that the policies presented by leading bodies are often little more than rhetoric. This is not surprising given that often such organisations are not part of the actual business sectors they seek to influence. Furthermore, such outcomes should also not be unexpected given the very limited awareness of such policies, a factor which not only brings into question their value, approaches to dissemination, and implementation but also poses the very question: Just who are such policies designed to serve?

The oft cited lack of awareness is also questionable. Certainly, owners/managers might not be aware of the information available through tourism organisations and professional bodies in this field. Even so, it is difficult to understand such a lack of awareness given the rise in media attention over the last few years to global issues—from global warming to food miles, protocols, and "energy" crises catalysed by fluctuations in the price of oil. At the same time we have witnessed increasing activity in promoting the reduction of waste and recycling and the introduction of "green taxes" on energy consumption and fuel. Thus irrespective of what one might anticipate of the knowledge and awareness of the owners/managers of these enterprises regarding sectorally based policy and initiatives, it is arguable that their awareness, and responsive action, in areas such as energy and waste management as a result of the preceding factors justify expectations of higher levels of awareness than are evident in these findings. The key point here is the need to raise awareness and knowledge of what can be done and that adoption and positive action follow this. As the various chapters identified, awareness does not always lead to positive action, and thus there is the need for measures that continue to promote and encourage such action. One approach would be to establish the support of local organisations such as tourism fora, chambers of commerce, business enterprise networks and other relevant bodies to promote the introduction of environmental management systems but not only to tourism enterprises but all businesses in the destination.

Quintessentially tourism enterprises are managed by people who predominantly live and work in the locality and have similar attitudes and values as others. It is a person's attitudes and values that lead to a particular environmental performance, yet awareness and concern tend to revolve around the home at best and rarely translate into actions in leisure-based behaviour outwith the home environment (Holmes et al., 2008). This arguably applies equally to their business. Therefore the overall aim by governments, consumer associations, tourism companies, and media should be to raise consumers' awareness with the aim of changing consumption behaviour and tourists' choices (Djerba Declaration, 2003). This is not as difficult as it might appear. For example, owners/managers are comparatively quick to introduce measures which are perceived to improve revenues, as demonstrated by the comparatively rapid introduction of e-mail facilities and Web sites. But whilst we consider tourism enterprises within the context of destinations, attention also needs to focus more widely on the destination itself and development. A generally recognised feature of tourism development is that in its primary stage the 'product' is essentially highly localised. However, as it develops, demand increases and supply expands, leading to inward investment by external companies and increasing imports to the area to expand supply and meet visitor needs. This pattern of development is increasingly rapid: witness Dubai. Thus, it is all the more important to investigate the extent to which tourism enterprises are locally owned and managed and the level of interconnections with other sectors of the economy and the community as well as considering the operational aspects of enterprises in terms of environmental performance—in other words, the triple bottom line. Tourism therefore should not be seen in isolation of the context—the environment—within which it takes place and hence a holistic approach to its development needs to be adopted. Yet, given the often rapid expansion of tourism, whilst a destination may be considered successful in terms of demand it may be not so well judged in terms of the way it has developed, as exemplified by Mensah (Chapter 8) and Erdrogan (Chapter 11). Precedence is all too often given to economic factors with socio-cultural and other environmental dimensions gaining comparatively limited consideration.

Thus, a key weakness in terms of progress towards sustainable development objectives in tourism is that much discourse, and indeed, approaches to tourism and development are predicated on economic factors. In this sense it is seen as 'industry.' In effect, tourism is "just tourism" (see Hultsman, 1995); or as Britton expressed: " . . . the capitalistic nature of the phenomenon . . ." (cited in Hall & Page, 1999). What could help progress is to consider tourism development from the perspective of the local residents; thus where a development clearly impacts on, for example, the visual amenity, it might be less likely to be promoted; other examples could be water usage by tourists and related facilities or the homogenisation of products and services for tourists. Such arguments are countered by the proponents of alternative forms of tourism, i.e., alternative to mass tourism, e.g., ecotourism, which are end-of-pipe solutions at best. As Butler argued " . . . too often, over-simplistic and naive views of the complex nature of tourism, and also of the environment, lead to misleading claims and hopes for alternative tourism" (cited in Romeril, 1994: 23). This implies a shift from a summative approach—for example—based on indicators for the three pillars of sustainability to a more integrative and adaptive approach such as the Plimsoll Model (see Greenwood et al., 2008). Technical and managerial approaches are not enough. Basically, and understandably from a business perspective, tourism enterprises are serving their own interests in the first place, which often contradicts with public interest (e.g., to protect/enhance the environment). To achieve real progress there is a need to adopt a political economy approach. The private sector must not be left to self-regulation. While voluntary initiatives should be encouraged, governments have to put in place and enforce environmental regulations. But, as the research studies presented in the foregoing chapters attest, questions must be asked as to why environmental governance appear to be so weak.

In total, the findings provide a valuable review of the current position of the environmental performance of tourism enterprises—their sustainability—and the incorporation of environmental management practices and systems. There are many owners who consider the environmental performance of their enterprise in some way(s) and who, along with potentially many other enterprises, may well respond positively to effective promotion of environmental management systems and initiatives designed to promote and further linkages with the economy, environment, and community, as long as such promotion is presented in the right way, i.e., positively with the right message. But further encouragement and promotion is needed. In effect, ways must be developed if substantial progress in the adoption of environmentally sustainable practices is to be achieved. As Von Geibler and Kuhndt argued: "Cooperation among information 'gatekeepers' at various levels is necessary to raise awareness of environmental and socially sound production patterns among SMEs, provide them with hands-on tools for integrating environmental and social concerns in day-to-day business, and establish economic conditions that reward such efforts" (2002: 63)

Tourism enterprises that do not recognise the value of such potential developments and fail to adopt proactive, long-sighted approaches may well find their development opportunities limited. In due course regulations on environmental matters will increase so there is a commercial imperative in addition to the environmental imperative. To be 'ahead of the game' today will save financial costs in the future and increased sustainability, ensuring stronger communities and better quality of life for all in the long term. In support of such objectives, the following areas for further study and discussion are proposed.

- In the context of awareness and action, what sources of information do owners/manager actually consider in terms of potential influence on their business practices?
- Small, local enterprises vis-à-vis the large multinational enterprises (e.g., re survivability) as well as the argument that large tourism companies (multinationals) are more open to adopt social/environmental responsibility projects (maybe because they have the necessary resources or is it just cost savings?).

- Tourism's fickle nature: as many enterprises (SMEs in particular) may not survive in the long term, there is poor interest in long-term environmental planning; as one manager stated: 'A tourism entrepreneur hardly ever plans his future more than five years in advance; in some cases, one year's forethought is sufficient . . . ' (Pleumarom, 2008).
- Marketing innovations seem to play a key role but what are the real innovations and what is "fantasy," i.e., greenwash?
- Question and investigate the underlying assumption that the behaviour/attitudes of tourism actors are similar; for example, the difference between Western and others, e.g., Asian, may be significant.
- The quality of "environmental innovations"; to illustrate: airlines offering carbon-offsetting schemes to help fund projects for biodiversity conservation; other tourism enterprises also offer compensation schemes instead of solving the environmental problems they produce. To illustrate, rather than properly treating wastewater before dumping it into the ocean, a hotel chain sponsors a turtle conservation project. A hotel company bulldozes a mangrove forest to build a golf course, while promoting water- and energy-saving measures. A resort chain works to reduce its carbon "footprint," while it depends on excessive water consumption for operating its spa businesses. Are these acceptable trade-offs or part of the aggravating environmental problems?
- Global environmental change vis-à-vis global economic liberalisation/deregulation.
- The effectiveness of environmental governance.

Whilst the outcomes of such discussion and research could contribute to progress towards more effective practices and promotion in the short term, their pursuance could contribute significantly to ameliorating some of the more unsustainable facets of tourism development in the longer term. Thus, at least, in some small way contribute to progress in the recognition and response of tourism enterprises to the quest for sustainable development.

REFERENCES

Djerba, 2003. *Declaration on tourism and climate change*. Available at: http://www.world-tourism.org/sustainable/climate/decdjerba-eng.pdf [accessed 18 March 2008].

Greenwood, J., Brothers, G. & Henderson, K., 2008. Don't sink the boat! The Plimsoll Model of tourism sustainability. In D. Leslie guest ed., Leisure, *Consumerism and sustainable development: "mission impossible."* Leisure Studies Newsletter 80, July, p.31–34.

Hall, C.M. & Page, S.J., 1999. *The geography of tourism and recreation—environment, place and space.* London: Routledge.

Holmes, K., Miller, G., Scarles, S. & Tribe, J., 2008. "I just don't think about it." Public attitudes towards sustainable leisure. In D. Leslie guest ed., *Leisure, consumerism and sustainable development: "mission impossible."* Leisure Studies Newsletter 80, July, p.27–31.

Hultsman, J., 1995. Just tourism: an ethical framework. *Annals of Tourism Research*, 22(3), p.553–67.

Mastny, L., 2002. *Redirecting international tourism. State of the world.* World Watch Institute. London: Earthscan, p.101–24.

Pleumaraom, A., 2008. Personal communication, October.

Romeril, M., 1994. Alternative tourism: the real tourism alternative? In C.P. Cooper & A. Lockwood eds., *Progress in tourism, recreation and hospitality management.* Vol. 6. Chichester: John Wiley, p.22–29.

Von Geibler, J. & Kuhndt, M., 2002. *Helping small and not-so-small businesses improve their triple bottom line performance.* UNEP Industry and Environment, July–December, p.63–66.

WTTC, 1996. *Agenda 21 for the travel and tourism industry: towards environmentally sustainable development.* London: World Tourism Organisation/ Earth Council and World Travel and Tourism Council.

Contributors

Kelly Bicker is Associate Professor at the University of Utah and serves as Executive Director for the International Ecotourism Society, specialising in research in sustainable tourism, natural resource management/recreation, and sense of place. She has worked all over the world, employed as guide, tourism manager, wilderness instructor, scuba and sailing instructor, professor, and researcher.

Ralf Buckley is Director of the International Centre for Ecotourism Research and Research Director of the Climate Response Program at Griffith University in Australia. He has published over a dozen books, over two hundred journal articles and over one hundred reports on various aspects of environmental science, management, policy, and law. For the past fifteen years his research has focussed on tourism and environment. He is a member of national and international advisory and award organisations in tourism, conservation, and heritage.

Nazmiye Erdoğan is a qualified landscape architect, who worked in this field before taking up a post at the Black Sea University. She is currently Assistant Professor at Baskent University, Ankara, and Assistant Director of the School of Tourism Management and Guide. She is the author of *the Environmental Problems: Causes and Solutions*, and *Environment and Ecotourism*.

Stefan Gössling is research coordinator at the Research Centre for Sustainable Tourism, Western Norway Research Institute, and an Associate Professor at the Service Management programme, Lund University/Sweden. He has been contributing author to the IPCC's 4th Assessment Report and has recently contributed to *Climate Change and Tourism: Responding to Global Challenges* (published by UNWTO-UNEP-WMO).

Chris Guilding: until 2007, Chris was the Director of Griffith's Service Industry Research Centre. He is a member of the Chartered Institute of Management Accountants and has taught accounting and finance in universities in England, Canada, New Zealand, and Australia. In recent years, he has developed a specific interest in accounting for tourism and hospitality issues. His book *Financial Management for Hospitality Decision Makers*, published by Butterworth-Heinemann, was notably translated into Mandarin in 2007.

Michael Hall is a professor in the Department of Management, University of Canterbury, New Zealand, and Docent in the Department of Geography, University of Oulu, Finland. Co-editor of *Current Issues in Tourism,* he has published widely in the fields of tourism, environmental history, and gastronomy, including research on social marketing, climate change, and sustainable consumption.

Albina L. Lara is a professor at the National University of La Matanza, environmental coordinator of Argentina's Binational Energy Projects, international consultant and Member of the Board of Environmental and Social NGOs: FARN, Naturaleza para el Futuro (Nature for the Future) and Amartya. She has worked extensively with the World Bank, USAID, IDB, UNESCO, and as a Cluster Manager with the UNDP Argentina office.

David Leslie is Reader in Tourism at Glasgow Caledonian University. His standing in the tourism field has been widely recognised; it is manifest, for example, by the award of a Fellowship of the Tourism Society, research commissions, and involvement in organisations such as the UK Roundtable Sustainable Development Forum, World Leisure and Recreation Association, and Leisure Studies Association.

Ishmael Mensah is a lecturer in tourism and hospitality management at the Department of Geography and Tourism, University of Cape Coast. His research interests are in tourism and the environment, destination marketing, and special events management.

Sophie Rainford is a sustainable tourism enthusiast and is passionate about the outdoors and looking after the natural environment. She currently works for Tourism New Zealand as Development Advisor, responsible for the international profiling of Qualmark as the official quality assurance system for New Zealand and supporting tourism business capability and regional tourism development in New Zealand.

Anita von der Thuesen-Pleumarom has an extensive career in the field of development, urban and environmental planning in Southeast Asia and for development education programmes such as ASA (work and study programme in Africa, Asia, and Latin America) of the German Carl-Duisberg-Foundation. Currently, she is Director of the Bangkok-based

Tourism Investigation & Monitoring Team and editor of their bimonthly news bulletin *New Frontiers-Briefing on Tourism, Development and Environment Issues in the Mekong Subregion.*

Anna Spenceley is an independent consultant and researcher based in South Africa who focuses on responsible tourism and sustainable development issues, mainly in emerging economies. Anna is a member of the World Conservation Union (IUCN) World Commission on Protected Areas, the IUCN's Southern African Sustainable Use Specialist Group (SASUSG), and is a director of the International Centre of Responsible Tourism–South Africa.

Jan Warnken is a senior lecturer in the Griffith School of Environment. He is particularly active in researching the specialist area of impact assessment and management of tourism complexes and activities. His current research activities focus on legal and environmental management issues of strata-title complexes in the context of sustainable tourism development and destination management.

Craig Wight is a business development consultant in the Moffat Centre, Glasgow Caledonian University. Craig undertakes business and academic project work for a range of public and private sector tourism organisations, specialising in visitor attractions and the role of heritage interpretation. Recently he has carried out research into narratives of Lithuanian and Jewish tragedy in museum interpretation and this research continues to underpin his evolving Ph.D. work.

Index